Healing Trauma:
The Power of Listening

Edited by
Evelyn Jaffe Schreiber

Healing Trauma: The Power of Listening

Edited by Evelyn Jaffe Schreiber

IPBOOKS.net
International Psychoanalytic Books

International Psychoanalytic Books (IPBooks)
New York • http://www.IPBooks.net

International Psychoanalytic Books (IPBooks)
Queens, NY.
Online at: www.IPBooks.net

ISBN: 978-1-7320533-1-1

Printed in the United States of America

For my parents and all shtetl ancestors

Table of Contents

Trauma Manifested in Social Spaces

Acknowledgments

The "Listening to Trauma: Insights &° Actions" Conference and therefore this edited collection would not have been possible without the tireless and stellar leadership of co-chairs Marshall Alcorn, Jr., Ph.D. and Arthur S. Blank, Jr., M.D., as well as guidance from the late Gordon Kirschner, M.D. of the Washington School of Psychiatry and the Forum on Psychiatry and the Humanities. The entire Conference Planning Committee, including Kate Black, Dart Center for Journalism & Trauma; Allen Dyer, M.D., The George Washington University Department of Psychiatry; Christine Erskine, LCSW, Washington Center for Psychoanalysis; Charles Gati, Ph.D., Johns Hopkins University; Nancy Goodman, Ph.D., Contemporary Freudian Society; James Griffith, M.D., The George Washington University Department of Psychiatry; Harold Kudler, M.D., Department of Veterans Affairs; Marilyn Meyers, Ph.D., Washington School of Psychiatry; and myself, Evelyn Jaffe Schreiber, Ph.D., The George Washington University Department of English, worked together seamlessly, volunteering time and energy to attend meetings, create the arc of the Conference, invite speakers, and organize panels. This interdisciplinary group of researchers, psychoanalysts, clinicians, and scholars demonstrates the creative and healing power of synergy. I thank Catherine Kushan, M.A., for her editing and research assistance for this volume, as well as Arnold Richards and Tamar Richards at IPBooks for their assistance and support.

On a personal level, I am indebted to Dori Laub's research on witnessing, which has significantly influenced my own research pursuits. Likewise, the work of Cathy Caruth has stimulated my thinking. The historians and teachers at the United States Holocaust Memorial Museum have provided me with the means of witnessing and creating witnesses through my work at the museum. I am grateful to my parents, Daniel S. Jaffe, M.D. (a psychoanalyst who treated traumatized soldiers on the European front in WWII) and Caroline Raifman Jaffe, M.A. (a clinical psychologist with astute insights into childhood trauma), for their guidance and inspiring work as witnessing clinicians. As always, I am truly thankful for my husband Scott, my empathetic listener who makes all things possible.

Preface

The study of trauma presents challenges not present in other fields of inquiry. We do not study trauma as we study geology, architecture, bridges, or livers. Trauma overwhelms and disorganizes experience. Researchers who investigate trauma take in the disorganization they study. Sensitive attention to trauma subjects the researchers or observers to forces similar to those that afflict the trauma survivor. Our capacity for sensitive observation is accosted. Our capacity to formulate instructive narratives and helpful analysis is made difficult by our encounters with suffering for which no verbal representation has yet been achieved. People and places at home and around the world call out to us for recognition and understanding. But trauma disrupts our understanding particularly in those moments of urgency when such understanding is most needed. For these reasons, research on trauma presents special problems. Trauma involves overwhelming affect and work on trauma subjects us to overwhelming affect. Because of these difficulties, work on trauma benefits greatly from collaborative, reflective, and respectful work.

Contributors to this volume, and participants at the conference held at The George Washington University in the Fall of 2016, joined successfully in this collaborative effort. And the fruits of these dialogues are here in this collection. This work began with extensive collaborative planning supported by the Forum on Psychiatry and the Humanities, and by our Forum Chair, the late Dr. Gordon Kirschner. Our planning group, led by Marshall Alcorn, Art Blank and Evelyn Schreiber, gathered psychoanalysts, scholars, clinicians, and local experts—Harold Kudler, James Griffith, Allen Dyer, Nancy Goodman, and Marilyn Meyers—for over a year to discuss the topic, select speakers, and develop a program that would give international representation and participation for all thinkers, scholars, and clinicians working with broadly psychodynamic understanding of trauma.

Evelyn Jaffe Schreiber's shrewd formulation of three areas of inquiry, "Definitions and Functions," "Intersubjective Engagements," and "Manifested in Social Spaces" represents the breadth and the depth of the collaborative contributions to current research. Formulating useful definitions of trauma is an ongoing process as human technology, belief, and practice change. Understanding person-to-person, face-to-face work with trauma becomes essential in a moment where our social world is increasingly virtual and mediated by cultural media. And finally, an understanding of the particular cultural and historical place of trauma can be absent in clinical work, but is crucial for a complex account of trauma affects. We are particularly lucky to have among our contributors, scholars and clinicians who write with a lifetime of thoughtful observant work, particularly Robert Lifton, Art Blank, Cathy Caruth, Françoise Davoine, and Dori Laub. They have seen, in some cases, 60 years of historical change and cultural shifts.

Nancy's Sherman attention to the moral injury of trauma gives emphasis to an aspect of trauma study often marginalized by most recent work in neuroscience in medical schools and work in the academy that concerns itself with Foucault's preoccupations with discourse and power. Trauma overwhelms, but much of its impact is upon our lived experience of meaning and ethical relations. These are experiences that require social discourse and engagement. Harold Kudler in this volume observes: "New diagnostic nomenclatures tend to emerge at pivotal moments in history: not just in the history of Science but in national history." Trauma has a nexis in the one who suffers, but trauma radiates outward into a culture. Cultures respond to trauma by seeking practices to avoid accidents, respond to catastrophes, and develop policies that eschew risk. When risk cannot be avoided, people pay the price for the wounds in multiple ways. Today, untold veterans of the wars of Afghanistan and Iraq cry out for help. Suicides have been precipitous, and while trauma is a popular word for labelling suffering, we face challenges in developing an effective supporting social structure spanning all the links that radiate out from the person suffering to all those places beyond the immediate—relatives and friends and associates. Putting this structure into place requires more work for clinicians, for academics, and for those working in media and public discourse. As a society we have much to do, but too often our capacity to listen to trauma and respond to its wounds is compromised by competing political demands and recurrent political crises.

In 1996 Cathy Caruth introduced trauma studies with her groundbreaking tome, *Unclaimed Experience.* That book had a powerful impact on clinicians and university researchers across the globe. This volume, bringing together eminent thinkers from clinical practice and from university research, offers opportunities for this continued dialogue between scholars and clinicians about this important subject.

Marshall Alcorn

Art Blank

Introduction

This collection of essays, with new contributions by Robert Jay Lifton and Cathy Caruth, as well as impactful work by leading psychoanalysts, researchers and clinicians in the field of trauma, memorializes the Keynote and Plenary talks at the interdisciplinary Washington Conference on Trauma, "Listening to Trauma: Insights and Actions," held at The George Washington University in Washington, DC, October 20–22, 2016.[1] For three days, interdisciplinary discussions among neuroscientists, researchers, practicing clinicians, and academics regarding manifestations of extreme trauma revealed forward-looking ideas about treatments that assist real people with evident trauma effects, including Holocaust survivors, war veterans, rape victims, and disaster survivors. The merging of biological underpinnings of catastrophic trauma with its clinical manifestations creates innovative and appropriate treatments to alleviate suffering. Dividing this volume into three sections illustrates how neuroscientists and therapists, working together, can listen across disciplines and respond in therapeutic ways in the treatment of people in pain. Working together in dialogue, these essays tackle the intricate network of psychological (including memory and affect) and physiological roots of trauma and the impact for individuals in social interactions.[2]

Trauma: Definitions and Functions

Evidence of trauma has been documented throughout time, from Homer's early literary depictions to documented accounts after the Civil War, World War I, World War II, the Korean War, the Vietnam War, and recent wars in Iraq and Afghanistan. Those who treat victims of severe trauma have detailed individual cases as well as larger

---

1. In 2010, The George Washington University Department of Psychiatry and the Department of English held a highly successful interdisciplinary conference, "Listening to Trauma." This first conference was, in part, inspired by Cathy Caruth's ground-breaking book, *Unclaimed Experience: Trauma, Narrative, and History*, wherein she investigates individual and collective trauma through the intersection of psychoanalysis, literature, and literary theory. Specifically, she explores the difficulty of narrating the "unsayable," of "knowing" the unknown or buried traumatic experience. Based on the success of the 2010 "Listening to Trauma Conference," a planning committee, in conjunction with the Forum on Psychiatry and the Humanities, the International Society for Traumatic Stress Studies, the Washington Center for Psychoanalysis, the Washington School of Psychiatry, The George Washington University Departments of Psychiatry and English, the Contemporary Freudian Society Washington, DC Program, and the Dart Center for Journalism and Trauma, organized the 2016 conference.

2. I am deeply grateful to Marshall Alcorn, Jr. and Arthur S. Blank, Jr. for their guidance in shaping the Introduction.

studies to record trauma's characteristics and successful methods of treatment. As recognition of trauma's existence in soldiers returning from World War II and Korea grew, the American Psychiatric Association published the Diagnostic and Statistical Manual (DMS-1) in 1952, which used the term "gross stress reaction" to describe war-related stress.

Having a diagnostic code enabled people suffering from traumatic stress to receive compensated care, and PTSD, the current descriptor, has become, according to Arthur Blank, "as well-researched and empirically validated as any disorder in DSM, now over 37 years. The very first validation study on the DSM criteria for PTSD, done just post-1980, produced an inter-rater correlation of .7, and validation studies have been upward since then, as the criteria have been further refined through the 3R, 4, 4TR, and Fifth Editions of the DSM." The varying DSM descriptions of trauma are consistent with Judith Herman's formulation in 1992: People suffering from trauma experience hyperarousal, intrusion, and constriction. While Richard McNally (2004) and others contend that the DSM-III diagnosis of PTSD arose from advocacy groups, it remains clear that physicians were treating a real illness that had been present since earliest records of combat in human history. Patients suffering from medically diagnosable traumatic conditions resulting from combat existed before the development of advocacy groups, and historical records indicate it has been observed during the Civil War as "soldier's heart," World War I as "shellshock," and World War II as "battle fatigue."

Psychoanalysts recognized the horrific effects of trauma after WWI and the Holocaust during WWII. The suffering of Vietnam War veterans brought more focused attention to understanding the intersubjective benefits of providing a listening other. Trauma began to be spoken of as "the black hole" in the mind and as unsymbolized and overwhelming. In talking treatments, symbolization of the trauma begins to take place in a witnessing surround. Powerful painful affects emerge and are metabolized within the witnessing context of an analytically informed therapy.

Clinicians and scholars may reflect different interests in their study of trauma and may mean different things when they use words like "dissociated" or "repressed' to describe traumatic memory. Indeed, different groups, depending upon their training and professional affiliations, may use the same word (dissociation, for example) differently. And there are thus many disagreements about the category trauma. Nonetheless, the core concept of trauma has had a stable meaning since Fenichel's 1945 *Psychoanalytic Theory of Neurosis*. This volume further supports this understanding of trauma, as it brings together cutting-edge physiological knowledge and accounts of effective clinical treatments that advance our increasingly complicated understanding of what trauma is and how it impacts its victims.

The establishment of the Society for Traumatic Stress Studies in 1985, later named the International Society for Traumatic Stress Studies as treatment for trauma spread worldwide, validated the growing need for publications and professional conversations regarding traumatic stress in treatment and culture. Research, such as that of Yehuda and McFarlane, establishes that "biological findings have provided objective validation that PTSD is more than a politically or socially motivated conceptualization of human suffering. Indeed, biological observations have delineated PTSD from other psychiatric disorders and have allowed a more sophisticated description of the long-term consequences of traumatic stress" (1997, p. xi). And Van der Kolk's work traces how "the affective power of people's passions arises from subcortical systems that are not under their conscious control" (2000, p.236). Discussing Charcot, Janet, and Freud, Van der Kolk outlines the history of trauma in studies of hysteria, where "memories of a traumatic event may become split off (dissociated) from ordinary consciousness and from voluntary control" (2000, p. 237); he designates Kardiner as first identifying the "psychobiological nature of traumatic stress" (2000, p. 242). Concerned with patients suffering symptoms of PTSD or severe trauma, this collection of essays connects the latest work in physiology/neuroscience with emerging clinical therapeutic methods for eliciting buried traumatic experiences from patients in order to offer vital and effective treatment of trauma.

The work of Robert Jay Lifton, Harold Kudler, James Griffith, and Allen R. Dyer classifies PTSD as a diagnosable entity and illuminates its manifestations. Progressive studies in neuroscience connect to diagnosis and treatment of catastrophic trauma, with implications for how people can live and function in the social world. Lifton's work describes the existence of long-term trauma connected to war and government upheaval, and his title, "Research as Witness," encompasses both the physiological aspects of trauma and the therapeutic response necessary to help patients by adopting the dual role of "scientific investigator and witnessing professional." His four studies of massive trauma—Chinese thought reform survivors; Hiroshima survivors; Vietnam veterans; and Nazi doctors—have done much to define catastrophic trauma and suggest approaches to healing. Lifton's work concludes that "PTSD is an expectable human reaction to an extreme and abnormal environment." Indeed, what we learn by studying past events can pave the way for those who have suffered to lead more meaningful lives. Tracing the early work in PTSD with veterans returning from the Vietnam War as well as the progressive inclusion of PTSD in the DSM III, Kudler suggests that effective diagnosis and treatment may require "neurochemical intervention (ketamine), a transcranial magnetic intervention (TMS), and talk therapy," working together to act on the same "essential pathology: a loss of normal signal processing secondary to psychological trauma."

In his study, James Griffith details the "physiological vulnerability of the prefrontal cortex and default mode network to extreme stress" as crucial to understanding the impact of these processes on "sense of self and relationships with others." He argues for the vital role of "existential neuroscience" in helping individuals to regain a feeling of being human. Likewise, Allen R. Dyer addresses the "biological (evolutionary), psycho-social (developmental), and Spiritual (ultimate concerns)" connected to PTSD. Further, through what he calls Ongoing Post Traumatic Stress Disorder (OTSD), Dyer considers how stress and trauma are related at basic biological and psychosocial levels. Dyer's worldwide research brings home the point that the on-going "[a]rtificial distinction between health and mental health obscures rather than clarifies the integral relationship of mind and body." Lifton, Kudler, Griffith, and Dyer acknowledge the necessary intersections of the biological and psychosocial to adequately heal those suffering from PTSD.

Treatment: Intersubjective Engagements

In accordance with these definitions of severe trauma and examples of the physiological and medical research contributing to understanding how to clinically work with survivors, the essays focus on clinician/patient psychoanalytic interactions that illuminate styles of traumatic suffering and provide effective therapy. A commonality among the papers in this section is that they reveal intersubjective engagements in a therapeutic setting that can elicit metaphoric narratives or enactments. Clinicians who heal patients describe their own involvement with the taking in of trauma from their patients. These intersubjective encounters lead to breakthroughs in therapeutic techniques. While the biophysical underpinnings of trauma help assess a patient's need for treatment, Dori Laub, Nanette Auerhahn, Arthur

Blank, Françoise Davoine, Marilyn Meyers, and Nancy Goodman discuss the one-on-one interaction between therapist and patient. Their methods indicate how traditional clinician-active models of treatment for those who suffer from trauma are giving way to relational, dyadic models. Rather than a one-way transfer of information from patient to therapist, the newest, crucial aspects of treatment define a therapeutic effect from a listener actually hearing what the patient is saying and being affected by it, so that traumatic events are perceived in an analogous way for the patient.[3] Psychoanalytical relational theory now is mainstream in psychoanalytic practice.

The specificity connected with this treatment involves a testimonial to a witness, for therapeutic effect. This therapeutic model posits that patients deserve to be heard in terms of their own particularity, and within the relational model, there are modes of relating that provide a prototype of what some skillful analysts do. Van der Kolk finds that "[p]utting an experience into words is one way in which people can regain the capacity to imagine alternative outcomes, besides the disaster of the trauma." (2000 p. 247); trauma represents the intersection of "emotional, cognitive, social, and biological forces that shape human development." (Van der Kolk, 2000 p. 255). The distinct ways that each therapist in this volume describes a relational approach have redefined traditional practice. Treatment through the concept of listening to a patient's testimony *per se* is therapeutic, and listening as important in therapy was implicit in Freud and in psychoanalysis. Currently, moving from an interpretation of events to a listening and hearing mode of therapy can lead to a therapist's response and interaction in a therapeutic way.

Dori Laub's experiences with Holocaust survivors and his founding work with the Fortunoff Video Archive for Holocaust Testimonies authenticate the need for an engaged, empathetic listener, eager to receive the testimony, who becomes a "witness to this dialogic process." In her clinical examples of traumatic enactment, Nanette C. Auerhahn illustrates how "the sensorimotor inscription of a traumatically absent object generates intergenerational and therapeutic reenactments" of trauma. She chronicles the releasing of bodily stored trauma as well as analyst absorption of analysand trauma. Likewise, Blank's therapeutic work is grounded in careful attention to the mind of another person, including creative, metaphorical thinking to in-

---

3. The International Association of Relational Psychoanalysis and Psychotherapy (IARPP) expresses this school of relational therapeutic practice, first brought to the fore by Ferenczi, which has had deep impact on the way most psychodynamic therapists work with trauma.

crease interaction between analyst and analysand, in order to move towards a symbolization of trauma. The crucial role of the analyst's reverie, which can be enhanced through meditation, suggests new ways of treating traumatized patients.

Françoise Davoine calls the two-way interaction between patient and analyst an "interference" that produces inscriptions of unknown traumas. Through dreams and metaphors, empathetic listening reveals what previously could not be accessed. In this process, according to Marilyn Meyers, the therapist serves as a containing and holding witness whose own dreams and nightmares help to process the patient's trauma. Through this "meta-witnessing" process, the therapist functions both inside and outside of the witnessing experience, which is particularly helpful to second-generation patients. Nancy R. Goodman also depicts the reciprocal transfer of traumatic material between patient and analyst by helping patients create a "museum in the mind" to explore together, allowing symbol and metaphor to take form, especially in the analyst's dreams that serve as witness to unconscious trauma.

Trauma Manifested in Social Spaces

Finally, clinical and literary depictions of how survivors process trauma suggest how people navigate trauma in the social world. Trauma exists not just in people who are suffering from traumatic experiences, but also exists in the social space where people try to work through trauma. Cathy Caruth notes the "centrality of the social and political realms in the production and maintenance of trauma." When communities are traumatized, traumatized individuals may suffer more and be more unable to work through suffering. Rather than promote healing, a traumatizing world exacerbates distress. Essays by Myra Sklarew, Gerard Fromm, Marilyn Charles, Nancy Sherman, Evelyn Jaffe Schreiber, and Jane Shore indicate how trauma lives in a particular time and place, interacting with, and being recognized by, cultural forces. That is, the social world—the world that people suffering from traumatic experiences live in—reflects the existence of trauma and its powerful effects on individual lives. In this third section, clinicians and academics describe how people make sense of, live with, and work through these symptoms of trauma. In his writings on trauma, Jeffrey Alexander explores how trauma has become a "new master narrative," validated on a cultural or collective level rather than merely on an individual one (2012, p. 17). Likewise, Fassin and Rechtman analyze how cultural discussions of trauma "have moved from a realm in which the symptoms of the wounded soldier or the injured worker were deemed of doubtful legitimacy to one in which their suffering, no longer contested, testifies to an experience that excites sympathy and merits compensation" (2009, p.5). The essays in this section represent cultural traumas and how people in the social world warrant treatment through a collective acknowledgement of traumatic wounding. Political forces need to understand, and make accommodations for, the social world in which patients are enmeshed.

The power of metaphor to represent and bring forth unconscious traumatic memory features in Myra Sklarew's three differing examples of Lithuania survivors of the Holocaust. Sklarew ties the experiences of these survivors to how the neuroscientists view the formation of these effects, giving examples of how hyperarousal and dissociation intersect with the role of the amygdala and hippocampus in connection to emotional memory. It is through metaphor and psychotherapy that the unseen physiological trauma comes into consciousness. Compassion helps those who inherit trauma to move beyond the effects of unconscious and unknowable events. Gerard Fromm's work with second-generation trauma portrays the difficulty of articulation for those who inherit trauma, rather than live through it. In his work with the descendants of Nazis, Fromm investigates second and third generations playing out the lives of their elder generations, rather than their own. Children of perpetrators must tell their stories so that "the picture of intergenerational transmission of trauma emerges, giving birth to narratives that reconstruct a prior generation's trauma so that it can be worked through rather than inherited as self-destruction." Marilyn Charles looks at this problem of accessing inherited trauma in legacy generations: children of the Aboriginal culture in New South Wales are caught in an inherited cycle of unarticulated trauma and shame. To gain narrative coherence, metaphors promote the playfulness necessary to discover a self and rebuild a life. Recovery from shame also features in Nancy Sherman's work on treating returning soldiers suffering from moral despair, moral anxiety, or moral disillusionment through the development of "compassionate self-empathy." Sherman outlines five common aspects of moral injury that can produce shame and require self-empathy to recover. A survivor of trauma can develop self-empathy by internalizing "the empathy of a therapist toward her." Developing an empathetic view of oneself can promote healing.

Shame, inherited trauma, and an erased past are central themes in the work of Nobel Prize winner Toni Morrison, and Evelyn Jaffe Schreiber provides a literary example of the power and process of testimony in *God Help the Child*. Characters responding to traumatic events create narratives to alleviate both individual and communal trauma. Their testimonies elicit unknown, unconscious trauma and facilitate movement from fragmented selves to people who can connect with others. They develop Laub's "internal listener" through testimony to an "external witness" to produce internalized knowledge. Morrison's novel becomes a holding space for African American trauma and intimates productive ways to work through it. Jane Shore's poetry provides another literary example of how the creative process of writing can articulate personal trauma. She explains how the metaphor of the formula for the TV series *Law & Order* provided her with a model of the crime and then the retribution. The show became a witness, offering a representation of her trauma (the crime) and the restitution that punishes the perpetrators. Her creative process of finding the "emotional center" of a poem, "what I didn't know I knew," leads her to the "unclaimed territory" of her trauma so that others may witness and share the burden of her trauma. The unfinished poem mirrors Shore's own lack of closure, but through the writing process she is building the "inner witness" that Dori Laub finds crucial to successful recovery from trauma.

In our current social and political historical time of global unrest and trauma-producing events, it is imperative to accurately diagnose and effectively treat people who suffer from the after-effects of severe trauma. The voices in this collection define where we are in the history of trauma's legacy of symptoms and emerging breakthrough therapeutic techniques that address personal stories in collective history. Trauma, defined here as physiological and social, exists. As the overwhelming response to the "Listening to Trauma: Insights & Actions" Conference suggests, the urgency of addressing trauma's devastating impact has led to interdisciplinary discourse regarding trauma's underpinnings and treatment. Physiological evidence and relational modes of therapy verify that the power of listening to trauma leads to healing.

References

Alexander, J. (2012). *Trauma: A Social Theory.* New York: Polity Press.

Blank, A. (2017). Personal communication.

Bloom, S. L. (2000). Our Hearts and Our Hopes are Turned to Peace: Origins of The International Society for Traumatic Stress Studies. *International Handbook of Human Response to Trauma.* New York: Kluwer Academic/Plenum Publishers. Edited by Arieh Y. Shalev, Rachel Yehuda, and Alexander C. McFarlane.

Caruth, C. (1996). *Unclaimed Experience: Trauma, Narrative, and History.* Baltimore: Johns Hopkins University Press.

———— (2014) *Listening to Trauma: Conversations with Leaders in the Theory & Treatment of Catastrophic Experience.* Baltimore: Johns Hopkins University Press.

Fassin, D. and R. Rechtman. (2009). *The Empire of Trauma: An Inquiry into the Condition of Victimhood.* Trans. Rachel Gomme. Princeton: Princeton University Press.

Fenichel, O. (1945). *The Psychoanalytic Theory of Neurosis.* New York: W.W. Norton & Co.

Herman, J. (1992) *Trauma and Recovery.* New York: Basic Books.

McNally, R. J. (2004). Conceptual Problems with the DSM-IV Criteria for Posttraumatic Stress Disorder. 1–14. *Posttraumatic Stress Disorder: Issues and Controversies.* Ed. Gerald M. Rosen. Chichester: John Wiley & Sons Ltd.

Van der Kolk, B. (2000). Trauma, Neuroscience, and the Etiology of Hysteria: An Exploration of the Relevance of Breuer and Freud's 1893 Article in Light of Modern Science. *Journal of America Academy of Psychoanalysis,* 28: 237–262.

Yehuda, R. and McFarland, A. C. (1997). Introduction. In R. Yehuda & A.C. McFarlane (eds), *Psychobiology of posttraumatic stress disorder* (pp. xi–xv). New York: New York Academy of Sciences.

Trauma: Definitions and Functions

Research as Witness

Robert Jay Lifton

Institutional Affiliation and Note

Robert Jay Lifton, M.D. is a psychiatrist, psychohistorian, and one of the United States' foremost public intellectuals. He was for many years associated with Yale University, and also with Harvard University and the City University of New York, and is now at Columbia University. His psychohistorical studies of Chinese thought reform, survivors of Hiroshima, Vietnam veterans, and Nazi doctors have illuminated the psychology of totalism and the experience of survivors of war and atomic bombing. He has also been concerned with the psychology of genocide, the impact of nuclear weapons, and the many-faceted influences of death in life. In the following contribution, he illustrates how his work has added to our understanding of psychological trauma.

Abstract

I will discuss four research studies from the standpoint of trauma: Chinese thought reform, the survivors of the atomic bomb in Hiroshima, antiwar veterans of the Vietnam War, and Nazi Doctors. In each case, I will explore the nature of the trauma; my own struggles with the work; my interview method as combined with a mosaic of culture and history; the broader, universalistic significance of the findings; and the relationship of each study to the various levels of healing and to our larger history. Throughout, I will examine the constructive interplay of scholarship and activism and will suggest the dual role of the researcher as both scientific investigator and witnessing professional.

Editor's note:

Dr. Lifton was scheduled to be the Keynote Speaker at the 2016 "Listening to Trauma Conference: Insights & Actions." He was to give an overview of his work in the field of trauma, but at the last minute fell ill and could not attend. Cathy Caruth graciously, and I might add brilliantly, pulled together Lifton's notes for the talk and "channeled Lifton" as she presented a thought-provoking paper. What follows is Lifton's paper with Caruth's comments on substance appearing in footnotes. Her comments on structure or process appear in the text below in italics.

Before presenting Dr. Lifton's talk, I would like to make note of the central theme of denial throughout Lifton's work, which ties to- gether a larger or collective history and what we think of as personal histories. In the case of Vietnam and in the case of the Holocaust, on both of which events Lifton has done pioneering work, denial is central, as a collective and, more specifically, as a political phenom- enon. In the case of Viet Nam, we might recall the struggles of Arthur Blank, as he opposed denial of PTSD, in psychiatry and the Veteran's Administration, in order to set up the Vet Centers; we might also think of the work it took to introduce PTSD into the Diagnostic and Statistical Manual (DSM) of the American Psychiatric Association (APA). One element to pay attention to in Lifton's talk, then, is the central function of denial that runs throughout the traumatic events he discusses, a problem that may be especially important to us at our particular historical moment [this talk was given the morning after the third debate between Donald Trump and Hillary Clinton in the 2016 presidential election].

I've known Dr. Lifton for more than 20 years. He is, of course, a path-breaking thinker in many areas. But it is this innovative em- phasis on denial in the traumatic field that leads, in the talk you will hear today, to the real opening of trauma to a rethinking of individual histories around what Françoise Davoine and Jean-Max Gaudillière refer to as "Big History": to an understanding, in other words, of the centrality of the social and political realms in the production and maintenance of trauma.

On these matters, I would like to make two remarks. First of all, the connection between individual and collective trauma is important to think about, now, in relation to the political realm. I read that the APA just gave out tips for people that are feeling stress, and per- haps even posttraumatic stress, from our current election season. Of course, most of you probably watched the third debate last night. We heard one of the candidates suggest that he might not honor the results of the election. The possibility of trauma emerging on the scene, if this were to be the case, might not necessarily be individual, but rather a collective response to damage in the political realm or to democracy. On the other hand, after the release of the "Access Hollywood" tapes this season, in which one candidate bragged about sexual molestation, many individual women reported having post-traumatic responses bound up with a public, political figure's, and possible president's, endorsing this kind of behavior, and with his subsequent enacting of aggressive behavior in the second debate with his female opponent. In the first case, then, we are dealing with a political wound felt concretely by many individuals, and in the second case we are dealing with individual wounds that emerge because of the political context. We are confronting in both cases what might be thought of as (potential) political trauma.

Secondly, as I have suggested above, we cannot pursue this exploration of the entanglement of individual and collective trauma without an exploration of denial, and this, too, touches on another central phenomenon we are all faced with in this election: the prevalence of lying. Lifton helps us see (and in this sense he echoes some of the insights of Hannah Arendt) that denial, in the context of political trauma, is not merely a matter of individual acts or attempts "not to know"; it is also a matter of political erasure. The denial of reality in the political realm is at the heart of trauma and is something that Lifton looks at from the very beginning of his work.

Editor's Note: The talk that follows is edited by Caruth, from Lifton's original notes, in order to fit into the timeframe of the Conference. Following the introduction to Lifton's text, Caruth's remarks are placed in footnotes on the material she is reading aloud.

***

Robert J. Lifton's talk is called "Research as Witness," and he asks us to think of research not just as a form of knowing, but as a form of witnessing. Witnessing does not simply concern the transmission of knowledge but the transmission of experiences that cannot be articulated as knowledge (at least that is how I would understand witnessing).

Introductory Remarks: Research, Thinking, Activism

Any research we do is an ethical enterprise, whether we are studying diabetes, the symptoms of depression, or the nature of Chinese thought reform (or brainwashing). The issues are twofold: first, we hold ourselves to rigorous standards of respect for evidence, for reporting what we observe—whether or not it is what we hoped for in connection with prior assumptions. The second ethical dimension is less thought about and has to do with the broad commitment to healing. I have in mind real healing, not just the healing of people's suffering from the conditions or events we study but a larger sense of combating the disruptive forces responsible for human suffering. The issue is especially vivid in our work with trauma. We try to offer help or relief and even a new beginning for people who have been traumatized. But we are also deeply concerned with combating the forces relating to killing and suffering.

And I would argue that this larger ethical impulse is not just a matter of being a concerned citizen but has much to do with us as professionals, in our case mostly psychological professionals. In that sense, we have, first of all, what we call research findings, or scientific observations, concerning our function of witnessing as professionals: we listen to what traumatized people tell us and then retell their stories as authentically as we can, but we do so from the standpoint of our professional knowledge. We are not the survivors in question and it is they who are the primary witnesses. But we are witness to their witness; and our version of the story can add useful dimensions to the whole issue, too. Moreover, witnesses can be the beginning of activism.[4]

Witnessing and acting are not necessarily the same thing, but bearing witness to destructiveness and evil cannot help but call forth feelings of opposition to that destructiveness and evil, and that can lead to activism in various forms, all having to do with sustained public advocacy. It is important to say a word here about scholarship and activism. There has long been a conviction that they are incompatible. One should be a pure scholar looking for truth or else an engaged activist seeking change, but never the twain shall meet. I want to suggest the opposite: that rigorous scholarship can inform and deepen activism, and that thoughtful expressions of activism can give meaning and motivation to scholarship.

There are four studies here. First, the study of Chinese Communist thought reform, or brainwashing, in the mid-fifties, which

---

4. Cathy Caruth: these notes were originally comments made as asides in the presentation of Dr. Lifton's text. For Lifton, I would elaborate here, "witness" doesn't just mean that you listen but that you also act—although sometimes witnessing, listening, can be acting.

provided me with the identity of a psychiatrist in the world who did studies out there and came home to put together his narrative about them (Lifton 1961). The second study is of atomic bomb survivors in Hiroshima in 1962 (Lifton 1967). The third study concerns anti-war veterans in the 1970s, mostly in New York and New Haven (Lifton 1973), and the fourth study details Nazi doctors in the '70s and early '80s, an immersion into evil that led ultimately to applying some of those lessons to Americans and others in connection with torture and genocide (Lifton 1988). Subsequent work I did, including research on the fanatical Japanese called Aum Shinrikyo in the late 1990s (Lifton 1999), mostly stems from my involvement in those four earlier studies. This later work concerned apocalypticism.

About each of these studies I will raise five questions. The nature of the experience; the trauma undergone by those involved; my own experience in studying the event and talking to survivors; the mosaic approach; and the psychological interview, all of which are modified toward the direction of dialogue. The interviewer, not the interviewee, is the seeker, the person who writes about the encounter, with both sides getting some benefit from the interview. But the mosaic, which extends the study to historical influences, is also integral to grasping what is going on in the interview: the universality of what is being gleaned from a historical and cultural interview moment, what is universal in the problem of the particular. Ultimately, I reflect on the direction of social healing emerging from the life-affirming insights that can be derived from the most destructive kind of behavior.

Chinese Thought Reform[5]

1. Nature of the trauma

In Chinese thought reform, the nature of the trauma is a mixture of coercion and exhortation that could be entirely psychological but was always threatening and sometimes included physical brutality or what amounted to forms of torture. Trauma, here, had to do with the pressure to believe and change through the manipulation of guilt and fear: guilt feelings having to do with condemnation and self-condemnation for not having served the Chinese people, for having served the régime, having been a landowner, etc. Perhaps the trauma can be characterized as control trauma, as being subjected to the total control of others. We humans have a considerable degree of freedom of the mind provided us by our symbolizing function. That symbolizing

---

5. See Lifton 1961.

process requires us to bring our imaginative contributions to every perception we take, so that we take in nothing nakedly, but reconstruct all that we see or hear or touch or smell. All of this psychic action takes place and contributes to one's overall narrative, the story of one's life that one constructs over time. Thought reform attacks that narrative and threatens one with very painful outcomes if one does not surrender it in favor of a different, in this case Communism, central narrative and symbolizations.[6] "The trauma could be reduced," he goes on, "if one were strongly responsive to the exportation, to the promise of a new life in a brilliant new society."

2. My reaction to studying Chinese thought reform

What, then was my reaction to thought reform? I was fascinated at two particular levels: that of individual change, but also of the larger national picture of tens or even hundreds of millions of Chinese, from elementary-school to old age, being subjected to a psychological and political process that could have considerable depth. There had been no historical precedent for this.[7]

As I got into the work, I found myself increasingly troubled by learning of the extent to which truth could be distorted, or denied, or reversed, and during the year-and-a-half I spent in Hong Kong, I had many American visitors who told me of similar tendencies under the malignant influence of McCarthyism.[8]

People subjected to false accusations and various punishments by a threatened society is another version of control trauma. I wouldn't say that I experienced control trauma—I was not being coerced or threatened—but I do remember undergoing a disturbance. The world had gone mad in these abhorrent quests for control of our psyches, a process in which I was somehow involved.

---

6. I would note what Lifton is saying here: symbolization is a kind of de-symbolizing process.

7. And I have to say that as I was reading this, I was thinking about what we're all learning, now, about how a country can change fairly rapidly, it seems, under certain kinds of pressures, like the ones that have been emerging in the US over the last year-and-a-half.

8. You know who the lawyer to Donald Trump was, correct? He was the lawyer for McCarthy, as well, so there is a curve back to that in our current political realm.

3. The Mosaic

In the context of the interview, I was always aware of the mosaic of profound cultural and historical forces within which my interviews took place. One aspect of thought reform—the extraction of false confessions with the use of various forms of physical pressure and torture—was derived from Soviet practice and hardly originated there, but the specific Chinese contribution was a systematic pursuit of what was called *reeducation*, which I came to recognize as a process of changing one's identity from that of the filial son or daughter to the filial communist. There is also a link of all things to Confucianism, looking toward the universal. My focus on the particulars of Chinese cultural and historical influence, in order to elicit what was universal in the traumatic project of thought reform, was essential.

4. Looking Toward the Universal

My focus on the particulars of Chinese cultural and historical influence was also aimed at eliciting what was universal in the traumatic project of thought reform. Here I made use of the concept of totalism, widely used in literary theory and applied in a specific psychological way by Erik Erikson. I elaborated eight themes of what I called ideological totalism, by which I meant the all-or-none claim to ultimate truth and ultimate moral virtue. One theme is milieu control, the control of virtually all communication in an environment including much inner communication with the individual self. Another theme is doctrine over person, meaning that should one find oneself disagreeing with the prevailing truths, the disagreement is viewed as a problem or deficiency in one's individual self. And the third theme, the most malignant of all, is what I call the dispensing of existence, which means that the world is divided into those who have a right to exist, and those who possess no such right. This could lead to being refused membership in the society's most central groups or in the most extreme, could lead to being accused of criminal offenses and even being executed.

I received an indication of universality. I heard that the chapter in which I described the eight deadly sins of ideological totalism has become a kind of underground document among those making their way out of fanatical American religious cults. These themes of milieu control and doctrine over person and the dispensing of existence— and the other five as well—seem to apply as much in the American cults as they did in the highly different cultural and historical environment of Chinese thought reform. I would say that there is a universal dimension to all forms of intense experience, including that of trauma, but one finds the weight of that universal dimension through the mosaic of culture and history.[9]

5. Directions of Social Healing

With regard to what I am calling social healing, certain findings confirm the limitations of thought reform. I recorded these findings not only in my original volume *Thought Reform and the Psychology of Totalism*, but in another book called *Revolutionary Immortality* (Lifton 1968). I found that people could react highly negatively to overdoses of thought reform in a pattern I call the hostility of suffocation. The control of communication in any environment was never airtight.[10] There is what I called a *law of diminishing conversions.*[11] What I found was that the Chinese Communists over-reformed to the point of harming their own cause by the negative responses that could be evoked.

We have recently encountered evidence of thought reform with the same kind of vengeance. There have been a series of show trials with former dissidents confessing the error of their ways. The totalism of ideology may, after stepping back from it for a considerable period of time, return vigorously in its most extreme elements. China's model may apply to others who engage in large-scale trauma to their own populations. They may be caught in the vicious circle of traumatizing on a large scale, then pulling back and modifying their behaviors to their own interests, but then finding that their sense of themselves has an essentially totalistic dimension—even an apocalyptic one, which will not let them cease carrying through subsequent ways of traumatizing behavior in order to reassert their own collective identity as bearers and teachers of truth.

What about the researcher's own ethical position in connection to what he or she learns about that reform? This becomes clarified by two encounters I had. During the rebellions on campuses of the 1960s and 70s, I was sometimes asked by radical students whether I

---

9. I would note, here, that there is a big debate in trauma theory concerning this question of universality. There are a number of ways we can formulate this notion.

10. That's his hopeful moment here.

11. Hannah Arendt seemed to think the same thing, but in the Internet age we might wonder whether or not there always is the same possible resistance to thought control.

wished to step back a little and renounce some of the critical things I had said about Maoist behavior. I could answer, but I did not, that from a universalistic standpoint, I was opposed to any such effort to manipulate and control people's minds. I also received perhaps the inevitable call from someone who represented a government agency, which turned out to be the CIA. It was the CIA, of course, and in that conversation and from other investigations it became clear that certain American and military groups wanted a piece of the action, wanted to learn from the country's adversaries how to do its own controlling of minds. So I could again say that, as I try to make clear in my book, I saw myself as attempting to expose patterns of ideo-logical totalism and not to embrace them for use by anyone. What I am saying here is that the investigator can experience his (or her) own trauma, not only by taking in, and in some measure sharing, the experience of survivors, but also in relation to his own sense of public responsibility for acting on what he has learned.

Hiroshima Study[12]

1. Nature of the trauma

The nature of this trauma would be included under the category of massive psychic trauma, which was originated for the study of Holocaust survivors, and I learned about this in my workshops with those who were treating and studying Holocaust survivors. In addi-tion to fitting into a general phenomenology of the psychology of the survivor, to which this work led, there are two specific patterns among Hiroshima survivors that are important to mention.

First, a confused sense of the end of the world.[13] Those who survived did not know what had happened to the city. They used such terms as "a large electrical event" or "the sudden appearance of a Buddhist hell." In either case, it was a sense of the world's coming to an end and the expected death of everyone there. This was part of the

---

12. The second study Lifton writes about is life-and-death survivors of Hiroshima, and this is the book for which he won the National Book Award and really came into public prominence. If we listen to Lifton and the symptoms that he finds in Hiroshima survivors, what he will call, in one of his essays "the image of atrocity" is specifically an image linked with the bomb (Lifton 1971). And that image linked with the bomb is then going to weave itself through all of his other ways of understanding trauma after his Hiroshima study (Caruth 2017).

13. Note that the image of atrocity here is apocalyptic, and I would reiterate that this element, which is linked to the bomb and to the totalizing element of the bomb, is going to weave itself through the rest of Lifton's work.

destruction that had no limit. It was infinite. There was one narrative, a man who had witnessed the effects of the bomb from a suburb—he looked down and saw that Hiroshima had disappeared. From this I came to the mantra, "one plane, one bomb, one city."[14]

A second sense of "inner taint" was very strongly experienced in response to observing in oneself and others acute and chronic radiation effects. Survivors in general may feel tainted by death, but here there is the sense of a poison that has entered one's body and could strike one down, indeed kill one, at any time, and even extend to endangering the next generation. I call this "fear of invisible contamination." From a split second in time, one was to experience a lifelong immersion in death.

In addition, the whole issue of psychic numbing, as lifesaving and mind-saving, was central to these survivors. Survivors described how their minds were shut down or turned off, but the danger of psychic numbing, becoming associated with a sustained inability to feel or experience one's experience, can be associated with withdrawal and depression. All people subjected to extreme trauma undergo a prolonged struggle with balancing how much to feel and how much not to feel.

Hiroshima survivors could also feel that their experience had given them what they called special knowledge. While they had difficulty saying what this special knowledge consisted of, it seemed to be knowledge of total destruction, or of the end of the world.[15]

2. My Own Experience and Reactions

My own experience, of course, is that we're influenced by what we find in our research, but we are inevitably drawn to do our research with trauma. I did not become anti-nuclear from my six months in Hiroshima; rather, I went to Hiroshima because I was anti-nuclear. And of course, what I learned there enormously intensified and expanded what became a lifelong confrontation with nuclearism[16].

There's an important difference between talking about trauma,

---

14. So, absolute annihilation. And that is really, I think, at the heart of Lifton's vision of trauma, both individual and collective. See Caruth 1995.

15. I think here is where Lifton draws his insight into survivors as not only psychologically damaged, but also as witnesses, including the veterans of the Vietnam War, who served for him as witnesses.

16. Indeed, I believe that trauma, for Lifton, is always linked to nuclearism in some symbolic way.

discussing with various leaders what the atomic bomb did, and pursuing the visceral experience of extreme trauma by means of intense psychological interviews. The significance of my own anxiety and uncertainty about completing the work, and then, after a few days, my having a calm sense of taking in psychological responses—was what I came to call "selective professional numbing."

In all this, I had a quick sense of responsibility to tell this story—to tell what had happened to people and the world at large. This is the sense of the responsibility of witness, which can include survivor-like feelings of one's own and anxiety about how to cope with them in a constructive way. At the time, I was very aware of a professional—one could say scientific—function that had to do with rigor and accuracy in reporting what I found. This is the researcher's struggle, to balance intellectual rigor and the requirements of witness.

3. The Mosaic

With regard to the mosaic of the interview, this had to do with Japanese culture and history and with the relative status of Hiroshima and Nagasaki. Hiroshima and Nagasaki became symbols of the use of nuclear weapons because they had little other than provincial identity, which became identified with their destruction. I also had to probe Japanese attitudes toward death, and toward their ancestors, who are ever present and converse with them, especially when they are sitting before household shrines.

4. Universality

Hiroshima survivors also became, for me, a model for the general psychology or phenomenology of the survivor.[17] In them, I could find such things as what I came to call the "death imprint."[18] In addition to the death imprint, the struggle with self-psychic numbing and suspicion of counterfeit nurturance, or of relationships in general, were, above all, efforts to give form and meaning to the whole experience. These struggles can be found in every kind of survivor,

---

17. We will see this also in his writing on Vietnam and in many of his other works.

18. I think that the word "imprint," here, is actually associated with the imprint of the light, of the bomb, and the figure of imprinting is associated with the fact that we know people were imprinted by the bomb, and their shadows were imprinted onto stones. Thus I think that the death imprint—the idea and even the phrase, for Lifton—carries with it the very specific kind of technology of the bomb.

including those who have lost close family members. I would particularly emphasize the issue of meaning. We are, as humans, meaning-hungry creatures, and survivors of severe trauma have experienced a shattering of a sense of the bonds of self, including those of meaning, and an urgency toward reconstructing a sense of meaning to help them through their subsequent lives. Survivors may do this through marriage and family, but quite a few people in Hiroshima sought meaning through their own witness: conveying to others what they had been through as both warning and wisdom.

So, I have spoken of seeking survivor meaning, and sometimes doing that through a survivor mission, as through a sense of conveying the story of Hiroshima to the outside world. This is parallel to the experience of parents of a child who died of leukemia devoting themselves to enhancing research in that area.

I did various kinds of anti-nuclear work, but especially became involved with Physicians for Social Responsibility and International Physicians for the Prevention of Nuclear War.

5. Directions of Social Healing

Hiroshima survivors—or *hibakusha*—underwent considerable healing in giving meaning to their experience by telling their story to the world. Their survivor mission benefited both their listeners and themselves. Trauma can lead to renewal only if some such meaning becomes associated with it. While we researchers should always be clear that we are not the actual survivors—that we are a step further away than they are in carrying through witness—still, that witness can contribute to our own sense of meaning and efforts at wellbeing. I believe that the Hiroshima experience helps us to confront trauma at all levels. Certainly, confronting massive psychic trauma has widespread reverberations in the direction of social healing. Social healing has to do with life-enhancing actions, on behalf of preventing the use of, and perhaps ultimately eliminating, nuclear weapons that endanger the human future. I believe there is an operative principle to the effect that just as one must imagine the idea of death in order to live fully, one must imagine the idea of a nuclear world's ending in order to keep the world going. What I am saying is that the use of interview studies of trauma to imagine future trauma in its most extreme form can contribute to avoiding that which one imagines.

Nuclear trauma derives from what I call nuclearism—the embrace of and exaggerated dependency upon nuclear weapons to maintain "national security," to keep the peace, and even to keep the world going. Nuclear weapons become the source of ultimate power, of power over death, to the point of near-worship. I've tried to make a psychological critique of nuclearism and apply it in my anti-nuclear activism. I have seen Hiroshima as valuable to us in providing genuine evidence of what a "tiny" nuclear weapon by present standards can do to our fellow human beings, as opposed to the abstract nuclear scenarios of strategists in which we fight and win nuclear wars and brilliantly recover from nuclear attacks. These scenarios can be as psychologically misleading as they are ethically repugnant.[19]

And finally, in my work in general, I've been concerned with what I've called malignant normality—creating environments in which what is considered the norm can be dangerous in the extreme.[20] I've been concerned with waves of nuclear normality, at times imposed with the help of psychiatrists and social scientists, in which opposition to weapons stockpiling and use can be framed as maladjusted or neurotic. Subsequently, a model of "living with nuclear weapons," with an advocacy for potential use, is what is ironically called "nuclear ethics"; and then we see various manifestations of the Strategic Defense Initiative (or "Star Wars"), a missile defense system serving as a "nuclear shield" and ostensibly rendering the weaponry ineffective or even obsolete, but replete with its own illusions and potentially serving as a stimulus to the nuclear arms race rather than as a restraint.

Imposing nuclear normality on a country is not without its own effects. Michael Carey (Carey 1982), a writer who worked with me some time ago, did an interview study of people subjected as children to the infamous duck-and-cover drills of the 1950s and 60s. What he found was that six-year-old kids were too smart to believe that putting a paper over one's head or ducking under a desk would enable one to survive a nuclear war. But they were confused by what the authorities told them and by authority in general, and they became susceptible to nuclear anxiety, including dreams of nuclear holocaust, particularly at times when there was talk of nuclear war.

We can say that a certain amount of nuclear anxiety was necessary for the waves of anti-nuclear movement, particularly during the early 1980s, and that anxiety was suppressed and repressed with

19. When Lifton came to Cornell a year-and-a-half ago, he talked about his recent work on environmental catastrophe, and he compared it to the issues surrounding nuclearism.

20. This is what Lifton talked about at Cornell with regard to climate change and our denial of it.

varying degrees of success.

Vietnam Veterans

1. Nature of the Trauma[21]

I realized that in all of my trying to get at the interaction between these men and this war, I tried to take into account what American soldiers experienced as the social. My term "the atrocity- producing situation" is a statement of that interaction. What I mean by an atrocity-producing situation is an environment, structured both militarily and psychologically, such that an average person—no better or worse than you or me—upon entering it could be capable of committing atrocities. In Vietnam, the military structure included counterinsurgency war in a far-off alien environment, involving a non-white culture in which it was often impossible to differentiate between soldiers and civilians, and also military policies that encouraged firing almost at random, as well as policies such as body counts, free-fire zones, and search-and-destroy missions. Psychological responses of the men included fear and helplessness in connection with deaths of buddies at the hands of an unseen enemy, and a state of angry grief and hunger for an enemy—or for people one could view as the enemy—as a target for revenge. There are undoubtedly atrocity-producing situations in all wars, but in Vietnam the war itself could be said to be defined by it.[22]

In the first edition of my book *Home From The War: Learning from Vietnam Veterans*, I used the subtitle *Neither Victims Nor Executioners*, which were the two roles or identities that Camus said we should never assume (Camus 1950). Many Vietnam veterans felt betrayed, sent to the war under false pretenses, and in that sense victimized. Moreover, the war to which they were sent, characterized as it was by atrocity-producing situations, caused participants to betray their own ethical standards. In that way, I understood the psychological experience of Vietnam veterans to be inseparable from their ethical experience. This merging was expressed in struggles with feelings of guilt.

Recent work by Jonathan Shay (Shay 2014) and others on what is called "moral injury" is very much in this spirit. We've al-

---

21. This is from Lifton's book *Home From the War: Learning from Vietnam Veterans.*

22. Of course, it's really prophetic here what Lifton said about this, in relation to our later wars.

ways been aware of moral aspects of trauma. But we do well to go further and recognize that the internal experience of trauma is never without an important moral component.[23] That recognition, I believe, changes our view of PTSD, in the efforts of veterans to overcome its painful effects.

With reference to PTSD, I was on the small committee that consulted with the Office of the Diagnostic and Statistical Manual—the DSM-III—in which the concept was given its expression. Chaim Shatan[24] was perhaps the central figure in organizing and pressing the case we made for it. Without going into detail, my sense is that despite the confusions and exaggerations that have surrounded the term, it has served a particularly useful function in acknowledging adult trauma and suffering. It is hard to believe now, but psychiatry has long ignored adult suffering, emphasizing instead other inherited tendencies towards such symptoms, or attributing adult suffering to childhood trauma, as in early expressions of psychoanalysis.

My own focus in the beginning was very much on adult trauma, and I was able to invoke my work with Hiroshima survivors as well as with Vietnam veterans, while arguing for the concept of PTSD. Even now, I think we always need to remind ourselves that PTSD is an expectable human reaction to an extreme and abnormal environment.[25]

Similarly, the rap groups that were formed by the coming together of anti-war veterans with psychological professionals who also opposed the war were an attempt to bring healing to groups struggling with painful affects. There was a commitment to making known the kind of war they'd been sent by their country to fight. In holding to the name "rap group" rather than "therapy group," we were keep-

---

23. Elsewhere, Lifton talks about this moral component in relation to "paradoxical guilt," a paradoxical guilt of survivors (Lifton 1979).

24. Chaim Shatan, 1924–2001, was a Canadian-American psychoanalyst, born in Poland with many extended family members lost in the Holocaust, whose OpEd in the *New York Times* in 1972 crystallized public awareness of PTSD in Vietnam veterans. He was a leader with Lifton and others in the installation of the PTSD diagnosis in the DSM in 1980.

25. And for Lifton, PTSD is really an attempt at witness. Lifton is proud—and should be—of helping to get PTSD made a diagnosis. We also know that it can be medicalized, and that people often don't want to be told they have PTSD because they feel they're being pathologized. But for Lifton, in *Home From the War*, the soldiers in the rap groups saw their "Vietnam Syndrome" as a moral witness (including even the flashbacks): a way of seeing things that couldn't be seen. So it's a very different understanding of symptomatology from the medicalized version. See Caruth 2006.

ing the effort non-medical, and recognizing that these groups had been initiated by the veterans themselves, and essentially belonged to them. The healing process was mutual, as we professionals were also struggling with our own anti-war feelings and failure to more effectively oppose the war. At the group sessions, veterans and professionals spoke about combinations of individual feelings and the nature of the war and its environment.

2. To My Own Reactions

For me, the rap groups were an opportunity to combine professional knowledge with passionate opposition to the war. Overall, my study of Vietnam veterans was a case of the activist tail wagging the scholarly dog, but it was still important to be rigorous about the findings.[26]

The rap groups also had an influence on me in terms of questioning the self-protective but distancing professional stance that we often assume. I also came to realize that one's status as a member of a healing group does impose the moral conversation. One makes choices as a professional about where, so to say, to hang out one's shingle. That is, what works for whom, and what work one does, and what the actual impact of that work is on other people and on the society.

There was an interesting development in that regard for our rap group progression. During the early 70s, you could reach at most a few hundred people. But our work could provide at least part of a model for a later outreach program of the VA, which was of course headed by Arthur Blank, and which could help thousands of veterans.

3. The Mosaic

(In the mosaic section, Lifton talks about one of the contributing factors to the experience of Vietnam vets: what he calls America's "superpower syndrome." He has also written a book about the superpower syndrome, which appeared in the early 2000s [Lifton 2003]).

The superpower syndrome in the US involved the idea that we

---

26. Lifton here offers examples of having to face his own assumptions and challenge them when he interviewed people. One example he gives is the case of someone he calls the "My Lai Survivor." This is one of the people who had been at the My Lai massacre, but did not shoot. Instead of coming to understand people's automatically being drawn in mechanically into massacres of that kind, he was able to discover that some of the soldiers actually abstained, and that there was the opportunity to abstain from shooting.

could be omnipotent and even take control of the historical process. Here, it was of the greatest importance that America emerge from WWII with unique power and authority—total authority. Unfortunately, the mosaic of counterinsurgency struggles, first against Communism and later against what we saw to be terrorism, continued, and still bedevils us. We have never recovered as a nation from the unacceptable loss of the Vietnam War.[27]

4. Universality

My findings that extended beyond the Vietnam War included the phenomenon arising in counterinsurgency wars, which of course has been true in Iraq and Afghanistan and beyond.

Another element that extends outward is the experience of young men being able to undergo significant change rather rapidly, and to find meaning in the meaninglessness of their war, even as they were still fighting it.

And also in universal terms, we could recognize the principle that war begets war. One direction of collective survivor meaning in relation to Vietnam was that we had to reverse the outcome.

5. Social Directions of Healing

But there is an alternate survivor meaning for Vietnam—that of the meaninglessness of war—at least as expressed by anti-war veterans. (*Instead of simply trying to express meaning, that is, one attempts to express meaninglessness.*) This basis for an anti-war movement has always been known, beginning with Homer's *Iliad*, where there are constant voices questioning whether all of the pain and suffering is justified.

Our observations on the atrocity-producing situation in Vietnam became part of the history of that war. We contribute, however limitedly, to the political version of what is called the "Vietnam syndrome"—the reluctance to become involved in distant counterinsurgency wars. In these ways, healing approaches to veterans are interwoven with healing approaches to our country in general, and in fact the world.

---

27. Lifton actually has formulated over the course of his work a kind of understanding of repetition compulsion on a collective level, as one war leads to another through the attempt to deny the loss of the previous war. And this repetition is entangled with the superpower syndrome as it appeared in the early 21st century.

The Nazi Doctors[28]

1. Nature of the Trauma

With Nazi doctors, one finds oneself self-investigating evil. As scientific researchers, we're uneasy with the word "evil" because of its subjectivity and resistance to quantification. But it would seem that the word is necessary for conveying sustained patterns of maiming, torturing and killing fellow human beings.

My focus in the work was not on the experience of victims and survivors, on which much work had already been done. Rather, I focused on the perpetrators and on the psychological and historical conditions that can call for or facilitate evil. Central to my findings was a pattern of socialization to evil. Most Nazi doctors were not fanatical ideologues—they belonged to the Nazi party and were drawn to Hitler's movement by the promise of revitalization, of renewed strength, that was not just collective and military but individual and psychological. But they did not believe in what I came to see as the Nazi biomedical vision. Hitler's theory, originally stated in *Mein Kampf*, was that the Nordic race was the only culture-creating race that had been dominant until infected and weakened by the Jewish race, a cultural-destroying race. The Jewish influence had to be destroyed for the Nordic race to once again become healthy and strong. That potentially murderous ideology—what I'm calling a biomedical vision—prevailed among Hitler's inner circle, and led to the creation of genocidal institutions such as Auschwitz, so that many, if not all, of the Nazi government's war-making murder could be understood as a racially-derived therapeutic project.

The German doctors in Auschwitz came to their behavior by adapting to that institution. I call this pattern a "socialization to evil," which starts with adapting to the Nazi regime, to the Nazified medical profession, and to the SS hierarchy in the town. It developed in Auschwitz what I have come to call a malignant normality. Thus, it was normal and expected and routine for German doctors in Auschwitz to send the great majority of Jews to the gas chambers and at times to perform fatal phenol injections on prisoners.

Nazi doctors used two defense mechanisms to do what they did: certainly psychic numbing, which meant setting up a mental barrier between self and behavior so that the behavior was blocked out, kept from registering psychologically in the mind of the perpetrator. The other mechanism was what I call "doubling"—meaning the creation

---

28. See Lifton 1988.

of a functional second self—so that Nazi doctors could carry through their murderous routine over the course of their week of work in Auschwitz or in Poland (consisting of selections and other activities contributing to the function of the death factory) but they could then go home to Germany for a long weekend or a few days, where they could be an ordinary husband and father. This is close to the psychoanalytic concept of splitting, but doubling emphasizes that each "self" had a functional structure, along with behavioral principles that were ethically at odds with the other self. I consider doubling to be part of the potential human repertoire and a very important source of adaptation or socialization to evil.

One can also observe doubling in victims who, in order to survive, must themselves undergo patterns of extreme numbing and brutalization so that some can say, "I was a different person at Auschwitz."

2. My Own Reactions

There's another experience of research in connection with the most extreme kind of behavior. It has to do with what Erikson called "actuality." I interviewed, on several occasions, a prominent Czech Jewish doctor who had been a prisoner in Auschwitz, where he was revered for the help he offered to fellow prisoners. After Auschwitz, he became a leading authority on survivors and their psychological difficulty with forms of treatment for them. We became friends, and in one of my last talks with him, he said "You know, Bob, I've been at this now for 40 years: first in Auschwitz, and then with survivors. I still can't believe that it really happened, that a group would try to round up all the Jews in Europe to take them to a place to kill them." There is something in one's state of mind that resists that truth as outside of all possibility. This is a protective mechanism for the most extreme and psychologically unacceptable behavior. Of course, one returns all too quickly to the actuality of things. The Nazis killed, Auschwitz was all too real, and I had encountered much of this as a researcher.

Of course, one has dreams that insist upon the reality of what one is studying.[29]

---

29. Lifton talks about the fact that he had nightmares in the first weeks of doing this; when he spoke to Eli Wiesel and said, "I don't know if I can go through with this, I'm having nightmares," Eli Wiesel responded, "Now you're ready to begin." See Caruth 1995.

3. The Mosaic

(Lifton turns to some examples of the historical and cultural effects of the genocide and of the context in which it took place. At one point he turns to an interview with the daughter of the Nazi Christian Wirth, which I summarize below).

Wirth's daughter was, at the time of my interview with her, a woman in her 40s, neither a doctor nor a Nazi, but the daughter of the chief camp doctor who had been told that her father had died in the war, though he had actually killed himself shortly after being taken into custody by the British army. She remembered him warmly, bouncing on his knee as a little girl, and had only recently found out that the bouncing took place in Auschwitz. Intent on trying to understand why her father had been part of what he had been a part of, she asked, "Can a good man do bad things?" Her father's history was that of a conscientious doctor who embraced Nazi ideology intensely. He was sent to Auschwitz to help them with the typhus epidemic, which he did. Horrified by what he saw, his reaction was to decide to bring death to them, which amounted to his setting up a systemized pattern of medicalized killing, insisting that doctors do the selection, performing the selection himself to display his own commitment to the system. That sounds like a twisting of what he thought was going to help people into murder. From letters I was given, love letters to his wife when she was not in Auschwitz, it became clear that family support for his work in Auschwitz gave him the strength to set up the situation of mass murder. Family support, as we know, is usually a good thing, especially in relation to trauma of any kind, but much depends on what the family support was for.

4. Universalization

This involves a malignant normality that includes the role of American doctors and psychologists in the use of torture.

5. Directions of Healing

When I finished my work on Nazi doctors and finally published the book, which was in 1986, I thought to myself that it would be ok if I died the next day. Of course, that was 30 years ago, and I am still going. My feeling then had not only to do with the extreme difficulty of the study, but also with the sense that it added something to collective healing. In an immediate sense, there was the behavior of many prison doctors, Jewish, Polish, and German, who remained healers despite everything in Auschwitz. They helped people to enable them to survive.

But more than that, my sense is that studying evil in nitty-gritty ways in itself suggests that we have alternatives. By exposing the reversal of healing and killing, I believe that one can deepen our sense of genuine healing and our ethical commitment to it. We reinforce our commitment to ethical examination of our behaviorist professionals, of what we do in the world and how it affects other people. The book *Nazi Doctors* has become part of what we call Holocaust literature, and that is a good thing. But it is also part of a broader literature of confrontation of evil in the service of larger social healing—and that, of course, blends the psychological with the political in terms of advocacy and institutions that so affect our work. We can learn from Nazi doctors how not to torture our own prisoners, and how instead to embrace policies and advocacies that enhance human life.[30]

A Few Concluding Thoughts

I think of these four studies as my basic ones on trauma and related matters. Later work tended to revert back to them in various ways. For instance, the study I did in Japan of Aum Shinrikyo in the 90s drew upon my thought-reform study, the Chinese Communism study, in terms of the cult's totalism and extreme apocalypticism; upon my Hiroshima and nuclear weapons work in terms of Aum's obsession with Hiroshima and with nuclearism in general and weapons of mass destruction; upon my Nazi doctors study in connection with Aum doctors who maimed and killed in the cult's interest or blackmailed patients in order to extort cash contributions from them. My point here is that work on the trauma of extreme situations requires both separate focus—each study is specific and particular—and at the same time can interrelate with other studies in the psychology of perpetrators and victims.

What is one's relationship to humankind after bearing witness to such extreme cruelty and evil? After I finished my work with Nazi doctors, some people would ask me, "what do you think of your fellow human now?"—expecting me to say, "not very much." But what I find myself saying is that we can go either way: we are not programmed for evil or for nonviolent behavior. We do have an evolutionary capacity, even genius, for adaptation, which means

---

30. This is something Lifton was publicly involved in confronting, especially in our last war.

sufficient cooperation for survival. Our research on trauma is in the service of that adaptation and survival.

In our research, we seek to apply scientific means of investigation in order to learn about and combat human suffering. But we also bear witness to the destructive behavior and evil causing or contributing to that suffering. We are both scientific investigators and witnessing professionals, and we seek an ethical path that combines those functions. Similarly, we are both scholars who seek knowledge and activists who advocate behavior that does not destroy, but contributes to human life.

To be sure, our influence is modest. Our work does not quickly transform collective violence into universal benevolence. Yet our work counts and contributes to a body of thought and advocacy that adds considerable importance to democratic society.

Our work is, in a sense, always too late: the destructive behavior and the trauma have occurred, the suffering is already there. But in another sense, it is never too late: the healing we struggle to bring about in individual people and in our larger society is always in great need and our efforts are never wasted. To put it more generally, everything counts. I will close with the phrase that has served me through all my work. It is a line from Theodore Roethke, one of America's truly great poets:

"In a dark time, the eye begins to see."

References

Camus, A. *Ni victimes ni bourreaux. In Actuelles: critiques politiques. Tome I: Chroniques.* 1944–1948. Paris: Gallimard.

Carey, M. (1982). Psychological Fallout. *Bulletin of the Atomic Scientists* (Volume 38, No.1).

Caruth, C. (1995). An Interview with Robert Jay Lifton. In Cathy Caruth, ed. *Trauma: Explorations in Memory.* Baltimore: Johns Hopkins University Press.

——— (2006). "Interview with Trauma Pioneer Cathy Caruth," conducted by Aimee Pozorski, in Connecticut Review 28/1.

——— (2017) "A Perverse Quest for Meaning": False Witness in Vietnam and Beyond. *Continuum,* special issue edited by Susannah Radstone and Felicity Collins.

Lifton, R.J. (1961). *Thought Reform and the Psychology of Totalism: A Study of 'brainwashing' in China.* New York: Norton. Reprinted 2014 by Martino Fine Books, Eastford, CT.

——— (1967). *Death in Life: Survivors of Hiroshima.* New York: Random House. Reprinted 1991 by University of North Carolina Press, Chapel Hill.

——— (1968). *Revolutionary Immortality: Mao Tse-tung and the Chinese Cultural Revolution.* New York: Random House. Reprinted in 1976 by Norton, New York.

——— *Beyond Atrocity.* In Richard A. Falk, Gabriel Kolko and Robert Jay Lifton, eds.

——— (1971). *Crimes of War: A Legal, Political-Documentary, and Psychological Inquiry into the Responsibility of Leaders, Citizens, and Soldiers for Criminal Acts in Wars.* New York: Random House.

——— (1973). *Home from the War: Learning from Vietnam Veterans.* New York: Simon and Schuster. Reprinted most recently in 2005 by Other Press, New York.

——— (1979). *The Broken Connection: On Death and the Continuity of Life.* New York: Basic Books.

——— (1988). *The Nazi Doctors: Medical Killing and the Psychology of Genocide.* New York: Basic Books. Reprinted by Basic Books in 2000.

————— (1999). *Destroying the World to Save It: Aum Shinrikyo, Apocalyptic Violence, and the New Global Terrorism.* New York: Henry Holt.

————— (2003). *Superpower Syndrome: America's Apocalyptic Confrontation with the World.* New York: Nation Books.

Shay, J. Moral Injury. (2014). *Psychoanalytic Psychology* (Volume 31, No. 2).

Repeating the Past in Pathology and Theory: Practical Suggestions for the Field of Traumatic Stress

Harold Kudler

Duke University

Author Note

Adjunct Associate Professor

Department of Psychiatry and Behavioral Sciences

Duke University

Chief Consultant, Mental Health Services

United States Department of Veterans Affairs*

Harold.Kudler@VA.GOV

*These remarks represent the personal views of the author rather than those of the Department of Veterans Affairs

Harold Kudler

Abstract

In trauma theory, as in the pathology of trauma, repetition rules. Certain core ideas and disagreements have defined more than a century of research and clinical effort. This chapter will put Traumatology, itself, on the couch in order to determine whether a careful analysis of the sometimes frustrating cyclic progress that has characterized the field might also serve to elucidate its underlying dynamics: biological, psychological and social. Persistent ideas and competing metaphors will be traced back to common elements in an effort to uncover and articulate fundamental principles of trauma. Once understood, these will be offered as the foundation for greater conceptual clarity and new opportunities in research and practice.

Repeating the Past in Pathology and Theory:
Practical Suggestions for the Field of Traumatic Stress

"The past is never dead. It's not even past."

William Faulkner

Faulkner's observation provides the theme for this discussion of the status of traumatic stress research, which can only be fully understood and projected into the future if we pay attention to our past.

Another, much older observation on progress in medicine by one of the founders of empirical science is also pertinent:

"Medicine is a science which hath been [...] more professed than laboured, and yet more laboured than advanced: the labour having been, in my judgment, rather in circle than in progression. For I find much iteration, but small addition."

Sir Francis Bacon (1605)

Bacon's remark is more of a rebuke. He suggests that medicine advances in circles rather than straight lines. This observation remains valid, but I think there may be an equally valid excuse for medicine, its researchers, and its practitioners: medicine, like all sciences, attempts to describe nature. And, as an applied science, medicine seeks to use that knowledge to promote health. But natural processes and the foci of medical studies tend not to be linear but, rather, are cyclic and dynamic. As an example, consider the complex feedback loops and multiple, interacting cascades involved in the physiology of the hypothalamic-pituitary-adrenal axis (just one of the many biological systems studied by researchers in psychological trauma and considered essential to its understanding). Therefore, I hope that medicine (and, in this case, the field of traumatic stress) can be forgiven if its advances fail to be simple linear progressions.

Still, as workers in the field of psychological trauma, we need to ask ourselves how best to attain advancement rather that circular reiteration. Santayana (1905) warned that "Those who cannot remember the past are condemned to repeat it." Another possible explanation for our circular tendencies in the field of traumatic stress may reflect a core human dynamic: it can be very difficult to remember your own past. One of the problems with remembering the past is that history, like nature, is dynamic and can't be reduced to straight lines even if we'd prefer them.

Such problems may only deepen and reticulate when humans try to work together, even when they do so under the banner of science or of medicine. Experience demonstrates that personal dynamics are often the most powerful and that they operate on multiple levels:

- Dynamics of the patient, his/her family and community
- Dynamics between patient and clinician
- Dynamics between mental health professionals
- Dynamics between clinicians and researchers
- Dynamics between studies in different systems (functions vs. structures) and at different levels
- Dynamics between followers of different disciplines/ perspectives/schools
- Just plain people being people

Just as dreams reflect the complex interaction of the neuropsychological systems that combine to produce them (Reiser, 1990), medical models mirror interactions and tensions (often intergenerational) which, as documented in Paul de Kruif's *Microbe Hunters* (1926), sometimes oppose and sometimes provoke discovery.

In considering our plight as traumatologists, it seems wise to start out by admitting that we can't advance human understanding without involving humans or approach the complexity of human biology and human experience simultaneously even if, as scientists, we would like to isolate the object of our study and control all known variables. For these reasons, we are stuck with dynamics, biological, personal, and social, for better *and* for worse. Because the tasks of remembering history and of making progress in medicine are as complexly layered and highly dynamic as are physiology, the structure and function of the brain, and the interactions among our thoughts, feelings and social systems, this discussion will, of necessity, range back and forth across time, people, systems and ideas in order to describe and contextualize the status of our field and articulate paths forward.

My own career has a certain cyclical relationship to the field of psychological trauma, so I'd like to begin with a personal history if only to lay out my biases. My experience in the field of psychological trauma began with my residency rotation in psychiatry at West Haven VA Medical Center in July 1980. My first Chief of Service was Dr.

Paul Errera, a psychiatrist who had, himself, begun his career as a first-year resident at that same VA medical center. Later, I was lucky enough to follow his career path to Washington where he served for nearly a decade as the lead physician for VA Mental Health. Although Paul taught us a great deal about the technical aspects of psychopathology and treatment, his key lesson was that psychiatry was about what happened within and between people, and that psychiatrists and other caregivers were just as human as the patients they sought to treat.

My first psychotherapy supervisor at West Haven was Dr. Art Blank, who was also a key organizer of the Trauma conference. Art had served as U.S. Army psychiatrist in Vietnam and introduced us to the concept of Vietnam Stress Syndrome as kind of shadow curriculum within the traditional syllabus. In that early phase of my psychiatric experience, most teachers and most of my fellow residents seemed to believe that the veterans we were treating were no different in their psychiatric problems from any patient we might encounter across town in the university hospital or community mental health center. They were simply in VA because they happened to have access to that system (as if it were their form of insurance). My training by Paul and Art helped me to grasp the then radical idea that, just maybe, the mental health problems which brought veterans to our wards and clinics might have something to do with the fact that they were veterans who had experienced massive psychological trauma in the course of military service. This made them unique indeed!

The third edition of the *Diagnostic and Statistical Manual of Mental Disorders* of the American Psychiatric Association (*DSM III, 1980*) was published a few months after my start at the West Haven VA. *DSM III* contained the first iteration of PTSD as a mental disorder. It established the diagnosis of PTSD while asserting an "atheoretical," descriptive approach as part of a new effort to "medicalize" mental health. Medicalization was another way of saying that, in order to progress, psychiatry needed to move past the dominant psychoanalytic premises of the time and recast itself in what many believed to be the more discrete and testable hypotheses of biology. The hope was that, through the compromise of dropping theoretical concepts in the psychiatric nomenclature and focusing on observable elements of mental disorders, it would be possible to improve the validity and accuracy of diagnoses as a foundational step in improving the treatment of those conditions.

New diagnostic nomenclatures tend to emerge at pivotal moments in history: not just in the history of science but in *national* history. The history of war has played a significant role in their timing. The first nationally accepted psychiatric nomenclature was *The Statistical Manual for the Use of Institutions for the Insane* (1918). This manual was developed by the National Committee for Mental Hygiene under the leadership of Thomas Salmon, M.D.. Salmon not only directed the National Committee for Mental Hygiene—a collaboration of leading consumers, family and community members, academics, practitioners, government agencies, and other stakeholders in the mental health of the nation—but he was also just returning from service as senior psychiatric consultant to General Pershing's American Expeditionary Forces in Europe in 1918 as World War I ended. The *Manual* met a key need of veterans as they dispersed to communities across the nation. Up until that time, there was no common language in which to frame or treat the mental health problems with which these Veterans were returning home.

The National Committee for Mental Hygiene continued to co-publish the *Statistical Manual* with the American Psychiatric Association (APA) until the APA published *DSM I* in 1952. *DSM I*, championed by the Army's lead psychiatrist in WWII, General William Menninger, was derived from the Army's manual of mental disorders, which had been developed to ensure that, no matter where in the world a service member or veteran might develop a mental disorder, there would be a common language to identify the problem and, hopefully, a common clinical understanding and therapeutic response.

These cyclic innovations in framing mental disorders shared similar motivations, yet they produced strikingly different ways of understanding and approaching mental health and illness. Recently, the National Institutes of Mental Health (NIMH, 2016) have encouraged a new, more neuroscientific approach:

> … research that seeks to define the neural bases of complex behaviors and mental illnesses. Because it is often difficult to foresee where significant, high-impact scientific advances are likely to emerge, NIMH will continue to support a wide range of research, including discovery-based and hypothesis-driven studies …

Research priority areas are identified within each of the following three strategies:

1.1: Describe the molecules, cells, and neural circuits associated with complex behaviors

1.2: Identify the genomic and non-genomic factors associated with mental illnesses

1.3: Map the connectomes [comprehensive maps of neural connections in the brain] for mental illnesses

NIMH emphasizes that "These research topics are not intended to be exhaustive," but still leans heavily on the idea of defining mental disorders in biological terms as a basis for scientific and clinical progress in psychiatry, replacing the more clinical and descriptive *DSM*.

Concurrent with the release of *DSM III* (and its inclusion of PTSD), was a rising awareness of post-deployment mental health issues among Vietnam veterans. Just as VA Medical Centers (VAMCs) began to embrace the *zeitgeist* of medicalizing mental health by recasting it in discrete biological terms, the Vet Center program (officially, Readjustment Counseling Service or RCS) was designed to engage veterans on their own terms: personal, family, and community. What was most innovative (and what remains most effective) about the Vet Center program is its insistence on approaching the mental health problems of veterans and their families in terms of their military experience and culture. Of note, Art Blank became the first National Director of the Vet Center Program soon after I trained under him at West Haven. The Vet Centers, now under the direction of an Iraq War veteran, continue to provide a critically important pathway for veterans of Vietnam and of other combat operations before and since.

To this day, clinicians, administrators and, most important, veterans and their families often segregate to either VA medical centers or the Vet Centers. Might this reflect the underlying tension of a conceptual bifurcation (medicalizing vs. personalizing) in American psychiatry's approach to psychological trauma? If so, then it is essential to point out that veterans and their families seem to sort themselves along divergent paths that originate within the internal conflicts of the field of psychological trauma. Must our paths bifurcate? Not necessarily—but the fact that they *do* points to an underlying dynamic which we will return to later.

Even though the vast bulk of current PTSD research is couched within biological, cognitive, and behavioral terms, it's important to remember that the establishment of PTSD as a diagnosis and the Vet Center model both derive from the work of psychoanalysts/psychiatrists Chaim Shatan and Robert J. Lifton. Both were invited by members of Vietnam Veterans Against the War to observe "rap groups" in which veterans provided peer-to-peer support and understanding long before mental health professionals were even aware that there were significant problems to discuss. Shatan and Lifton recognized an evident psychiatric disorder and argued for its recognition by APA. They also brought attention to the value of peer groups as a means of readjustment and emphasized the importance of sharing personal perceptions, understandings, and responses in recovery from trauma.

The work of Lifton and Shatan aligned well with the contemporary efforts of their colleague, Henry Krystal. Krystal, a psychoanalyst/psychiatrist who was also a concentration camp survivor, convened workshops on late sequelae of overwhelming experiences resulting in the 1968 publication, *Massive Psychic Trauma*. His 1988 book *Integration and Self Healing* suggests that psychological trauma overwhelms the mind/brain's capacity to employ affects as useful signals. This was an important extension of Freud's theory of signal anxiety which, in essence, says that once anxiety can no longer flexibly mobilize defense, the psyche becomes incapable of managing new experiences or processing old ones. The survivor is left without words for feelings, a condition Krystal called "alexithymia."

Within Krystal's formulation, psychological trauma occurs at the interface between the individual and the environment. Trauma distorts that interface, making it difficult to keep the outside world out or the internal psychological world in. Worse yet, there is no reliable communication between the two. One can think of PTSD as the clinical expression of this mind/brain dilemma. Dr. Krystal's son, John Krystal, a leader in PTSD research, also focuses on signaling systems in traumatic stress, but he pursues them at the level of neurobiology through the glutamate system. Glutamate, a message-carrying molecule, is the most important and prevalent of the excitatory neurotransmitters. Since the 1980s, John Krystal has been thinking about PTSD in terms of disruption in the brain's capacity to appropriately manage signals. This has led him to study ketamine, an N- methyl-D-aspartate (NMDA) glutamate receptor antagonist, as a potential treatment for PTSD.

One of ketamine's effects is an increase in neuroplasticity. Krystal suggests that PTSD may, at least in part, reflect a loss of neuroplasticity: "Where the brain is concerned, sometimes in order to get better, it is necessary to restore the capacity of the neural circuit to remodel itself. Sometimes it is the deficit in that capacity—neuroplasticity—that is part of what we think of as the illness. In the case of stress disorders, we've learned that traumatic stress can cause the retraction of knob-like input centers called dendritic spines, which are the places where signals come into nerve cells. This is particularly true in glutamate neurons in the brain." Dr. Krystal points out that there is evidence of spine retraction in symptoms seen in stress and anxiety disorders, including impaired memory function and impaired capacity to learn to respond to stressors in new and therapeutic ways. "If your capacity for neuroplasticity is impaired, in other words, the capacity of these networks to learn and adapt is compromised." (Brain & Behavior Research Foundation, 2011).

If we conceive of PTSD as a pathological alteration of brain circuitry (which has already been suggested by anatomical and functional neuroimaging), then increasing neuroplasticity might facilitate the creation (or, perhaps, the re-creation) of adaptive neural pathways which could resolve the problem. Transcranial Magnetic Stimulation is also hypothesized to alter the activity of different brain circuits and, possibly, to increase neuroplasticity in order to re-tune or re-route dysfunctional brain circuits (such as might exist post-trauma) in ways complementary to ketamine's purported effects.

If this is, in fact, the therapeutic mechanism of these more biological approaches to the treatment of psychological trauma, it is also well in line with Eric Kandel's (1979) early intimation of neuroplasticity within the context of psychotherapy:

> "… I would argue that it is only insofar as our words produce changes in each other's brains that psychotherapeutic intervention produces changes in patients' minds. From this perspective, the biologic and psychologic approaches are joined." (p. 1037)

These considerations may provide a practical step towards synergy in our theories and treatments. Perhaps a neurochemical intervention (ketamine), a transcranial magnetic intervention (TMS), and talk therapy all act on the same essential pathology: a loss of normal signal processing secondary to psychological trauma, resulting in a residual pathological response to external and internal stimuli. Further, we could understand a common mechanism of treatment: restitution of flexible, adaptive signal processing through the development of new neural networks/connections/facilitations with consequent therapeutic effect on thought, feelings, and interpersonal relations. If all of these superficially disparate approaches act by engaging the same brain capacity for neuroplasticity (a capacity which even neuroscience has only just begun to appreciate), then they only differ in their route of approach. Our task as clinicians could then be framed as coming to understand our patients and their preferences well enough to know which approach best fits each individual.

In saying this, I want to emphasize that this conception does not diminish the importance of the mind. It simply supplies a common denominator (altered signal processing and the need to stimulate therapeutic neuroplastic repair) in order to advance the dialectic between mind and brain that, up until now, has been more inclined towards circular reiteration than progression.

One proof of concept would be in applying this approach to other facets of research and clinical work with survivors of psychological trauma, to see if it would fit there as well. In recent years, studies have demonstrated posttraumatic epigenetic changes in trauma survivors that may be passed along to offspring (Yehuda, 2009). This intriguing discovery indicates that Lamarck (1809) may have been partially correct in his theory of the inheritance of acquired characteristics.

While many in the field may view epigenetic changes as actual wounds in the genetic code of individuals and their descendants, it is equally reasonable to consider that these discrete genetic changes may be part of a cascade of adaptive responses to trauma, meant to reset signal processing of mind and brain in a "fast track" evolutionary response to an overwhelming experience in a dangerous world. Such consideration extends the concept of neuroplasticity to the level of protein transcription underlying neuroanatomic and functional interactions of neurons at synaptic and even sub-cellular levels. Epigenetics is only one new perspective on the mechanism(s) underlying psychological trauma, its persistent effects, and potential treatment approaches. The value of proposing altered signal processing as a common mechanism for the pathophysiology and persistent clinical effects of psychological trauma is that it provides a unifying approach, stimulates new research ideas, and opens new opportunities to explore novel therapeutic approaches.

Curiously enough (and in keeping with the theme of this chapter), the core ideas expressed above in 21st-century terms were already represented in Freud's 1895 *Project for a Scientific Psychology*. That title for this radical essay (which wasn't published until 1950, more than a decade after Freud's death) was provided by his translator, James Strachey. Freud's own title was *Psychology for Neurologists*; and his aim was to build a solid foundation capable of supporting the study of hysteria within the context of his experience, professional identification, and ambitions as a neurologist and neuroscientist.

Freud's conception of psychopathology as a disruption of neural networks is best represented by the schematic in Figure 1, which was drawn in his own hand.

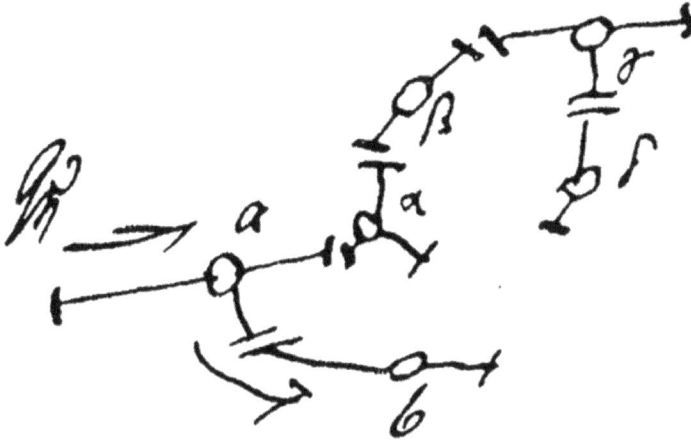

Figure 1. Figure 14 in Freud's Project (p. 323)

In order to approach an understanding of the clinical presentation of hysteria, Freud tried to apply the terms of contemporary neuroscience. He understood the mind/brain system as an evolutionary and individual effort to remain resilient in the face of stress. He therefore hypothesized that humans had evolved neural systems for managing the toxic "unpleasure" associated with traumatic experiences. The interactions of these systems underlay the psychological phenomenology of traumatic neuroses. In much the same way that Henry and John Krystal would later postulate their respective approaches, Freud believed that an overwhelming stressor could alter the connections of mind/brain systems such that normal processing becomes unavailable, resulting in persistent posttraumatic biological and psychological changes. This, then, is the central idea that the field of psychological trauma has spent a century circling around.

In considering Figure 1, the lower loop describes the path of traumatic anxiety. Freud conceived this as the direct path which a "hostile" perception or memory, represented as **Qή**, can take to produce noxious "unpleasure" in the psychic system. The upper loop demonstrates how a neural network can serve to modify the passage of a powerfully toxic experience or memory—and thus succeed in preventing the mind/brain from becoming overwhelmed. Freud suggested that this upper loop could be overwhelmed and altered or even deactivated by massive psychic trauma.

There is value in letting Freud speak for himself on this subject (p. 323 of the Project):

Inhibition of this kind is, however, a decided advantage to [the psychic system]. Let us suppose that a is a hostile mnemic image [memory] and b a key-neurone [sic] to unpleasure. Then, if a is awakened, primarily unpleasure would be released, which would perhaps be pointless and is so in any case [if released] to its full amount [which would overwhelm the mind and brain]. With an inhibitory action from α [the upper loop] the release of unpleasure will turn out very slight and the nervous system will be spared the development and discharge of Q [the toxic quantum of traumatic stress], without any other damage. It is easy now to imagine how, with the help of a mechanism which draws the ego's attention to the imminent fresh cathexis [pull] of the hostile mnemic image, the ego can succeed in inhibiting the passage [of the psychological trauma, Q] from a mnemic image to a release of unpleasure by a copious side-cathexis which can be strengthened according to need. Indeed, if we suppose that the original Qή release of unpleasure is taken up by the ego itself, we shall have in it itself the source of the expenditure which is required by the inhibiting side-cathexis from the ego. In that case, the stronger the unpleasure, the stronger will be the primary defense.

Despite valuable nuggets still to be mined in the *Project*, there were many flaws in Freud's early conceptual model. For example, in 1895, cutting-edge neuroscience understood the nervous system in terms of a reflex arc (Kudler, 1989). If you look back at Figure 1, you can easily substitute a tap on the knee for the quantum of psychic trauma, **Qή**. The neural circuit (and the patient) can either perceive the traumatic experience, process it and discharge it (as 19th-century neurologists believed the energy transmitted into the body by a tap on the knee was released back out through the resulting kick) or struggle to repress the response. Freud believed that, should the repressive effort fail to fully contain the traumatic quanta, they would leak out as hysterical symptoms. Freud was trying to understand posttraumatic mental disorders within the laws that govern the conservation of energy. Within this view, hysterical symptoms were "powered" by a quantum of energy that could neither be entirely expressed (because of the attendant pain that would accompany the full expression of traumatic perception or memory into consciousness) nor released back into the external world through direct action. It would, instead, have to reside in repressed, unconscious form, which could, when triggered by reminders, act as an irritant. It becomes easy to understand that, at this point in his thinking, Freud understood abreaction as quite literally releasing excessive neural energy in order to restore homeostatic balance in the mind/brain system.

Because Freud couldn't see beyond a series circuit model of nervous function (the reflex arc), he could not understand how the same neural circuit could accurately retain past memories while processing new ones. On the other hand, he could not accept the idea that established memory would be overwritten by each new experience. This was the rock upon which his *Project* foundered. Freud didn't realize that the brain might function in parallel neural networks managing different memories and responses to them within multiple, neuroplastic connections and adaptive levels of facilitation rather than in simple arcs. Further, even though the idea was already nascent in his *Figure*, he had not made the leap to understanding neurons as signal transmitters rather than simple conduits for energy that had to be passed from perceptual to motor systems in order to observe the laws of thermodynamics. Had he done so, the course of psychology and neuroscience might have been very different. Instead, Freud shelved his *Neurology for Psychologists* and accepted a position now known as *Dualism*, which held that psychological and biological systems function as an integrated whole, which could not (as yet) be studied in an integrated fashion (Gay, 1988). It is only recently that new technologies and fresh discoveries have enabled new conceptualizations that once again offer the promise of integrating the study of mind and brain.

Given that these concepts have been around for more than a century, it would be to everyone's advantage for modern workers in the field of psychological trauma to find new ways to talk with one another about them—and new ways to translate shared concepts into clinical interventions. Leon Eisenberg (1986) decried a shift (I would amend that to a cyclic oscillation) from a brainless psychiatry to a mindless one. Can we progress as a field from splitting to synergy? If we are to understand and advance our field, we need to re-examine our history and our basic concepts. We also need to remember that neither science nor medicine is a competitive sport.

Further, we need to appreciate that, while they are intimately connected and frequently overlapping domains, science and medicine are not the same thing. Sharp focus and scrupulous control of variables are required in science, but when we apply our findings to the care of an individual human being or to the development of systems of care, we need to accept and think in more complex terms. Otherwise, we will continue to fall into the unproductive pattern of reiteration in medicine that Bacon chided us about centuries ago.

References

American Psychiatric Association & National Committee for Mental Hygiene (1918). *Statistical Manual for the Use of Institutions for the Insane.* New York: National Committee for Mental Hygiene.

———— (1952). Diagnostic and Statistical Manual of Mental Disorders (1st ed.). Washington, DC.

———— (1980). Diagnostic and Statistical Manual of Mental Disorders (3rd ed.). Washington, DC.

Bacon, F. (1605). *The Advancement of Learning.* In James Spedding, Robert Ellis and Douglas Heath (Eds.), The Works of Francis Bacon (1887–1901), Vol. 3, 373. *http://www.worldcat. org/title/works-of-francis-bacon-volume-3-philosophical-works-3/oclc/889954859/viewport.* Accessed June 25, 2017.

Brain & Behavior Research Foundation. (2011). Linking brain and behavior: Gifted researcher advances understanding of the brain's biology that leads to breakthroughs in treatment of anxiety and other disorders. *https://www.bbrfoundation. org/content/linking-brain-and-behavior-gifted-researcher-advances-understanding-brain's-biology-leads.* Accessed June 25, 2017.

De Kruif, P. (1926). *Microbe Hunters.* New York: Blue Ribbon Books.

Eisenberg, L. (1986). Mindlessness and brainlessness in psychiatry. The Eli Lilly Lecture, Winter Quarterly Meeting. Royal College of Psychiatrists, London, 21 January 1986. *British Journal of Psychiatry* 148: 497–508.

Freud, S. (1895/1950). Project for a scientific psychology. In J. Strachey (translator and Ed.), *The standard edition of the complete psychological works of Sigmund Freud,* Vol. I (pp. 281–391). London: Hogarth Press and the Institute of Psychoanalysis.

Gay, P. (1988). *Freud: A life for our time.* London, England: Norton.

Kandel, E. (1979) Psychotherapy and the single synapse: The impact of psychiatric thought on neurobiologic research. *NEJM* 301(19): 1028–1037.

Kudler, H. (1989). The tension between psychoanalysis and neuroscience. *Psychoanalysis and Contemporary Thought,*

12:599–617.

Krystal, H. (1968). *Massive Psychic Trauma*. New York: International Universities Press.

——— (1988) *Integration and Self Healing: Affect, Trauma, Alexithymia*. Hillsdale, N.J.: Analytic Press.

Lamarck, J.B. (1809). *Philosophie zoologique: ou Exposition des considérations relative à l'histoire naturelle des animaux*. Dentu et L'Auteur, Paris.

National Institutes of Mental Health (Updated September, 2016). Research Priorities for Strategic Objective 1. *https://www.nimh.nih.gov/about/strategic-planning-reports/strategic-research-priorities/srp-objective-1/index.shtml*. Accessed June 25, 2017.

Reiser, Morton F. (1990). *Memory in Mind and Brain: What Dream Imagery Reveals*. Basic Books, New York.

Santayana, G. (1905). *The Life of Reason: Or, the Phases of Human Progress*. Volume 1. New York: Charles Scribner's Sons. (p.224).

Yehuda, R. (2009). The relevance of epigenetics to PTSD: Implications for the DSM-V. *Journal of Traumatic Stress* 22(5):427–434.

Trauma, Neuroscience, and Narratives of Lived Experience

James Griffith

Dept. of Psychiatry and Behavioral Sciences

The George Washington University

Author Note

James L. Griffith, M.D.

Department of Psychiatry and Behavioral Sciences, The George Washington University.

Correspondence concerning this chapter should be addressed to James L. Griffith, M.D., 2120 L Street, NW, Suite 600, Washington, DC 20037 or jgriffith@mfa.gwu.edu

James Griffith

Abstract

Trauma—an event that evokes terror, horror, helplessness, or humiliation, too severely for too long—can produce lasting changes in a person's sense of identity and relatedness with others that extend beyond any specific posttraumatic symptom, such as nightmares of the event. These changes are commonly experienced as "I'm no longer the person I've always known," as a loss of trust in the goodness of other people, or as a sense of alienation from feeling "at home" with others. Existential neuroscience and evolutionary psychology propose that trauma induces a physiological, and potentially reversible, shift in brain information processing that maximizes speed and force of reaction to threat. This shift occurs at the expense of impaired executive functions and person-to-person processes of social cognition. Loss of the latter is reflected in a disabled capacity for creating narratives of personal experience, leading to a sense of fractured identity, alienation from one's familiar world, and inability to bear witness either to one's own suffering and that of others. Recovery from these impacts of trauma upon personhood can begin by strengthening emotion regulation, which enables recovery of executive functions and social cognition. Narrative competencies then can also recover, freshly enabling a sense of being fully human. Contributions that existential neuroscience make toward understanding impacts of trauma upon personhood contrast with common views of neuroscience research as necessarily reductionistic when applied to human experience.

Trauma, Neuroscience, and Narratives of Lived Experience

Trauma—an event that evokes terror, horror, helplessness, or humiliation, too severely and for too long—can produce lasting changes in a person's sense of identity and capacity for relatedness with others that extend beyond any specific posttraumatic symptoms, such as nightmares of the event. The existence of posttraumatic symptoms lay forgotten throughout the middle 20th century but burst into cultural awareness as soldiers returned home from war in Vietnam. After Vietnam, "PTSD" became a household word. PTSD became associated with images of Vietnam veterans jumping into manholes at the sound of a car backfiring, nightmares about combat, and frightening eruptions of violence upon slight provocations. Medical science responded by defining a new psychiatric illness, Posttraumatic Stress Disorder, or PTSD for short (American Psychiatric Association, 2013). As colloquial usage of PTSD spread through American society, there came wide familiarity with its core symptoms- nightmares and intrusive memories as "flashbacks," behavioral avoidance of reminders of the trauma, and hyperarousal, manifested as poor sleep, irritability, and avoidance of bright lights or loud sounds. An expanding psychiatric research literature on PTSD has focused almost entirely upon treatment of these core symptoms (Friedman, Keane, & Resick, 2014).

Posttraumatic Stress Disorder

Exposure to Threatened Death, Injury, or Sexual Assault Leaves Chronic Symptoms—

- Re-Experiencing Symptoms— Nightmares, Intrusive Memories
- Behavioral Avoidance— Constricted lifestyle avoids contact with reminders of trauma
- Emotional Numbness— Detached, "empty"
- Hyperarousal— Irritability, Intolerance of bright lights or loud noise, Light and fragmented sleep

However, close examination of those who endured traumat-

James Griffith

ic events described a more complex story. In a moment, traumatic events altered some survivors' sense of self and relationships with others in ways that became life-changing. Rather than feeling that "I suffer from symptoms," a traumatized person felt "I'm changed as a person—I no longer recognize who I am." These impacts upon personhood sometimes happened even when residual nightmares, flashbacks, avoidance, and hyperarousal symptoms were insufficient to merit a PTSD diagnosis. Patrick Mondaca (2017), a writer and Iraqi veteran, stated:

> *"I do not have PTSD the way it is traditionally defined. . . . I have sustained an adjustment of my person, of my sense of self, of my relationships, and of what would have been my common surroundings in any peacetime society. This is less a traumatization than it is a casualty of war. It is a detachment from the rest of society— an inability of the soldier to come home completely.*
>
> *Our society is focused on PTSD and the identification of specific occasions of trauma and its treatment. But I am less injured than displaced. I will never belong, most because I have been something that most of my fellow citizens have not been and cannot be: a soldier.*

Even when trauma is severe and intentionally afflicted, as in cases of political torture, the major PTSD symptoms have not necessarily accounted for the greatest suffering. For example, a woman living under a totalitarian government was "disappeared" by secret police, hooded, beaten, and threatened with rape and death. After her release, she stated, "What I feel most when I talk about it is shame. . . . I was in there only 24 hours and that was enough to make me suffer bad nights a long time. I'm no heroine." (Agger, 1992, p. 69). While shame is regarded as expectable after sexual violence, it has puzzled trauma psychotherapists that it can be a prominent *sequela* for most types of traumatic events. Survivors of catastrophes ranging from ship sinkings to wild animal attacks report feelings of alienation and displacement as common *sequelae* of trauma (Gonzales, 2012, p. 4). This shame typically leads to social withdrawal from other people (Rothschild, 2000).

A survey of persons seeking outpatient psychotherapy for posttraumatic stress symptoms, often insufficient to merit a full PTSD diagnosis, collected a sample of comments about the impact of trauma upon their personal lives:

- "I feel strange."

- "I feel buried alive."
- "I felt to blame. I must have done something wrong."
- "I felt betrayed by my city. I always felt safe there."
- "Something was taken from me. I just turned 21, just felt comfortable in my own skin— that was taken from me."

Across all these accounts, a common theme is a persistent sense of alienation, no longer belonging. This "not belonging" suggests that focus of recovery from trauma may need to extend beyond reduction in PTSD symptoms to include restoration of a relational world, both with self and with other people.

Impact of Trauma Upon Person

Beyond Symptoms of PTSD—
- **Broken sense of identity**
- **Loss of sense of living in a trustworthy world**
- **Disappearance of joy**
- **Paradoxical guilt**

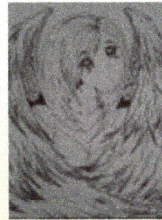

Existential Neuroscience— Trauma Shifts the Brain's Information Processing from New to Old Brain

Existential neuroscience provides a neurobiological perspective for understanding how trauma can so dramatically reconfigure personhood (Iacoboni, 2007). Existential neuroscience studies how functional brain circuits shape a person's subjective experience as that person interacts with a physical world and in relationships with other people (Griffith & Gaby, 2014). A functional brain circuit is a "family" of interconnected brain cells, or neurons, that work together to accomplish a common task, such as focusing attention or holding an item in memory. Intrinsic connectivity networks (ICNs) are large-scale neural networks associated with characteristic functions and behavioral correlates (Spripada, 2012; Hermans, Henckens, Joels, & Fernandez, 2014). ICNs might be likened to a "clan" or "family of families" of functional neural networks that share a common class of functions. Executive functions, social cognition, and emotion regulation are functions of ICNs whose operations can be altered by traumatic experiences (see Figure I). They appear to play central roles in the sense of fractured identity, psychic numbing, or alienation following a traumatic experience.

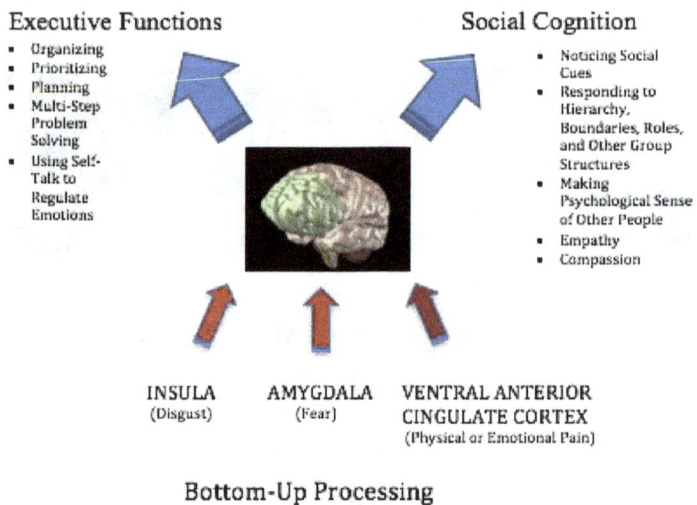

Executive Functions
- Organizing
- Prioritizing
- Planning
- Multi-Step Problem Solving
- Using Self-Talk to Regulate Emotions

Social Cognition
- Noticing Social Cues
- Responding to Hierarchy, Boundaries, Roles, and Other Group Structures
- Making Psychological Sense of Other People
- Empathy
- Compassion

INSULA   AMYGDALA   VENTRAL ANTERIOR
(Disgust)   (Fear)   CINGULATE CORTEX
                                 (Physical or Emotional Pain)

Bottom-Up Processing

FIGURE I. The Prefrontal Cortex and Associated Intrinsic Connectivity Networks (ICN's)

Over the past two decades, an enormous amount of neuroscience research has studied how chronic PTSD represents long-term structural changes in the brains of symptomatic individuals. Some of these have been regarded as adaptive biological changes in response to chronic stress, such as expansion in size of the amygdala from fresh growth of dendritic spines and terminal axons. Other changes have been regarded as structural damage from stress effects, such as shrinkage in size of the hippocampus. Delineating these structural changes has contributed to a better understanding of the neurophysiological underpinnings of PTSD symptoms and chronic effects of extreme stress upon brain tissue (Lanius, 2006; Rauch et al., 2000; Bremner et al., 2003).

However, these chronic structural changes in the brain do not account for acute symptoms of trauma from which people typically recover within a few days, such as difficulty concentrating, light sleep, edginess, and a sense of feeling surreal. They also would not account for changes in sense of self and relatedness to the surrounding world that can happen in a moment. Such rapidly occurring and transient changes suggest physiological alterations in the brain's functional state, rather than structural damage to brain tissue. It is as if the brain suddenly shifted gears in its information-processing.

Trauma produces an immediate physiological change in brain state that has been characterized as a shift from "new brain" to "old brain." This shift seems to mark the felt impact of trauma upon a person. Its meaning appears best explained by the biological evolution of the human brain. The dramatic expansion in size of the prefrontal cortex most distinguishes the human brain compared to that of all other animals. Over the course of evolution, the prefrontal cortex expanded from only a small ribbon in lower mammals to nearly 25% of the entire human brain (*see Figure II*) (Kolb 2006). This "new brain" brought to humans its capabilities for executive functions, *i.e.*, planning, organizing, prioritizing, focusing attention, multi-step problem solving, using self-talk to regulate emotional state; as well as social cognition, *i.e.*, the ability to notice social cues, to make psychological sense of other people, to organize cohesive groups; and to experience empathy and compassion for others (Cacioppo & Patrick, 2008). Executive functions and social cognition together made human beings

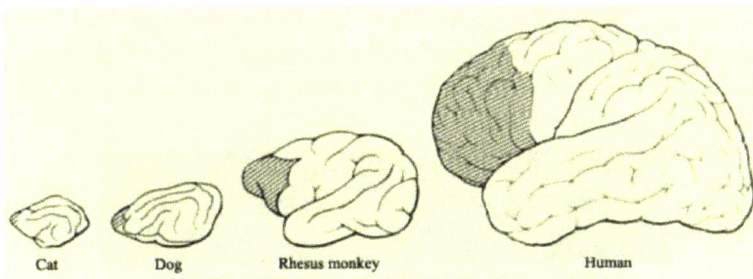

Figure II. Evolution of the Prefrontal Cortex from Cats to Humans

ascendant over other mammals, which might be otherwise stronger, faster, or more agile.

Evolution of the brain proceeded by placing new systems on top of older systems with the latter still operational, analogous to Microsoft Windows' sitting upon the older DOS operating system in a desktop computer. One can still use the old DOS keystroke commands rather than the point-and-click mouse— the latter is more sophisticated, but the key strokes are still there. For the human brain, this layering of operating platforms was significant in that it provided a backup system for the newly evolved prefrontal cortex. Faced with a threat, the prefrontal cortex, relying upon its executive functions and social cognition, would first attempt to problem-solve an impending threat while also reaching out to other people for assistance. However, the prefrontal cortex had two major vulnerabilities, one functional and the other structural, both leaving situations when older systems might preferably take command. Functionally, prefrontal cortex had a slower processing speed. The more complex operations of executive functions took time, which could be problematic in a life-and-death emergency when time was of the essence. Structurally, the prefrontal cortex would become the most vulnerable region of the brain for instability under extreme stress (Arnsten, 2009; Arnsten, Mazure, & Sinha, 2012). When flooded by an incoming burst of information from subcortical alarm systems, the prefrontal cortex would go off-line. Combined, these two drawbacks meant that the "new brain" functioned optimally during emotional quietude, but could shut down under conditions of extreme stress, and older limbic and basal ganglia systems would then need to take over crisis management. These older systems would produce either a rapid fight-or-flight attempt to escape, or, when trapped, a freeze response that would mimic death, presumably in the hope that a predator would lose interest. The prefrontal cortex was located at the front of the brain, while these older systems were located towards the back of the brain. Researchers using functional brain imaging have documented how a front-to-back shift in brain metabolic activity occurs in response to a traumatic event.

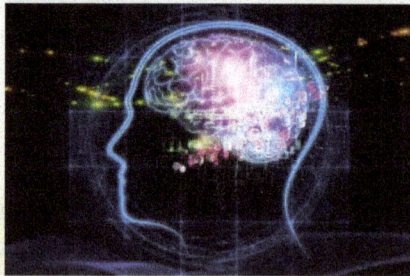

Existential Neuroscience: Trauma Shifts From New to Old Brain

However, this front-to-back shift in brain activation also re-shuffled which functional brain circuits could figure prominently in information processing and which would be relegated to the background. A review of this re-ordering takes a first step towards explaining how trauma can change so dramatically a person's sense of self:

- Implicit Cognitive Processes Become Dominant— "Implicit" describes cognitive processes that are rapid, automatic, and operating largely outside conscious awareness. These include attention, memory, pattern recognition, and emotional reactions to events. Importantly, implicit memory codes memories of body sensations, emotions, and mood. Extreme stress, such as a traumatic event, strengthens the efficiency and durability of implicit memories. These implicit memories become the nightmares and flashbacks of PTSD (Siegel, 2012).

  "Explicit" cognitive processes utilize volition and conscious awareness, but are slower. Explicit cognitive processes include narrative memories, logical analysis, and focusing concentration upon one item at a time. Explicit memory, which codes memories in language as narratives, is suppressed by extreme stress.

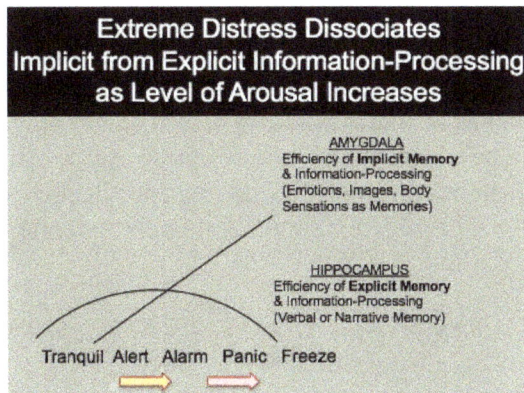

Mr. Kasim, for example, was a college professor who survived imprisonment and torture in a Middle Eastern country due to his family's political activities. Seeking treatment for nightmares and anxiety, he told about a problem that puzzled him. "Any time I see someone in a uniform, a policeman or even a fireman, I start running— but I don't know why. It makes no sense." Mr. Kasim's flight from a fireman represented implicit memories of uniformed police in his country of origin, but disconnected from any particular narrative memory that would give it context.

Less extreme, transient illustrations of stress-related impairment of explicit memory are common in everyday life. For example, Ms. Whitaker and her partner were both highly successful professionals who sought couple therapy due to conflicts in their relationship. Both couple partners grew frustrated with the couple therapy, because neither could clearly describe the back-and-forth interactions that became angry arguments. Each could only remember how it felt and a few angry statements that stood out. When consumed with anger, both partners lost capacities for narrative memory.

• Relating to Other People as Group Members, Not as Individual Persons— Categorical social cognition supports relatedness to others based only upon signs of group membership, *e.g.,* skin color, accent, other physical features that mark racial, ethnic, religious, gender, or socioeconomic group membership. Categorical social cognition appears to have evolved as a rapid detection system for ascertaining who is a safe in-group member or potentially unsafe out-group member (Griffith & Kohrt, 2016).

A second social cognition system, person-to-person social cognition, is slower but can apprehend unique features of individuals one person at a time. Person-to-person social cognition, but not categorical social cognition, can attune empathically with other people. Person-to-person social cognition is suppressed by the extreme stress of trauma (Griffith & Kohrt, 2016).

Trauma Produces Shift from Person-to-Person to Categorical Social Cognition

John Cacioppo's social neuroscience research program at the University of Chicago has studied how empathy and accuracy of social judgments both rely upon intact emotion regulation. Traumatized persons lose emotional awareness of others, resulting in more frequent *faux pas* in social settings and failures of empathy in relationships (Cacioppo & Patrick, 2008). This also happens at population levels. Nationally, the September 11 terrorist attacks heralded a transformation within the United States from valuing ethnic diversity as a societal resource to political campaigns against immigrants, Muslims, or other minority groups.

- Loss of Ability to Use Feelings to Monitor Emotional State— Trauma can reduce emotional awareness to the level of raw body sensations and impulses to act. Use of feelings for monitoring emotional states may dissipate, particularly for complex feelings (*e.g.*, wonder or feeling gratified) or blends of feelings (*e.g.*, melancholy, bemusement) (Frewen et al., 2008). Victor Frankl described how he and other prisoners felt no joy when first liberated from the Nazi concentration camp. "Although they passed through fields of flowers, they were unable to form an emotional reaction to them." (Gonzales, 2012, p. 4). Under extreme stress, a person may feel numb or empty, detached and non-reflective about impulses driving actions.

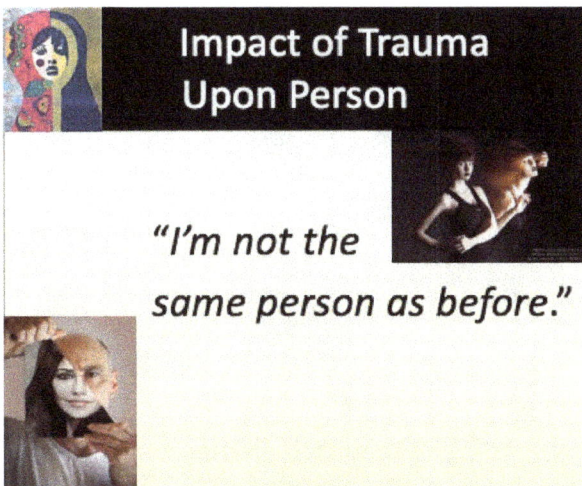

Impact of Trauma Upon Person

"I'm not the same person as before."

- Loss of Creativity, Self-Reflection, and Clarity of Identity—

The default mode network is the resting state of the brain, which shows slow, rhythmic waves of activation while musing, daydreaming, self-reflecting, or imagining perspectives other people might hold (Raichle, 2010). The default mode network is active only while no goal-directed actions or problem-solving thoughts are in progress. Although seemingly at rest, 80% of the brain's energy expenditures are utilized by the default mode network. The default mode network appears to serve as the primary neural infrastructure for self-experiences. It appears to synchronize other brain systems to be ready to meet expectable demands of the environment. It plays central roles in creativity, self-awareness, and sense of identity. Trauma-induced shifts in the brain's metabolic state disrupt connectivity among the different components of the default mode network (Spripada, 2012). Such loss of connectivity has been postulated to produce impaired awareness of self. Detachment or a sense of alienation may be a result. For example, a Marine captain had survived three tours of duty in Iraq and numerous firefights, killing enemy fighters, and experiencing close encounters with death. After rejoining his U.S. family and community, he felt as if "I'm without my compass." He lacked major symptoms of PTSD, such as nightmares or avoidant behaviors. However, he felt overly controlled, detached, lacking any deep desires, and uncertain of a direction for his life.

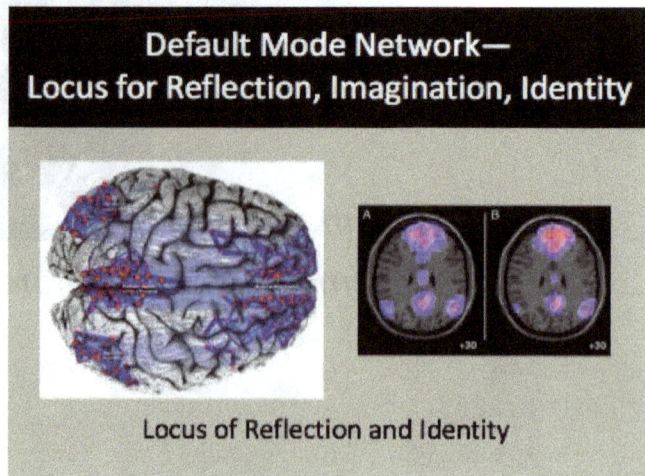

Default Mode Network—
Locus for Reflection, Imagination, Identity

Locus of Reflection and Identity

Collectively, such shifts in relative dominance of the brain systems appear to have held survival value by speeding reactions to threats in crisis situations and heightening their force. Minimal information would be required prior to acting. Cognition would be stripped to a perceived threat (alarm) that triggers an emotion (fear) and a motor response (fight-or-flight). From a neurobiological perspective, trauma broadly re-sets the brain for survival in an unsafe world (Spripada, 2012).

The cost of living primed for survival is a loss of richness in one's experience of living due to impairments in the capacity to form complex narratives out of lived experiences. Narratives are the fundamental units of human experience. Inchoate experiences are articulated into language through the telling of narratives (Bruner, 1986; White, 1992). A narrative is more than a factual record of remembered events. A narrative has a plot, characters, context, and a point to be made (Cobb, 2013). Its characters have a landscape of consciousness, consisting of thoughts, feelings, intentions, choices, and identity, as well as a landscape of action, consisting of actions taken in response to a surrounding environment and relationships (Bruner, 1986; White, 1992). Identity can be regarded as a canon of first-person narratives in which oneself is the protagonist.

Composing a narrative requires language, explicit memory, focused attention, and self-reflection. When elemental cognitive processes are impaired, narratives lose complexity and depth of meaning. It is common that a traumatized person recites affectless facts about what happened but misses appropriate feelings or the meaning of what happened. For example, a woman after a rape described being pulled into an alley at knifepoint, then being beaten and sexually assaulted, until dragging herself to a street where she could flag down a taxi. Although her account was factually detailed without gaps in memory, it was told as if a newspaper reporter's third-person account, detached and omitting inferences for how she was personally impacted. When trauma is extreme, explicit memory and language can be shut down entirely, leaving lapses into which disconnected traumatic images and body sensations intrude as nightmares and flashbacks (Rothschild, 2000; Roozendaal, McEwen, & Chattarji, 2009).

An impaired capacity to narrate experience has profound consequences. Meaning cannot be generated from events of daily life. People remain isolated from their own pain. Living in communion with others loses vitality, whether in relationships or communities. As Cobb (2013, p. 27) has commented:

"Separated from narrative, people do not have access to the pro-

duction of meaning; as a result, neither protest nor politics is possible. People are disabled from participation in public deliberation and cut off from the reflective processes through which not only healing but also social mobilization and change are possible."

Loss of narrative competencies has moral consequences. Witnessing requires awareness of a suffering person's emotional experience, as well as self-reflection that juxtaposes that awareness of other with awareness of one's own being. It requires a voiced response to the injured person that acknowledges the meaning of the suffering. It is through the telling of narratives that witnessing occurs. As Agamben (2002, p. 121) has noted: "Human beings are human insofar as they bear witness to the inhuman." Without narratives to give form and meaning to raw experiences, traumatized people can be rendered unable to bear witness to inhumanity that has afflicted either themselves or others. A traumatized person then feels jaded and empty, unable to muster empathy or compassion.

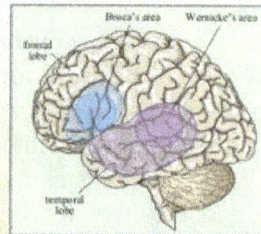

With Trauma, An Event Can Occur That Cannot Be Witnessed

With trauma, neurophysiological impairments appear in systems for—
- Language
- Person-to-Person Social Cognition
- Narrative Memory
- Experiencing complex feelings as expressions of emotion

Existential neuroscience can contribute a physiological perspective to Dori Laub's discussion of trauma as an event that cannot be witnessed (Felman & Laub, 1992). Functional impairment among key brain systems can so disable composition of complex narratives that essential prerequisites for bearing witness are missing.

Existential Neuroscience Can Help Guide Recovery of the Person from Trauma

Existential neuroscience helps explain the sense of fractured identity, numbness, and alienation that trauma can impose. It also helps organize a plan for recovery. There must occur a forward shift in brain metabolic activity so that the prefrontal cortex again comes on line with its executive functions and social cognition that are essential for narrating experience and enabling a social world. As Bloome (2013, p. 133) has summarized:

> *Trauma robs us of whole chunks of our experience, and in doing so, appropriates all or part of our identity. To achieve psychological safety, victims must regain the power of speech, a narrative of memory, and the symphony of modulated feelings that constitutes full humanness.*

Achieving a back-to-front shift in brain metabolic activity is the initial agenda for recovery from trauma. This shift depends upon robust emotion regulation. Emotion regulation is a set of mechanisms whose mission is to keep the level of activation of emotion-generating subcortical networks within a range that protects effective functioning of the prefrontal cortex. Emotion regulation operates in a manner analogous to the cooling system of a motor or the fan blowing over a computer hard drive. A wide variety of potential mechanisms for achieving emotion regulation exist. *Figure III* illustrates six major pathways. Each of these pathways can draw upon literally dozens of cognitive techniques, lifestyle choices, activities, and life practices for keeping emotional intensity within bounds. *Figure IV* displays the dynamic relationship between adequacy of emotion regulation and access to executive functions and social cognition.

Figure III. Strategies for Emotion Regulation

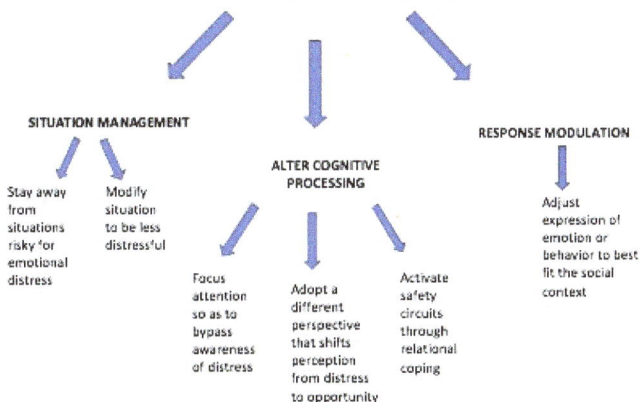

SITUATION MANAGEMENT

RESPONSE MODULATION

ALTER COGNITIVE PROCESSING

Stay away from situations risky for emotional distress

Modify situation to be less distressful

Focus attention so as to bypass awareness of distress

Adopt a different perspective that shifts perception from distress to opportunity

Activate safety circuits through relational coping

Adjust expression of emotion or behavior to best fit the social context

Figure IV. Emotion Regulation and Top-Down Cortical Regulation of Arousal.

Robust Emotion Regulation

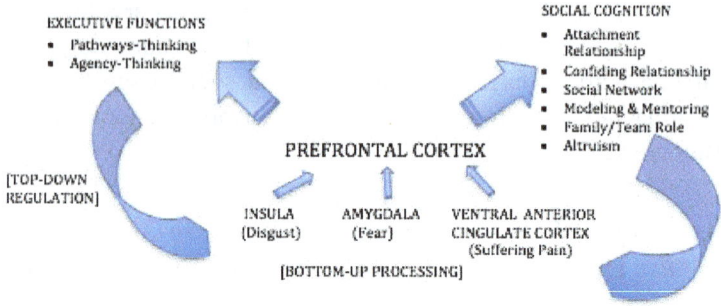

Loss of Emotion Regulation

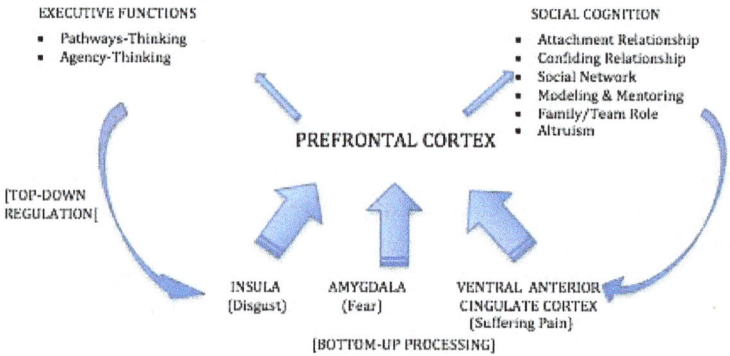

As shown earlier in *Figure I*, sensory information about the external environment and internal body organs is conveyed upward through the brainstem into subcortical systems that activate in response to threat (amygdala), disgust (insula), and physical or emotional suffering (insula and ventral anterior cingulate cortex) (Griffith, 2018). This upward transmission of sensory information is referred to as "bottom-up processing" of information (Hermans, Henckens, Joels, & Fernandez, 2014; Roozendaal, McEwen, & Chattarji, 2009).

This bottom-up sensory processing is regulated in "top-down" fashion by nerve fibers from the prefrontal cortex and dorsal cingulate cortex that descend to inhibit activation of the subcortical systems. Although modest activation of prefrontal cortex can speed information processing and focused attention, excessive activation produces disorganization and loss of prefrontal functioning. As illustrated in Figure IV, it is critically important that top-down regulation by the prefrontal cortex and dorsal cingulate gyrus keep the level of arousal within a workable range (Hermans, Henckens, Joels, & Fernandez, 2014; Arnsten, Mazure, & Sinha, 2012).

There are as many methods for emotion regulation as there are ways that different people use to calm themselves emotionally when afraid, angered, disgusted, or hurting. Shifting focus of attention away from what feels upsetting is a simple but useful technique for moment–to-moment emotion regulation. Spiritual practices, broadly, are methods developed over centuries to restore equanimity through breathing, prayers, recitation of sacred scriptures, or rituals (Griffith & Griffith, 2002). Other people turn to exercise or to repetitive activities that require focused attention, such as knitting or playing a computer game (Gonzales, 2012). Most people turn to relationships to restore emotion regulation.

Three "safety networks" are a particularly potent group of circuits for restoring emotion regulation in the wake of trauma response. These circuits are activated by relational interactions with other people. When activated, they quieten subcortical alarm systems (Eisenberger, 2013):

- A "relief circuit" utilizes information streams from the brain's mirror neuron system to deactivate alarm responses of the amygdala. Mirror neurons are cells in the brain that track facial expressions and hand movements of other people, providing information necessary for making psychological sense of other people. The inner, dorsomedial surface of the prefrontal cortex processes mirror neuron information to determine that protective people are nearby. It then inhibits subcortical alarm responses (Eisenberger, 2013; Hornstein, Fanselow, & Eisenberger, 2016);

- A "maternal caretaking system" is organized around the septal nuclei, hypothalamus, and ventral striatum (Eisenberger, 2013; Eisenberger et al, 2011). When activated by an attachment relationship, the maternal caretaking system inhibits alarm responses within the salience network, while also activating reward systems in the ventral striatum. As result, fear is diminished and approaching the other person feels pleasurable. Evolutionarily designed to connect parents with their young, the system appears adaptable to other relationships as well.

- The "ventral striatum" houses the reward circuitry of the brain (Eisenberger, 2013). The ventral striatum is densely populated with dopamine and opiate receptors. When activated, the gratification is sufficiently intense that fear is overridden.

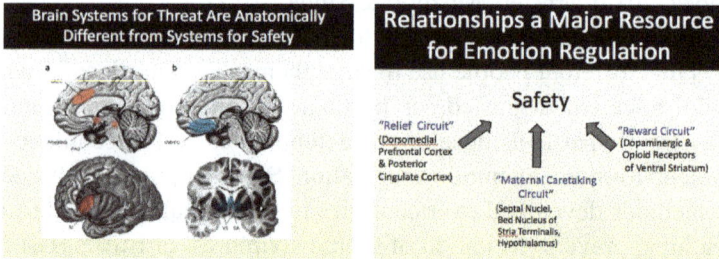

Robust emotion regulation is critical for restoration of memory, language, and self-reflection that are prerequisites for formation of narratives. Narrative competencies are necessary for experiencing life in a richly textured way. They are essential for clarity of sense of self. While there are many mechanisms that provide emotion regulation, activation of the safety circuits may be foremost in their potency.

How People Recover from Traumatized Personhood

This neurobiological map points to pragmatic interventions that can facilitate recovery from trauma. Through education about trauma, a person can learn the significance of numbness and detachment as a clinical condition— a solvable problem, not a representation of reality. This awareness externalizes the trauma by separating its effects from one's sense of self.

A second step is a robust program of emotion regulation using as many arms of *Figure III* as it is possible to employ. Such a program permits a re-stabilized prefrontal cortex to regain its functional status. Committed adherence is required to a program that might include yoga, spiritual practices, and aerobic exercise alongside reconciliation and renewal of important relationships.

A third step is simultaneous engagement of both executive functions (problem-solving, goal-seeking) and social cognition (turning to relationships and groups for support) in an effort to eliminate stressors and reduce threats. Assertive coping, rather than avoidant coping, underpins effective use of executive functions. Assertive coping entails facing and dealing with stressors, rather than avoiding them. It requires envisioning a better future, planning a pathway towards that future, finding do-able steps along that pathway, and holding to a perspective that change is possible. As these steps are taken, a sense of personal agency is enhanced, and fear of an unsafe world is diminished.

Engaging social cognition means taking stock of one's relationships, instituting repairs when needed, and adding new relationships when possible. The aim is never to meet overwhelming stressors alone. There then are multiple relational pathways through which the safety circuits can be activated. First among these are attachment relationships, such as parent-child relationships and love relationships. Presence of an attachment relationship quietens activation of amygdala threat circuits. Other relationships include confiding, family or team roles, social networks, and altruistic relationships.

The final step is self-witnessing and feeling ownership for the return of creativity, self-reflection, person-to-person relationships, and a life organized by rich complex narratives, both those that are lived and those shared in community. As the default mode network regains its efficiency, brain systems can be orchestrated for responding to a safe, more predictable world and with a clear sense of personal identity available for living in that world.

Studies of individuals who have recovered from severe traumas illustrate the initial primacy for emotion regulation strategies that can enable other steps of recovery to follow. These emotion regulation strategies are often idiosyncratic and unique to the individual. They frequently are found through self-discovery. Laurence Gonzales's *Surviving Survival: The Art and Science of Resilience (2012)* provides detailed case studies of individuals who survived life-threatening catastrophes. What is notable in narratives of these individuals' recoveries is the broad variety of emotion regulation strategies that they employed and the uniqueness of each person's preferred methods. For one survivor, it was learning to knit; for another, it was learning to lay bricks; for another it was writing. Most of these emotion regulation strategies originated out of daily life, not trauma psychotherapy by mental health professionals. Relationships with other people and spiritual practices were perhaps the most reliable resources for emotion regulation.

Conclusion

Existential neuroscience and evolutionary psychology tell our human story as a story of executive functions, social cognition, and creative actions that helped human beings compete for survival against reptiles and mammals who were stronger, faster, and often better equipped by bodily armor. The mechanical challenge was how to design a "cooling system" that would keep an overheated prefrontal cortex and default mode network on line despite excessive arousal from stress. Installing multiple redundant mechanisms for emotion regulation provided an answer to stress management for the usual range of stressors during normal times. Trauma results from stressors that lie outside that range. Understanding this physiological vulnerability of the prefrontal cortex and default mode network to extreme stress is key to understanding how trauma impacts one's sense of self and relationships with others. Restoring emotion regulation and activating safety networks are the first steps to recovery.

Neuroscience research has been critiqued as a new positivism that attempts to reduce human experience to physical events within brain tissue. However, understanding brain mechanisms that enable or constrain what language and relationships can create is a non-reductionist approach to psychiatric humanism (Griffith, 2014). It can be argued that language and physiology meet at the level of functional brain circuits. Poetry cannot be reduced to physiological events among the synapses and neurotransmitters of brain circuits. However, a poem cannot be imagined and composed without intact brain circuits for language, memory, attention, and processes of identity and self-reflection. What has not been sufficiently appreciated is that functional integrity of these brain circuits exists along a continuum, and unprotected exposure to stress plays a role in whether brain circuits are more intact or less intact in their functioning. The downstream effects of extreme stress impact core aspects of being human, such as emotional awareness, empathy, compassion, and bearing witness to suffering.

The perspective of existential neuroscience does not replace other clinical perspectives for assessing, formulating, and treating posttraumatic symptoms. It can help explain dramatic alterations in sense of self and relationships with other people that can bring greater distress than the nightmares of PTSD. It contributes to our repertoire of strategies for helping a traumatized person regain a richly experienced sense of being human.

References

Agamben, G. (2002). *Remnants of Auschwitz: The witness and the archive*. Cambridge, MA: Zone Books.

Agger, I. (1992). *The Blue Room: Trauma and testimony among refugee women, a psycho-social exploration.* (M. Bille Trans.). New Jersey: Zed Books Ltd.

American Psychiatric Association. (2013). *Diagnostic and statistical manual of mental disorders, 5th edition: DSM-5.* Washington, DC: American Psychiatric Publishing.

Arnsten, A. (2009). Stress signaling pathways that impair prefrontal cortex structure and function. *Nature Reviews Neuroscience,* 10, 409–421.

Arnsten, A., Mazure, C.M., & Sinha, R. (2012). This is your brain in meltdown. *Scientific American,* 306(4), 48–53.

Bloom, S.L. (2013). *Creating sanctuary: Toward the evolution of sane societies*. New York: Routledge.

Bremner, J.D., Vythilingam, M., Vermetten, E., Southwick, S.M., McGlashan, T., Nazeer, A., & et al. (2003). MRI and PET study of deficits in hippocampal structure and function in women with childhood sexual abuse and posttraumatic stress disorder. *American Journal of Psychiatry,* 160(5), 924–932.

Bruner, J. (1986). *Actual minds, possible worlds*. Cambridge, MA: Harvard University Press.

Cacioppo, J.T., & Patrick, W. (2008). *Loneliness: Human nature and the need for human connection.* New York: W.W. Norton.

Cobb, S. (2013). *Speaking of violence: The politics and poetics of narrative in conflict resolution.* New York: Oxford University Press.

Eisenberger, N.I., Master, S.L., Inagaki, T.K., Taylor, S.E., Shirinyan, D., Lieberman, M.D., & Naliboff, B.D. (2011). Attachment figures activate a safety signal-related neural region and reduce pain experience. *PNAS,* 108(28), 11721–11726.

Eisenberger, N.I. (2013). An empirical review of the neural underpinnings of receiving and giving social support: Implications for health. *Psychosom Med,* 75, 545–556.

Felman, S., & Laub, D. (1992). *Testimony: Crises of witnessing in literature, psychoanalysis, and history.* New York: Routledge.

Frewen, P., Lane, R.D., Neufeld, R.W., Densmore, M., Stevens, T., & Lanius, R. (2008). Neural correlates of levels of emotional awareness during trauma script-imagery in posttraumatic stress disorder. *Psychosomatic Medicine,* 70(1), 27–31.

Friedman M.J., Keane T.M. and Resick P.A. (Eds.) (2014). *Handbook of PTSD: Science and practice.* (Second ed.). New York: Guilford Press.

Gonzales, L. (2004). *Deep survival— who lives, who dies, and why.* New York: W.W. Norton.

———— (2012). *Surviving survival: The art and science of resilience.* New York: W.W. Norton.

Griffith, J. L. (2014). Neuroscience and humanistic psychiatry: A residency curriculum. *Academic Psychiatry,* 38, 177–184.

———— (2018). The hope modules: Brief psychotherapeutic interventions to counter demoralization from daily stressors of chronic illness. *Academic Psychiatry,* 42, 135–145.

Griffith, J.L., & Griffith, M.E. (2002). E*ngaging the sacred in psychotherapy: How to talk with people about their spiritual lives.* New York: Guilford Press.

Griffith, J.L., & Gaby, L. (Nov 28, 2014). Brief psychotherapy at the bedside: using existential neuroscience to mobilize assertive coping when patients are demoralized. *Psychiatric Times,* 1–8.

Griffith, J.L., & Kohrt, B.A. (2016). Managing stigma effectively: What social psychology and social neuroscience can teach us. *Academic Psychiatry,* 40(2), 339–347.

Hermans, E.J., Henckens, M.J., Joels, M., & Fernandez, G. (2014). Dynamic adaptation of large-scale brain networks in response to acute stressors. *Trends in Neurosciences,* 37(6), 304–314.

Hornstein, E.A., Fanselow, M.S., & Eisenberger, N.I. (2016). A safe haven: Investigating social-support figures as prepared safety stimuli. *Psychological Science,* 27(8), 1051–1060.

Iacoboni, M. (2007). The quiet revolution of existential neuroscience. In E. Harmon-Jones, & P. Winkielman (Eds.), *Social neuroscience: Integrating biological and psychological explanations of social behavior.* (pp. 439–453). New York: Guilford Press.

Kolb, B. (2006). Do all mammals have a prefrontal cortex? In J. Kass (Ed.), *Evolution of nervous systems: A comprehensive reference.* (Vol. 3 ed., pp. 443–450). New York: Elsevier.

Lanius, R.A. (2006). A review of neuroimaging studies in PTSD: Heterogeneity of response to symptom provocation. *Journal of Psychiatric Research,* 40(8), 709–29.

Mondaca, P. (February 18, 2017). Not injured by war, but displaced. *The Washington Post,* pp. A17.

Raichle, M.E. (2010). The brain's dark energy. *Scientific American,* 302(3), 44–49.

Rauch, S.L., Whalen, P.J., Shin, L.M., McInerney, S.C., Macklin, M.L., Lasko, N.B., & et al. (2000). Exaggerated amygdala response in masked facial stimuli in posttraumatic stress disorder: A functional MRI study. *Biological Psychiatry, 47(9),* 769–776.

Roozendaal, B., McEwen, B.S., & Chattarji, S. (2009). Stress, memory, and the amygdala. *Nature Reviews Neuroscience,* 10, 423–433.

Rothschild, B. (2000). *The body remembers: The psychophysiology of trauma and trauma treatment.* New York: W.W. Norton.

Siegel, D.J. (2012). Chapter 2: Memory. *The developing mind.* (Second Edition ed., pp. 46–90). New York: Guilford Press.

Sripada, R.K. (2012). Neural dysregulation in posttraumatic stress disorder evidence for disrupted equilibrium between salience and default mode brain networks. *Psychosomatic Medicine,* 74(9), 904–911.

White, M. (1992). Deconstruction and therapy. In D. Epston, & M. White (Eds.), *Experience, contradiction, narrative, & imagination* (pp. 109–151). Adelaide, South Australia: Dulwich Centre Publications.

Mind-body Adaptation to Adverse Experiences

Allen R. Dyer
The George Washington University

Author Note:

Professor of Psychiatry and Behavioral Sciences, Vice-chair for Education, Department of Psychiatry and Behavioral Sciences, The George Washington University

Allen R. Dyer

Abstract

Trauma is often understood as either a psychological phenomenon (as in PTSD) or a physical phenomenon (as in a broken bone) though in fact mind and body are closely interrelated. Much of our understanding of trauma comes from the careful studies of veterans of the Vietnam War, and from those studies came the recognition that survivors of childhood abuse suffer similar symptoms. Civilians in war zones have been less studied, but similarly experience stress-related disorders with both psychological and physical concomitants. This paper looks at health issues in Iraqi civilians in light of research on adverse childhood experiences (ACE) to better appreciate the mind-body impacts of traumatic experiences.

Mind-Body Adaptation to Adverse Experiences

In this discussion, I would like to look at how adverse experiences inform our understanding of mind and body, health and illness. I will draw on my educational and humanitarian experiences in the areas of war, conflict, and complex emergencies (particularly in Iraq), to suggest a broader understanding of what has economically come to be called PTSD, posttraumatic stress disorder, a term that I believe fails to encompass the complex impact of traumatic war experience or other adverse experiences. My reflections will be biological—in an evolutionary sense; psychosocial—in a developmental sense; spiritual—in the sense of ultimate concerns; and they will be semantic in the attempt to clarify how we try to communicate about some of the more elusive and troubling aspects of human experience.

Susan Sontag reminds us in her important book, *Regarding the Pain of Others*, that those beset by war and murderous politics are located on the same map as those of us who are less directly affected by such wars and murderous policies. Our privilege, she suggests, might be linked to their suffering—in ways we might prefer not to imagine—much as the wealth of some might imply the destitution of others. My comments take up Sontag's challenge to look closely at the invisible wounds that wars and civil conflicts impose on those involved; everyone is involved—both soldiers and civilians alike.

Nomenclature, the names we give things, can help us understand how we conceptualize these situations, the ones we call "traumatic" as a linguistic shorthand for experiences that may be so painful that even talking about them accentuates the pain. It has become convenient to talk about PTSD as a diagnostic entity that encompasses the psychological difficulties many soldiers have after war experiences.

The "symptoms" of this "disorder," PTSD, were not just suffered by soldiers, we came to recognize. People who had experienced sexual "abuse" in childhood had similar symptoms, notably flashbacks and intrusive memories. They experienced not just these symptoms, but also identified as the similar disorder, which we have come to call complex-PTSD (See *Table1*) (Herman, 1992, Cloitre, *et al.*, 2011).

Civilians in war zones have been less studied, but certainly no less affected. My own experiences, both working with Iraqi health professionals since early 2001 and teaching in Iraq since 2007, have impressed on me the ongoing stress that people have endured. On my first trip to Iraq in 2007, I was impressed by the stories people told about the horrors of uncertainty of possible loss of one's own life, coupled with the inevitable loss of friends and murders of family

Allen R. Dyer

members, often in the most gruesome manner. As a physician, I was also impressed by these narratives about the anxieties people faced, as well as the associated health impacts they experienced, including extraordinary incidence of heart attacks, cancer, headaches, difficulty sleeping, dermatologic conditions, diabetes and difficulty controlling weight. These stories were told as directly part of the stress under which they were living. Also of note was the extraordinary resilience of the Iraqi people, strong family and community ties and strong religious faith, even as communities were disrupted, families dislocated, and faith challenged—or, perhaps worse—politicized.

The association of physical health problems in the context of ongoing stress situations impressed on me that there was a dimension of the health impact that was not captured by the moniker PTSD. This led me to suggest that when stress is ongoing rather than a single traumatic event, it might be useful to identify it as Ongoing Traumatic Stress Disorder, OTSD, in order to emphasize both the physical and the psychological health impacts on those affected. While we have long recognized the importance of a bio-psycho-social medical model and even a bio-psycho-social-spiritual model, in practical reality these dimensions are usually seen as separate concerns, often addressed by different people. Simply stated, war is bad for your health.

War is often cast as a moral struggle, two opposing sides, Us versus Them, or Good versus Evil. In the words of Carl von Clausewitz, the famous Prussian general and student of warfare—who gave us perhaps the most accepted definition of war as "the extension of policy by other means" — "military action is never directed against material force alone: it is always aimed simultaneously at the moral forces which give it life, and the two cannot be separated." (Clausewitz, 1984: p. 137). Whatever moral forces give rise to conflict, the effect is disastrous on ordinary people, soldier or civilian, caught in the crossfire. It may also be disastrous for humanitarian workers, whatever their moral persuasions regarding a particular conflict.

Iraq Population Profile

- Extraordinary stress x 30 years
- Incredible resilience
- Decreased life expectancy
- Increased infant mortality
- Resurgence of tuberculosis

- Higher than expected incidence of cancer →(7-8 times world rates) ←
- Higher incidence of heart disease, diabetes, etc.
- High rates of depression, other psychiatric disorders, and substance-use disorders

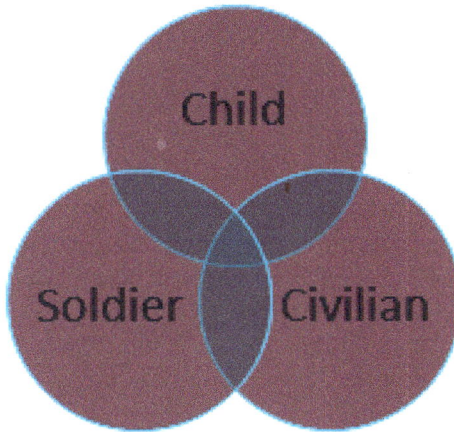

Table 3 Alternative nomenclatures for describing traumatic stress experiences

PTSD	OTSD	Complex PTSD
Post-traumatic Stress Disorder	Ongoing Traumatic Stress Disorder	
A: Stressor (experienced or witnessed) Reaction of fear, helplessness or horror B: Anxiety C: Dissociation D: Hyper-arousal E: Nightmares F: Flashbacks	• Stress endures in time • Person experiences psychological symptoms plus • Physiological correlates • Changes in vital signs: temp, BP, heart rate, respiratory rate, pain • Endocrine/ Metabolic changes • Difficulty maintaining internal milieu	• Severe relationship impairments • Disturbances of mood regulation (e.g. outbursts of anger)

The definition of trauma is subjective. The dictionary defines trauma as a deeply distressing or disturbing experience. More recently, trauma has come to be understood as an emotional shock following a stressful event, which may be associated with a physical shock and sometimes lead to long-term distress. In medicine, trauma may be a physical injury, belying the etymological origin of the word (from the late 17th century, Greek origin), which literally meant a wound.

The interrelationship of the physical and mental aspects of trauma hints at the stigma associated with PTSD (and any emotional distress). This stigma is particularly likely in war situations wherein "heroism" is the expectation, and anything less may be associated with some overt or implicit culpability, or even an inability or unwillingness to hide one's vulnerability or to pretend it doesn't exist. Considered from the perspective of mental health (wellbeing) rather than illness, this may be an inability or unwillingness to recognize and acknowledge the reality of this condition. Thus, PTSD is the heir of misunderstandings of previous wars, when the psychological symptoms were identified as "shell shock", and treatments (often coercive behaviorist conditioning and shaming tactics) were aimed at getting the soldier back to the front. Current attempts to better understand Traumatic Brain Injury help us to appreciate earlier misunderstandings of shell shock, and to redress this disservice to those who serve.

Recently, the "D" in PTSD has come under question, which suggests that posttraumatic stress is not a disorder, but rather, an injury. Particularly in military circles, there has been advocacy for replacing the "D" for disorder with an "I" for injury, based on the argument that soldiers and veterans would be more likely to seek treatment and treatment would be less stigmatized. While PTSD is enshrined in the *Diagnostic and Statistical Manuals*, the abbreviation "posttraumatic stress" is gaining some currency over the more controversial acronym, PTSD.

Indeed, calling the response people have to any disaster, natural or man-made (human made), a disorder is probably a misnomer. These are NORMAL RESPONSES TO ABNORMAL SITUATIONS. From a scientific point of view, looking at psychopathology in the way we look at pathophysiology from an ecological standpoint (that is, a systems view or a bio-psycho-social-spiritual view), it only makes sense to realize the normalcy of these responses that are being labeled pathological. We'd all be conflicted, too, if we had to adapt to such a conflicted environment.

Natural history of PTSD

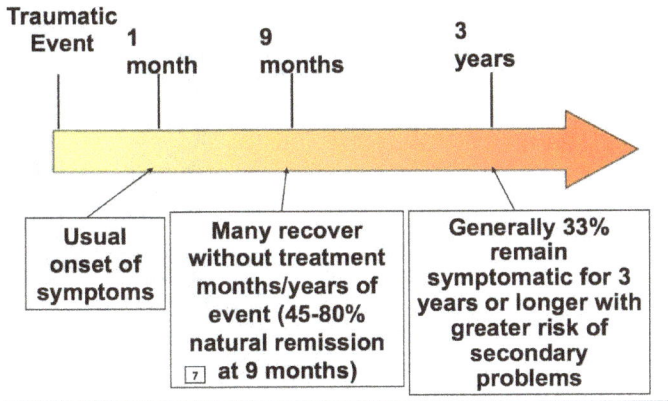

This diagram suggests that PTSD is a result of a single traumatic event. Not everyone who experiences a shocking event develops PTSD. Some people, however, develop secondary problems, including the following:

- Substance-use Disorders

- Depression, including the risk of suicide

- Other Anxiety Disorders, e.g., panic attacks

Stress and trauma are related concepts and experiences at both basic biological and psychosocial levels. It is worth remembering that "stress" was originally an engineering term that was applied to materials, which entered the biological lexicon with Walter B Cannon's *The Wisdom of the Body* (1932) and Hans Selye's classic studies of the *Stress of Life* (1956). Stress involves the complex interactions of mind and body mediated through the endocrine and immune systems. Trauma also has physical roots, namely damage to materials. Understood psychologically, trauma refers to experiences, such as experiencing or witnessing an event that involves threatened death or serious injury, which are overwhelming and thus change the person in profound ways. Because stress and trauma are not synonymous, and because not everyone who experiences stressful situations becomes traumatized, *IASC Guidelines* (Inter-Agency Standing Committee on Mental Health and Psycho-Social Support, 2011) recommends not using the word "trauma" when one really means "stress."

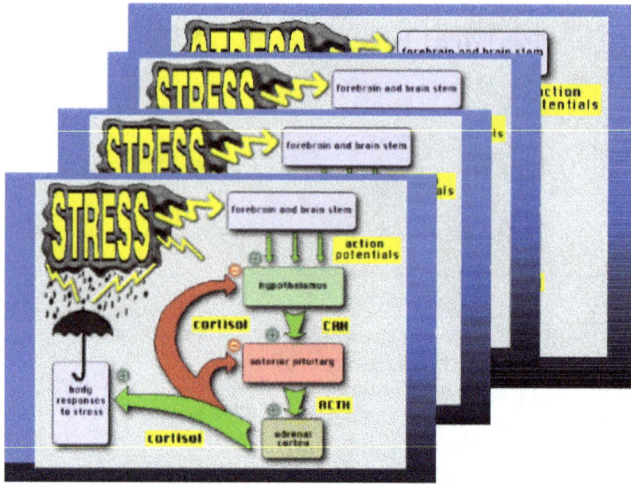

In an evolutionary sense, the body has selected mechanisms to survive stressful experiences. The fight-or-flight mechanism of the autonomic nervous system has enabled our ancestors to survive encounters with sabertooth tigers; increased heart rate, increased blood pressure, and the conversion of stored glycogen in the liver to ready-energy glucose, adaptive in a short-term situation, keeps you alive long enough to pass your genes to another generation. Repeated stresses, however, with the exaggerated cortisol response, lead to adverse health outcomes, including hypertension, diabetes, hypercholesterolemia, asthma, decreased immune function, increased infections, depression, attempts to solve these imbalances with drugs, possibility of neoplasms, and early death.

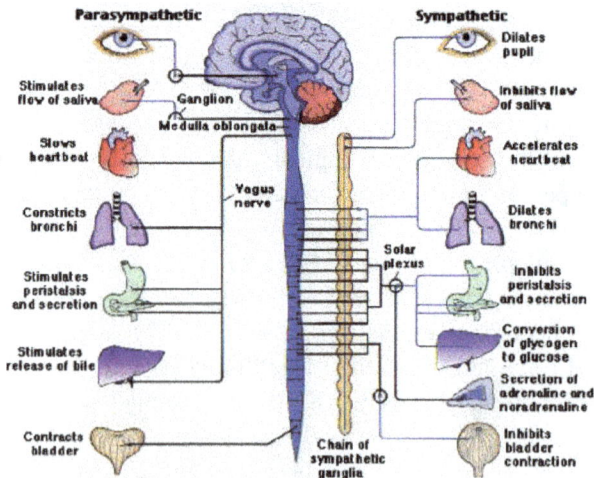

- The sympathetic nervous system pictured on the right is the fight or flight mechanism.

- The parasympathetic nervous system on the left is the rest and relaxation response.

- All of these physiological changes are automatic and out of our direct control – except breathing.

Ancient traditions have long recognized that we can calm our nerves by deep, slow breathing, which provides oxygen to the lungs, heart, brain, and restores equilibrium. One of the most compelling demonstrations of the impact of traumatic experiences—or adverse experiences—on health (outcomes) is the famous ACE (Adverse Childhood Experiences) study (Felitti, *et al.,* 1998). Significant is the direct, rigorous, graded correlation of adverse childhood experiences with (physical) symptoms and illnesses, leading causes of death including ischemic heart disease, cancer, chronic lung disease, skeletal fractures, and liver disease. Such adverse experiences include psychological, physical or sexual abuse; violence against mother; living with household members who were alcohol and/ or substance abusers or someone who is chronically depressed, mentally ill, institutionalized or suicidal, mentally ill or suicidal, or even imprisoned; having only one or no parents; and emotional or physical neglect. Perhaps even more important is the intermediate association with a number of maladaptive attempts to cope with the trauma including increased health risks for alcoholism, drug abuse, depression, and suicide attempts; 2-4-fold increase in smoking; poor self-rated health; sexual grazing (>50 sexual partners) and sexually transmitted disease; and increase in physical inactivity and severe obesity. These intermediate symptoms may be considered in isolation as problems in themselves, thus overlooking their multiple and antecedent causes and failing to respond appropriately and effectively to the patient's real need. Briefly, the more types of adverse childhood experiences (*Column 1*), the greater the neurobiologic impacts and health risk behaviors (*Column 2*), and the more serious the lifelong consequences to health and wellbeing (*Column 3*) (Feletti, 1998). Notably, the intermediate column of Health Risk Behaviors lists smoking, obesity (or eating disorders), alcohol or drug misuse, and other compulsive behaviors, which are often seen as isolated problems, rather than understood as unsuccessful attempts to ease the pain of dealing with the memories of adverse childhood experiences. Furthermore, a large array of chronic "medical" conditions may be

Allen R. Dyer

understood biologically as entitles unto themselves, when in fact they have complex psychosocial antecedents.

People with an ACE score of 4 were seven times more likely to be alcoholics as adults than people with an ACE score of 0. They were also six times more likely to have had sex before age 15, twice as likely to be diagnosed with cancer, and four times as likely to suffer emphysema. People with an ACE score above 6 were 30 times more likely to have attempted suicide. Later research suggested that only 3 percent of students with an ACE score of 0 had learning or behavioral problems in school. Among students with an ACE score of 4 or higher, 51 percent had those problems.

Table 4 – Adverse Childhood Experiences (ACE) Study Findings

Adverse Childhood Experience* ACE Categories (Birth to 18)	Impact of Trauma and Health Risk Behaviors to Ease the Pain	Long-Term Consequences of Unaddressed Trauma (ACEs)		
Abuse of Child 　▪ Emotional abuse 　▪ Physical abuse 　▪ Contact Sexual abuse **Trauma in Child's Household Environment** 　▪ Alcohol and/or Drug User 　▪ Chronically depressed, emotionally disturbed or suicidal household member 　▪ Mother treated violently 　▪ Imprisoned household member 　▪ Not raised by both biological parents (Loss of parent – best by death unless suicide, - Worst by abandonment) **Neglect of Child** 　▪ Physical neglect 　▪ Emotional neglect * Above types of ACEs are the "heavy end" of abuse. *1 type = ACE score of 1	**Neurobiologic Effects of Trauma** 　▪ Disrupted neuro-development 　▪ Difficulty controlling anger-rage 　▪ Hallucinations 　▪ Depression - other MH Disorders 　▪ Panic reactions 　▪ Anxiety 　▪ Multiple (6+) somatic problems 　▪ Sleep problems 　▪ Impaired memory 　▪ Flashbacks 　▪ Dissociation **Health Risk Behaviors** 　▪ Smoking 　▪ Severe obesity 　▪ Physical inactivity 　▪ Suicide attempts 　▪ Alcoholism 　▪ Drug abuse 　▪ 50+ sex partners 　▪ Repetition of original trauma 　▪ Self injury 　▪ Eating disorders 　▪ Perpetrate interpersonal violence	**Disease and Disability** 　▪ Ischemic heart disease 　▪ Cancer 　▪ Chronic lung disease 　▪ Chronic emphysema 　▪ Asthma 　▪ Liver disease 　▪ Skeletal fractures 　▪ Poor self rated health 　▪ Sexually transmitted disease 　▪ HIV/AIDS **Serious Social Problems** 　▪ Homelessness 　▪ Prostitution 　▪ Delinquency, violence, criminal 　▪ Inability to sustain employment 　▪ Re-victimization: rape, DV, bullying 　▪ Compromised ability to parent 　▪ Negative alterations in self perceptions and relationships with others 　▪ Altered systems of meaning 　▪ Intergenerational trauma 　▪ Long-term use of multiple human service systems	**ACE>4** AlOH　　x 7 Sex<15　x2 Cancer　x2 Emphysema x 4 **ACE>6** 　suicide attmp x30	

The World Health Organization has designed an *ACE International Questionnaire—ACE-IQ*. Questions cover family dysfunction; physical, sexual and emotional abuse and neglect by parents or caregivers; peer violence; witnessing community violence, and exposure to collective violence. *ACE-IQ* is currently being validated through trial implementation as part of broader health surveys. The *WHO Iraq Mental Health Survey* conducted in 2008 indicates the types of violence experienced by Iraqis at the height of the war. Note that in Kurdistan, where many people fled, people experienced higher values for the categories of life-threatening illness.

Table 5 Trauma Experience

WHO Iraq Mental Health Survey (2008)

Exposure to traumatic events

- *Capture/kidnapping*
- *imprisoned*
- *purposely causing harm to others*
- *arrest*
- *being beaten by spouse*
- The south/center shows higher values for the following categories: *refugee, internal displacement, exposure to bomb blast, capture, public humiliation, accused of collaboration, beaten by parents as child, beaten by someone else, sexual assault, causing accidental harm to others, witness to killing, death of dear one, family member kidnap, any war-related trauma, any trauma* and *other.*
- The Kurdistan region shows higher values for the categories *life-threatening illness.*

Resilience is a person's positive capacity to cope with stress and adversity. The term "resilience," like "stress," also derives from engineering (the ability of a strained body to recover its size and shape after deformation caused by stress). Like Selye's "stress of life", resilience has a biological parallel in what Selye called the "General Adaptation Syndrome." Psychologically, as well as physically and biologically, resilience is understood as the ability to "bounce back" from adversity (Bonnano, 2004). Across cultures, recognized factors that promote resilience include family support, social support, civil society, religion, and spirituality. Humanitarian assistance may be seen as one of those factors, in which instances the international community allies with local support systems to tip the balance from distress to adaptation and promote resilience and recovery.

While families in communities are among the most robust resilience factors, the world is currently facing a global refugee crisis, the largest since WWII. *Médecins Sans Frontières* (MSF) has organized an exhibition on the refugee crisis focused on three desperate situations: the so-called Syrian refugee crisis; Burundi, the long-standing ethnic tensions where currently 170,000 Burundians have fled to Tanzania; and Hondurans, fleeing organized crime and murders into Mexico in hope of reaching the United States (or Canada).

The George Washington University is an innovator in Global Health and Global Mental Health programming, recognized internationally for preparing students, residents and faculty to respond to global crises and complex emergency situations. GWU has touched the lives of vulnerable populations worldwide through programs that foster community support and healing. The GWU community approach builds medical infrastructure through education and consultation and strengthening civil society institutions.

This photo was taken by one of our GW psychiatry residents, Dr. Nicole Nguyen Perras, who was part of a team that did a psychiatric-needs assessment in November 2015. Another resident, Dr. Fatima Noorani, was part of the faculty for our GW Resilience workshop in Athens in June 2016. This workshop, sponsored by the U.S. Embassy with support from the Greek NGO Metadrasi, addressed vicarious trauma, stress, and burnout in humanitarian workers, employing mindful meditation, Hope modules, and Psychological First Aid (PFA) in small group exercises. More information is available at "GW Resilience Workshop":
(https://sites.google.com/site/gwresilienceworkshop/)

Summary

In consideration of the relationships between stress, trauma, and resilience, both psychologically and physiologically, I would like to suggest that health is an integrative concept involving biological, psychological, and social factors, which are all interrelated. Disaster situations, such as tsunamis, earthquakes, and especially wars, remind us that physical health cannot really be separated from mental wellbeing. Trauma has health consequences, physical and mental, and coping with trauma requires an integrated understanding. In Iraq, people have shown extraordinary resilience; yet they suffer increased susceptibility to cancer, heart disease, and a host of physical manifestations of stress-related conditions.

Conclusion

- The World Health Organization recognized the importance long ago of not only biological but also psychosocial factors in illness, when it offered its significant definition of health as "bio-psycho-social well-being, not just the absence of disease." (WHO,1946).

- Because of the dynamic interactions between biological and psychosocial factors we witness in global disasters and complex emergencies, I believe that there is a stronger statement that needs to be made. The artificial distinction between health and mental health obscures, rather than clarifies, the integral relationship of mind and body. There is no real difference between health and mental health. Health is health.

- The bio-psycho-social approach is not just a good idea; it is a reality based on an increasing body of scientific evidence.

- The challenge now is to apply that knowledge to practice in both resource-rich and resource-poor settings.

- "Global" health is not just about health somewhere else.

- "Global" in this sense means "comprehensive."

Allen R. Dyer

References

Alhasnawi, S., Sadik, S., Rasheed, M. et al. The Prevalence and Correlates of DSM-IV Disorders in the Iraq Mental Health Survey (IMHS). *World Psychiatry* 8: 97–109.

Bonnano, G.A. (2004). Loss, Trauma, and Human resilience: have we underestimated the human capacity to thrive after extremely aversive events? *AM Psychol* 59(1), 20–28.

Cannon, W.B. (1932). *The Wisdom of the Body.* New York: Norton.

Clauzewitz, C.V. (1984). *On War.* (Howard, M. and Paret, P. ed. and trans.) New Haven: Princeton University Press.

Cloitre, M. Courtois, C.A., Charuvastra, A. Carapezza, R. Stolbach, B.C., Green, B.L. (2011). Treatment of Complex PTSD: Results of the ISTSS Expert Clinician Survey on Best Practices. *Journal of Traumatic Stress* 24(6): 615–627.

Dyer, A.R., Bhardra, S. (2013). Global Disasters: War, Conflict and Complex Emergencies. In E. Sorel, (Ed.) *21st Century Global Mental Health.* Burlington, MA: Jones & Bartlett Learning.

Dyer, A. (2016). George Washington University Resilience Workshop. *http://sites.google.com/site/gwresilienceworkshop/*

Felitti, V.J., Andam, R. F., Nordenberg, D. et al. (1998). Relationship of childhood abuse and household dysfunction to many of the leading causes of death in adults. The Adverse childhood Experiences (ACE) Study. *Am J Prev. Med.,* 14(4): 245–258.

Griffith, J.L. (2010). *Religion that Heals, Religion that Harms: A Guide for Clinical Practice.* New York: Guilford Press.

Herman, J. (1992). *Trauma and Recovery: The Aftermath of Violence—From Domestic Abuse to Political Terror.* New York: Basic Books.

Inter-Agency Standing Committee (IASC). (2008). *Mental Health and Psychosocial Support in Emergency Settings Checklist for Field Use.* Geneva, Switzerland: IASC.

Miller, K.E., Rasco, L.M. (2004). *The Mental Health of Refugees: Ecological Approaches to Healing and Adaptation.* New York: Psychology Press.

Ministry of Health. (2007). *Ministry of Health Report.* Baghdad, Iraq.

92

Sadik, S., Abdulrahman, S., Readley, M. et al. (2011). Integrating Mental Health into Primary Healthcare in Iraq. *Mental Health Family Medicine* 8: 39–49.

Sadik, S., Al-Jadiry, M. (2006). Mental Health Services in Iraq. *Int Psychiatry* 3: 11–13.

Selye, H. (1956). *The Stress of Life.* New York: McGraw-Hill.

Snyder, Leslie. *Psychological First Aid.*

Sontag, Susan. (2003). *Regarding the Pain of Others*. New York: Farrar, Straus, and Girroux.

World Health Organization. (1946). *WHO Definition of Health, Preamble to the Constitution of the World Health Organization.*

——— (2007). *Iraq Mental Health Survey.* [Internet] [cited 2011 September 29]. Available from *http://www.emro.who.int/ iraq/pdf/imhs_report_en.pdf http://www.emro.who.int/iraq/pdf/imhs_report_en.pdf.*

——— (2008). *Iraq Mental Health Survey.*

——— (2015). *Adverse Childhood Experiences International Questionnaire—ACE-IQ.*

Treatment: Intersubjective Engagements

Testimony as Part of the Therapeutic Process in Psychoanalysis

Dori Laub
Yale University School of Medicine

Author Note

Dr. Dori Laub, M.D., was a practicing psychoanalyst in New Haven, Connecticut. He was a Clinical Professor of Psychiatry at the Yale University School of Medicine and Co-Founder of the Fortunoff Video Archive for Holocaust Testimonies. He served as Deputy Director for Trauma Studies for the GSP since 2001. He was Acting Director of Genocide Study Program (GSP) at Yale from 2000–2003.

Abstract

This essay is composed of three parts. Part one is the author's autobiographical journey into discovering the process of testimony both personally and professionally. Part two consists of reflections regarding the process of testimony to trauma. It is an event that is set in motion by the traumatic experience "out there"; the memory does not consciously preexist the process of testimony and there needs to exist an actively very-present listener—a witness, who is eager to receive it. It is a restoration of communication whose breakdown defines the traumatic experience itself. This experience is relived in the testimony and manifests itself through the multiple parapraxes that can occur in a testimony. Part three is a comparison between psychoanalysis and testimony, highlighting commonalities and differences. When moments of traumatic experience are relived in psychoanalysis, it is the process of testimony that carries forward the therapeutic action.

My Journey into Discovering Testimony

As a child five years of age, I was deported with my parents to Transnistria, the Romanian version of the camps to which Jews were sent during World War II. Romania was a military ally of Nazi Germany, and Transnistria was located in the territories it had occupied in the Ukraine. The river Bug was the demarcation line between the German and Romanian occupied territories, and the Einsatzgruppe "D," which operated there, regularly transferred Jews from the Romanian to the German side for execution.

My mother and I survived the camps and returned home. We hardly ever spoke about the experiences in the camps to each other, or to friends and relatives. Although I had clear and vivid memories, I hardly allowed myself to think or dwell upon them for any length of time. They came in a flash, which was always terrifying, and I promptly turned my attention away from them. When I was about 12 years old, I wrote those experiences up and posted them in weekly installments on the school billboard. I cannot remember whether anyone ever spoke to me about them. My mother tore them up before we crossed the border leaving Romania. She was afraid that they would be considered "suspicious documents" by the border guards.

The Eichmann trial held in Jerusalem in 1961 was a powerful jolt. I remember listening with awe to the opening statement of the public prosecutor, Gideon Hauser. His words sounded extraordinarily familiar, and in some way, they belonged to me. I was riveted, hearing on the radio excerpts from the testimonies of 111 witnesses. I felt very much a part of their world. Yet it was a world set apart, unreal, and located on another planet, which I could freely enter but did not want to stay in for a moment longer. I remember repeatedly passing the courthouse on my way to classes in medical school, seeing the long queues of people waiting for the doors to open. I felt drawn to join those queues, but in the end, I never set foot in the courtroom and never attended a hearing of the Eichmann trial.

Another very noteworthy incident happened a few years later, when I was finishing medical school. It involved one of my classmates—Levy Neufeld. His parents had placed him with a Polish couple before they were deported and murdered during the Holocaust; this is how he survived. He was an eccentric young man, sociable but difficult to get along with. As we approached final exams, he felt increasingly terrified. He only passed the first exam in dermatology, for which he had studied together with another colleague. He showed up to the other exams, but left in terror before they began. Eventually, he gave up trying.

There were rumors that he was seen roaming the streets of Jerusalem by motorcycle. Then, he just disappeared. Months later a series of murders occurred in various parts of the country. A man with an Uzi gun was shooting from behind bushes, killing people at random. The police suspected Neufeld to be the serial killer. I was warned that my life was in danger, because he had made threatening remarks about me. The biggest manhunt in the history of Israel took place in 1963, involving more than 4,000 policemen searching for "Levy Neufeld" and combing the country, to no avail. What was most striking about this situation was the simultaneous generosity and shortsightedness of the medical school. It was willing to allow this student many opportunities to take his exams, but to my knowledge, never considered him to be in need of psychiatric help. No one made the connection between his history as a child survivor and his present difficulties in facing life and taking his final exams. This simply was not an item on anybody's agenda at the time, nor was it on my own. I knew the history of his survival, but gave little thought to it. Paradoxically, he was seen not as a victim, but as the attacker from the dark of the night. Levy Neufeld's body was found more than a year later. He had hanged himself in the attic of an abandoned house, months before the first Uzi murder occurred. There was a letter on his body, apologizing to his friends. The Uzi murderer has not been found to this day.

My avoidance of the Eichmann trial and the psychic reality of Levy Neufeld are just two examples of a widely shared cultural blind spot. While the Holocaust was regularly memorialized and tangibly present in everyday life, it was not the topic of inquiry for those studying human behavior. It was not even mentioned in my psychiatric rotations in medical school. In my own analysis, three years later while already in the U.S., I described my concentration camp experience as a sun-bathed vacation in a green meadow, on the bank of a blue winding river, arguing with a girl my age about whether one can or cannot eat grass. Luckily, my analyst was European and quite familiar with the events of World War II. He stopped me in my tracks and told about the depositions given by women who had been liberated by the Swedish Red Cross in Theresienstadt: "Some of them insisted that the conditions were so good, that the women were served breakfast in bed by SS officers" (a particular way in German culture whereby love is demonstrated to a woman), he said to me. This interpretation of my denial was quite effective. I stopped talking about meadows and rivers and started remembering my real camp experiences.

It took, however, a major historical event several years later for me to fully realize the impact of the Holocaust experience on survivors and their offspring. I was able to get to Israel on the fourth day of the Yom Kippur war in 1973. I was stationed in a military base near the Golan Heights, ready to receive psychiatric casualties from the Syrian front. They poured in by the hundreds, having decompensated because of the brutality and suddenness of the war and because they served in makeshift units and not in their own organic reserve units. I noticed that the most frequent and severe psychiatric casualties, suffering either from depressive coma or from psychotic agitation, were soldiers who were children of Holocaust survivors. A radio operator heard the last utterances of a tank commander who had passed his station to refuel and get ammunition a few hours before: "I knocked out nine Syrian tanks; if I had more shells I could continue." Then the voice went silent. In this soldier's family, there was an abundance of shadows of people that had been murdered in the Holocaust, yet they were hardly mentioned. The front-line experience resonated with the familiar sense he had grown up with of having the knowledge of close people who had died, but not having been able to directly experience such knowledge.

Another soldier suffered from psychotic agitation after he had booted a Syrian POW officer in his chin. He grew up in a family with a father who talked of German brutalities—of soldiers smashing babies against the wall. The patient had been a military policeman trying to prevent civilians from approaching the front line—but he couldn't stop a car with two civilian passengers who wanted to join the fighting. A few hours later, he saw the car destroyed with two mangled bodies in it.

Reflections on Testimony

Testimony is the transmittal of information about an injury of such magnitude that it refuses both comprehension and registration. Survivors experience a powerful inner urge to transmit, to share this information both with themselves and with a committed, totally present listener. They are fully aware of its presence, but what is accessible to them are broken sensory fragments and overwhelmingly powerful affects. In the process of testimony, through the dialogue they produce with themselves and with their listeners, they narrativize these fragments, turn them into a coherent story with a before and an after, a beginning, a middle, and an end.

At its core, traumatic experience is ahistorical. It does away with the dimensions of place and time. It all happens in the here and now. Survivors may even speak in present tense. Accompanying affects are immediate and intense. The survivor may be at a loss for words when he/she feels incapable of re-imagining and expressing an experience. The narrative flow may be interrupted, and a gap may result. When the re-experienced emotions are too intense, the testimony may be broken up into discrete fragments. The supportive intervention of the interviewer is crucial at such moments to help rebalance the narrative, so it can resume its flow. In survivors who were psychiatrically hospitalized in Israel for most of their lives, the interviewer had to be much more present and active in order to make the testimony happen. On their own, they were unable to initiate or sustain the narrative flow.

Trauma theory helps both to generate and decode the testimony. In the first place, it informs the interviewer how to listen and how to respond. It identifies the moments in which what has been experienced exceeds the capacity to symbolize, to form a transmittable memory. The interviewer can offer his own symbolizing capacity, to create the words the witness cannot find. The viewer of the testimony becomes himself the witness to this dialogic process, and can thereby grasp the full dimension of the experience. She can capture it in the text or in the testimony she co-creates.

It is evident by now that I do not consider testimony to be a monologue—one person's telling a story. It is rather the product of a dialogic interaction. The witness/survivor has experienced a real event "out there" and is under strong internal pressure to transmit it to someone who wants to know it. The interviewer has that willingness to be totally present to the survivor, and receive as well as experience what he/she wants to transmit. It comes as no surprise, therefore, that the interviewer experiences strong countertransference feelings during the testimonial process. Such countertransference feelings and enactments are an invaluable source of information about the traumatic experience that has been testified to. These enactments sometimes take the form of sweeping countertransference parapraxes, such as: 1. an analyst's not knowing for more than a year-and-a-half of analytic work that her patient's family had the same Holocaust background that her own family had; or 2. an interviewer's not noticing that a mother and a daughter, testifying in each other's presence, to the scene of the murder of a baby by the camp Commandant, ended up telling quite differing versions of the same event. Neither the witnesses nor the interviewer picked up on that difference. In another example, an interviewer misrepresenting the survivor's age when the latter discovered that his father had died in the bunk next to him (describing him as a boy of seven and not 14, which was his real age), and the survivor's not correcting him. These are a few examples of the "memory parapraxes" one encounters in the testimony of trauma survivors. Trauma theory informs us as to what questions to ask and how to turn them into rich sources of information. As far as the survivors go, our engagement with their testimonies helps them alleviate a doubt they always had: whether what was experienced and remembered really happened or was merely a product of their imagination. One can detect here the effect of the German intent at erasure. Our willingness to listen and our interest serves as a confirmation of their inner reality. Survivors always wanted to speak and be heard. Not only the "writings from beyond the grave" attest to that. Between 1945 and 1950 about 20,000 testimonies, mostly in writing, were given. The flood of testimonies dried up once survivors realized that no one was interested in them. When the interest came back, testimonies were given again. While it's possible that survivors can be retraumatized through giving their testimony, especially when the listening conditions are not optimal, the risk of remaining silent is much greater than the risk of speaking up.

What distinguishes testimony in the first place are the very distinct and indispensable conditions under which it comes into existence. A protected space has to be provided, which contains not only the physical place and the necessary time, but also a totally present, committed, and attuned listener, willing to accompany the witness on the journey upon which he/she is about to embark. What has not been fully explored and articulated is the role of the camera in this endeavor, although experts in media studies (Pinchewski, A., 2012) have started to do so. What is needed to complement these external conditions is a readiness in witnesses to confront what is inside them, the real event of their lives, an experience, even if it covers a lifetime, that is known to be there, although it had hitherto not been consciously formulated. Throughout their lives, the witnesses could not avoid its presence, consciously aware of it only as discrete fragments, and they were both relentlessly drawn to it and recoiled in terror when coming near it. Each witness is therefore in possession of information that has yet to be recorded and brought to an addressee, to a party interested in receiving it. Testimony is thereby a transmittal of information, and there is an internal unrelenting pressure to convey that is met by an external person of readiness and eagerness to receive it.

It is in this setting that testimony can assume a life of its own in that witnesses' memories exponentially increase. Many Holocaust survivors I have interviewed over the years stated that by the end of their testimony, they were amazed about the extent to which they did remember, and about how much they could actually put into words. In this sense, the giving of testimony was in essence a process of creating new information. They had always pushed their knowledge to the side and considered it to be information that would be too upsetting and too frightening to themselves and too burdensome to others. In that sense, the experience of giving testimony was new and left them surprised by their own stories. In spite of the terror and the sadness they encountered during their testimony, they experienced a powerful urge to continue and to bring their narratives to completion.

In order to tell their stories, Holocaust survivors had to partially relive them. It is due to the nature of extreme trauma that memories of the atrocities experienced cannot always be related as past events, but break through the coordinates of time and place in which we commonly organize what we experienced. That is why survivor testimony often has a quality of immediacy to it, as though what happened is happening all over again, in the here and now. Massive trauma is fundamentally ahistorical, and testimony is an attempt to create a narrative in a sequential framework, which allows events to be arranged along a timeline with a before and an after. In this respect, testimony provides a level of historicization.

Therefore, what sets testimony apart from other instances during which survivors speak of or allude to their persecution experiences is its conception as a "whole," in the intimacy of a dialogue with a totally present and attuned listener. Its purpose is as a relief from a threatening, oppressive burden and as a transmission to a receptive audience.

Testimony and Psychoanalysis

The uniqueness of the testimonial intervention lies in the fact that there is always an event, an experience, even if it covers a lifetime, that is known to be there, even if it has hitherto not been consciously formulated. It is thus information that has yet to be recorded and brought to an addressee, a party interested in receiving it.

When transmittal of testimony has been accomplished, the survivor no longer is or feels alone with the inexpressible extreme experience. He/she is less helplessly prey to its devastating impact. The internal cauldron of sensations and affects has been put into the frame of a sequential narrative. They are now remembered, transmitted, and can also be forgotten. Such narrative is, however, never complete, and highly charged blank spots of the inexpressible (almost unimaginable) experience persist, exerting their magnetic power on the survivor, who feels compelled to endlessly revisit them while at the same time constantly fleeing their proximity.

It is these intense, affect-laden voids of memory, which can initially obliterate the traumatic experience in its entirety, that constitute the power source that drives testimony and exerts the pressure for its deliverance. This holds true for a broad range of experiences of extreme trauma. In more recent observations, cancer survivors, when feeling safe in the company of other survivors, are also driven to "tell their story" of their encounters with death. A group of chronically hospitalized "psychotic" Holocaust survivors who were interviewed in Israel in recent years experienced the same internal pressure to bear witness. Unfortunately, their capacity to symbolize, free-associate, reflect, and verbalize had been so profoundly damaged by the chronicity of their condition (lasting for decades), their social isolation, and their somatic treatments (insulin shock, ECT, and psychotropic medication), that all they were able to create was a constricted, static, and fragmented narrative.

The goal of traditional psychoanalysis, on the other hand, is to allow for the emergence of the unconscious through the method of free-association and the elucidation of the transference experience. There is no particular force, no inner compulsion that drives it, no story that reaches for words. It is rather a surrender to the wanderings of the mind, while feeling protected by the analyst's nonjudgmental presence and neutrality. It has a rhythm set by the frequency of the sessions and it lacks an endpoint in time. Dreams, parapraxes, transference experiences and enactments, and, last but not least, remembrances provide the scaffolding along which the analytic narrative unfolds. Although there is no explicit addressee in traditional analysis, the analyst's emotional presence implicitly fulfills that function, thus becoming the equivalent of the testimonial "thou."

Psychoanalytic literature is indeed replete with references to the internal good object, usually highlighting the infant's relationship with its mother. Beginning with Freud's (1930) concept of the oceanic feeling—being one with the universe—that arises from the oneness with the mother, and continuing with Margaret Mahler's

Dori Laub

(1963) developmental phase of symbiosis, Winnicott's (1953) "transitional space," Henry Paren's (1970) "inner sustainment," Mahler's (1975) "object constancy," and Kohut's (1971) "self object"—all of the above deal with processes that are essential for internal representation and symbolization to occur. The latter constitutes core components of the testimonial intervention.

Within the spectrum of psychoanalytically informed therapeutic interventions, the testimonial process possesses three unique elements: the internal pressure to transmit and tell; the real story that is "there"; and the yearning for and the presence of a listener who receives it. On closer scrutiny, these three elements do not place testimony in a category that is separate from psychoanalysis. Both processes—testimony and psychoanalysis— are in essence dialogic. The analysand does not speak to a void, even if he speaks to himself. In such a case, it is his/her own internal good object, projected onto the analyst, that he/she addresses. In both processes, the narrative deepens and branches out, taking turns that may come as a surprise to the narrator. Freud's (1933) dictum "where id was, there the ego shall be" applies to both, although in lengthier psychoanalysis this can go much further than in single-session testimony (p. 30). Furthermore, a process is set in motion in both, which can continue on its own, far beyond the time frame of the psychoanalytic or the testimonial event. This process includes, but is not limited to, symbolization, self-reflection, and remembering. While it is not a particular event that serves as an organizing principle, as in testimony, psychoanalysis also leads to the recovery of memories that may emerge as organizing principles and thus become building blocks of the psychoanalytic narrative. What may remain the basic difference between testimony and traditional psychoanalysis may be limited to the inner intense pressure to transmit and the experience of transmittal itself that are at the center of the testimonial intervention. The latter can, therefore, be seen as a piece of psychoanalytic work that is limited in scope and that does not include parapraxes, transference, or dream work.

The testimonial momentum may be also operative, in traditional psychoanalysis, when traumatic experience is involved. At such a juncture, it becomes the process that fuels the therapeutic action and provides the impetus for clinical movement and flow. It would be methodologically very difficult to isolate and study this in the context of such traditional psychoanalyses; therefore, the nontraditional modality of the testimonial intervention is needed in order to provide the most suitable research setting that can capture the testimonial momentum for its in-depth investigation. When the goal of the intervention is treatment and not research, it comes to be true that testimony takes the upper hand. When it comes to the treatment of severe traumatic experience, it is the testimonial process, and not the psychoanalysis, which counts most.

References

Kohut, H. (1971). *The Analysis of the Self.* New York, NY: International Universities Press.

Mahler, M.S. (1963). Thoughts about development and individuation. *Psychoanalytic Study of the Child,* 18, 307–324.

Mahler, M., Pine, F., & Bergman, A. (1975). *The Psychological Birth of the Human Infant: Symbiosis and Individuation.* New York, NY: Basic Books.

Freud, S. (1961). Civilization and its discontents. In Strachey (Ed.), *The Standard Edition of the Complete Psychological works of Sigmund Freud* (Vol. 21, pp. 57–146). London, England: Hogarth Press. (Original work published 1930)

Pinchevski, A. (2012).The Audiovisual Unconscious: Media and Trauma in the Video Archive for Holocaust Testimonies. *Critical Inquiry.* 39(1) : 142–166.

"I Could Eat You Up:"
Philomela, Trauma, and Enactment

Nanette C. Auerhahn, Ph.D.

Author Note

Nanette C. Auerhahn, Ph.D.

Winner of the Cleveland Psychoanalytic Center 2016 Essay Prize
Earlier versions of this paper were presented at "Listening to
Trauma: Insights and Actions: The Second Washington Conference
on Trauma," George Washington University, Washington, DC,
October, 2016, and at the Cleveland Psychoanalytic Center, January,

2017.

24800 Highpoint Road

Beachwood, OH 44122

Nanetteca@aol.com

Nanette C. Auerhahn

Abstract

The myth of Philomela is used as a paradigm for taking possession of traumatic knowledge via enactments that engage the other/therapist who feels with the survivor. Cannibalism in the myth is shown to be an apt metaphor for visceral affective knowing and for recruitment of the body in the metabolization of trauma. A time before speech is rekindled in trauma, when relating occurred in the matrix of bodily contact between mother and child as each hungered for the other, and attachments were formed by eating each other up. Cannibalism is explored as a terrifying, necessary act of bonding with mother and analyst. Along with the myth of Philomela, the Oedipal myth and clinical examples that include parallel process are used to illustrate how the sensorimotor inscription of a traumatically absent object generates intergenerational and therapeutic reenactments.

"I Could Eat You Up:" Philomela, Trauma, and Enactment

"What the patient puts on your plate, that is what you eat."
Maurits Katan, M.D.

The following paper explores how trauma that is neither symbolized nor represented is made known to the self and other. How
do we tell ourselves and others what has happened to us when formulation is not yet possible, and when knowing, making known, and
being known bring terror? For instruction, we turn to the myth of
Philomela, discovering a paradigm for taking possession of traumatic
knowledge via enactments that engage the other/therapist who feels
with the survivor. The action in the story of Philomela turns around
cannibalism, which is shown to be an apt metaphor for visceral affective knowing and for recruitment of the body in the metabolization
of trauma. It harkens back to a time, rekindled in trauma, "before
speech…when relating and being were in the matrix of bodily contact
between mother and child" (McLaughlin, 1987, p.578) and the infant
feared both eating and being eaten. We approach the myth not literally, but like a dream in which characters can represent parts of the
self, contiguity may suggest causality, and reversibility of sequence
is possible. (For an earlier discussion of the myth of Philomela, see
Laub and Auerhahn, 2017).

The most famous rendering of the story of Philomela is that of
Ovid. In the fifth year of her marriage to Tereus, King of Thrace,
Procne asks her husband to let her see her sister Philomela. Tereus
travels to Athens to bring Philomela to visit, and lusts for her upon
seeing her. At the end of their voyage, he forces her into a cabin in the
woods where he rapes her, threatens her to remain silent, and cuts out
her tongue in response to her defiance. Unable to speak, Philomela
weaves a tapestry that tells her story and has it sent to Procne who,
enraged, kills her son by Tereus, boils him, and serves him as a meal
to her husband. Procne and Philomela confront Tereus with the boy's
severed head, making Tereus aware of his cannibalism. He pursues
them with an ax. To escape his revenge, they pray to the gods to be
turned into birds. Procne is transformed into a swallow, Philomela
into a nightingale, and Tereus into a hoopoe.

The narrative repeats a theme twice: there are two events of
which someone is unaware. Procne does not know about the rape,
while Tereus is unaware that he has eaten his son. In each instance,

something happens that changes ignorance into knowledge. Procne learns of Philomela's rape from the tapestry that tells the story. Tereus learns of his cannibalism when Procne and Philomela present his son's severed head. The first carrier of knowledge, the weaving, is an artistic representation. The second, the presentation and eating of the body, is an enactment. The enacted realm is "where all experiences that cannot be symbolized in words…find their expression…not only those that are preverbal and have no words, but also those whose overwhelming nature necessitated their dissociation or disavowal" (Katz, 2014, p. 43). The murder, boiling, ingestion and presentation of Tereus' son can all be understood as enactments of the original rape that bring horror and tragedy to awareness and are necessary for knowing.

Aristotle refers to the weaving that tells the story as the "voice of the shuttle" – an example of a poetic device that aids recognition of what happened earlier in the plot. Literary critics see in the weaving a metaphor for the artistic process. Little has been written about the similarly communicative functions of the cannibalism and presentation of the severed head. All bear on our topic: the manner in which trauma that cannot be fully narrated nevertheless is made known to self and other (Laub and Auerhahn, 2017).

A Myth for Trauma: Philomela, not Oedipus

The myth of Oedipus has been a central organizing myth for psychoanalysis, framing how we know what we don't know and what we shouldn't know. It is about the child's initiation into language and triadic relationships, and how we take possession of forbidden knowledge. In the Oedipal myth, the hero is split horizontally, with what he does not know actively repressed "below" into the unconscious. The myth provides a paradigm for repression and for distinction between conscious and unconscious selves; it has been useful in understanding creation of the dynamic unconscious and critical for conceptualization of conflict and defense. With the peak of the Oedipal complex's occurring between the ages of three and five, at a time of achievement of object constancy and consolidation of the ego and language, fantasy from that period has been viewed as activating symptoms and as critical in development of the personality and psychopathology. For Kleinians, the Oedipal complex is associated with the depressive position and the ability to relate to the whole person (Laplanche and Pontalis, 1973). While Oedipus did have a history of trauma, the myth's focus on language and defense has limited our understanding of trauma in which a different kind of doubling occurs, and in which deficit more than defense determines the emergence of knowledge of events that defy representation. Pre-Oedipal trauma, as well as adult trauma that activates annihilation anxiety, both require a different metaphor.

The myth of Philomela is a metaphor for the vicissitudes of trauma that elude language. While Procne, on first reading, appears to have repressed her maternal love for her son, the myth's storyline is a paradigm for a more primitive process—that of dissociation and the vertical split between the traumatized self and the apparently normal self, as represented by the two sisters, Philomela and Procne, who illustrate that the traumatized self is a fragmented, divided self. A vertical split is initiated during trauma when the mind is severed from the brain's speech centers, creating experience that is recorded in sensorimotor percepts, not remembered in words. The severed tongue and head are eidetic presentations of severance from language; the conscious mind is disconnected from unsymbolized, unmetabolized trauma and cannot process what has not been represented, narrated, or shared with a witness and which instead makes itself known through semiotic as opposed to symbolic presentations (*cf.* Kristeva, 1980). After the rape, the traumatized self, Philomela, is hidden from the part of the self, symbolized by Procne, that attempts to live in the normal world, not thinking about or even knowing what happened.

Severing of the connection with language and reason is depicted many times over in the myth, even as its manifest content narrates eventual movement into voice and communication. The death of language is symbolized in the cutting out of Philomela's tongue and in her transformations. Early Greek sources have Philomela turning into a swallow, which has no song. And although most depictions of the nightingale in art and literature are of female nightingales, female nightingales do not sing. Only males do, undercutting the ubiquitous use of the nightingale as an archetypal symbol for the oppressed woman who finds her voice in a beautiful, sorrowful lament that stands as a metaphor for art and literature.

If trauma is cut off from language and hence the symbolic, how does it emerge? A first reading of the myth suggests that weaving, *i.e.,* symbolization, leads to action and dénouement. But while artistic creation is the idealized means for processing, communicating, and transforming experience, the less "tasteful" aspects of the myth typify the way trauma emerges in life and therapy—as somatic enactments that engage and involve the other/therapist who feels with the victim. The vicissitudes of trauma follow the path of enactment first, including swallowing (insertion) and digestion (metabolization,) and only then creation of a narrative. The semiotic precedes the symbolic; Philomela is earlier than Oedipus. Thus, while the Oedipal myth has been used paradigmatically to understand fantasy as "an imaginary scene in which the subject is a protagonist, representing the fulfillment of a wish (in the last analysis, an unconscious wish) in a manner...distorted...by defensive processes" (Laplanche and Pontalis, 1973, p. 314), the myth of Philomela is illustrative of a process prior to language and the symbolic, in which early formative childhood experiences encoded in preverbal, sensorimotor forms of memory are reactivated by trauma, which likewise is registered on the sensorimotor level. These experiences belong to a time when the infant, in his earliest days, does not distinguish between words and actions and experiences his fantasies as actually happening, *e.g.,* the baby does not merely want to destroy the breast but feels that he is doing so.

Early sensorimotor experiences emerge in psychoanalytic treatment of survivors of trauma where "the regressive constraints of the analytic frame...potentiate an intensification of the action intent of words, silences, actions, and nonverbal communications in both parties" (Katz, 2014, p. 38). Melanie Klein's view of *phantasy* as psychic representatives of bodily impulses and feelings that have not yet been formulated in words is relevant here. Klein viewed phantasies as mental expressions of instincts originating in the first two to three years of life. She was concerned with primary fantasies, representative of the earliest impulses and desires, that are bound up with sensation and that later in life operate independently and alongside Oedipal fantasies and words. These fantasies are activated in trauma and reactivated in analytic treatment in the form of enactments and semiotic presentations, *e.g.,* bodily posture, facial expression, and manner of speaking. (See Isaacs, 1948). The view of traumatic enactments in this paper is different from that of Chused (1991, p. 615) who defines enactments as "symbolic interactions between analyst and patient which have unconscious meaning for both" and which are perceived by the patient as an actualization of his fantasies. This paper focuses on traumatic enactments as pre-symbolic eruptions of shards of sensorimotor and affective memories that are digested by patient and analyst.

At a time when the infant experienced attachment as involving hunger for another, and internalization and introjection were synonymous with swallowing a mothering other, creation of relationships was physical, feelings and words were experienced as bodily sensations, and "the mouth was the beginning and center of the child's developing ego" (McLaughlin, 1987, p. 578). It is no accident that the action in Philomela turns around a meal, as the nature of analytic treatment necessitates that the analyst make room internally for the analysand and that the analysand make room internally for the analyst. This reciprocal swallowing can kindle traumatic enactments around issues of eating and being eaten, especially in victims of trauma.

Emergence of Trauma via Enactment

All my therapies begin with enactments on my part. Feeling depleted from concentrating all day on my clients' psychic realities, I find that sipping coffee during sessions helps me feel nurtured, as if I am putting something back inside. I offer coffee to clients as well. My office suite has a kitchenette, and my office has a Keurig machine. Patients help themselves. Only while writing this paper did I recognize the underlying fantasy of emptying myself out so as to be able to hold what patients pour into me and the seductive aspects of inviting patients into my kitchen. Thus it was with Greg, whose analysis has been characterized by a series of enactments.

As Greg and I walk down the hallway from the waiting room to my office, he often cracks jokes; there is an air of informality, as if we were not analyst and analysand. I have a sense of something that belongs in my office overflowing into the hallway, in violation of rules of confidentiality. The most dramatic enactment occurs six months into our work, when I pick up Greg in the waiting room and he asks if he might have a cup of tea. We walk to the kitchenette, and I direct him to the water cooler, where a complicated maneuver for eliciting hot water is required: a button must be pushed toward the back while simultaneously held down. I explain this, but Greg appears not to listen and hurriedly manipulates the button with difficulty. I try to help, but he ignores what I say, takes a small amount of water with jerky motions, and quickly tells me, "It is fine." I feel disregarded, shoved aside and unheard, as if I am an insignificant bystander watching someone else's scene.

Greg and I walk to my office, whereupon he stops outside the door of the office next to mine and leans his head against the door as if listening to conversation inside. I worry that a colleague might see or that the therapist inside might come out and be annoyed at the boundary violation. "Don't do that," I plead, embarrassed, as I try to redirect him away from my colleague's door, as if he is a little boy acting out. When we get to my office, Greg asks for more water, as he realizes that he has very little in his cup. Feeling irritated, I direct him to the Keurig, cautioning that adding water to his cup might cause it to overflow, given the level already there. I watch anxiously as the water pours into his cup; he suddenly and without warning jerks it away, calling to me to quickly put a second cup there to catch the overflow. I am not quick enough to prevent water from pouring out of the machine and am annoyed as I clean up the "mess." In contrast, Greg lies down on the couch and begins the session, as if the foregoing interactions are outside of the hour and not part of our work.

I am left disoriented and confused, having difficulties getting my bearings, feeling as if I have been picked up, played, and then dropped. What has just happened? I wonder, feeling as if Greg and I had an interaction that left me stimulated and alone by the wayside, while he moved on. After a titillating interaction, he had dropped me and was now starting over, ignoring what had happened between us and my excited state, as if we could now start anew, as if we had just begun now. I am left unsatisfied and having to tend to myself by myself so as to calm down. I feel that he embarrassed me by trying to listen in on my colleague's therapy, thereby exposing me as an inept therapist to any colleague who might have overheard the goings-on in the hallway. He also disregarded my feedback, not allowing for a shared, smooth and coordinated filling of his cup that left a mess for me to clean up. I note all this without realizing what any of it means, what his actions have communicated, but determine to bring it into our discourse to examine together. I reflect on my anger at the mess caused by his failure twice to listen to my instructions and my embarrassment at his behavior outside a colleague's door. I am struck by our misattunements, as I seemed unable to guide him and he did not adequately cue me when he intended to withdraw his cup to prevent an overflow which he instead caused. I eventually recognize that in pulling out early, Greg and I had lost the opportunity to think and talk together, to connect. It took months for me to recognize my agitated arousal as similar to that of a sexual partner of a lover who suffers from premature ejaculation. We have enacted a sexual scene.

Once Greg lies on the couch, he speaks about depression. I point out that he has brought other emotions into the room—*e.g.,* playfulness and hostility—by his actions prior to the session. He admits to having been upset the day before by sounds emanating from the therapist's office next door: "I felt intruded upon in our space, making it hard for me to hear and think," he says. I wonder if his anger at the disruption in our work makes him not trust me, hence the miscommunications. "I knew it wouldn't overflow and was watching, but maybe didn't communicate that clearly. And you pulled out without warning me," I say. "Yes," Greg admits, "This happens all the time because of my problem in hearing. I don't hear well and can't think clearly, make mistakes and then get blamed...I hear part of it and think I should know it and don't hear it all and try to do things quickly."

Several themes emerge over the next sessions that bear on the meaning of the foregoing interactions. We had previously discussed his attraction to the therapist next door, whom he had seen a number of times as we walked to my office and who was the type of "hard, beautiful, bitchy woman" he used to be attracted to. He and I now speak about the disorganization that had been evident in him the day before when we could hear voices next door. These he now relates to the sounds of his parents' fighting and the vomiting of his alcoholic, seductive mother, which he heard growing up in a bedroom that shared the parental bathroom. Greg recalls seeing his mother naked through the open door of her bedroom and relates stories about boundary violations with colleagues including a sexualized relationship with a co-worker's wife. He recounts his sexual history, which includes encounters that he experienced as anxiety-provoking and shameful, a pattern that consolidated in problems with premature ejaculation that culminated in an avoidance of intimacy. After a girlfriend aborted his child, he "no longer trusted a woman's contraception and would pull out early," compounding performance problems. He recounts the sexualized atmosphere created in his family home by the promiscuity of his brothers and their flirtatious friends. He talks about girlfriends who had been victims of incest and whose sexual energy excited and frightened him, making him angry about having to satisfy them.

The themes of intrusion, boundary violations, hearing and being disturbed by fearful goings-on next door, misattunements, premature spilling, spoiling, overstimulation, sexual violation, anger—all had been present as implicit memory and were made manifest in the analysis in the form of an enactment that engaged sensorimotor memories. Over the following sessions, these were elaborated via associative networks and details in explicit memory, creating a narrative history that contextualized what had been a burst of procedural memory, resulting in an enactment that told in actions what he could not yet fully tell in words. The enactment was a kind of condensed performance that was unpacked over several weeks. It took the form initially of an eruption, a vomiting, which had to be regurgitated and digested before being articulated in words. Literally and figuratively, Greg pulled out his cup early and expected me to catch the overflow in an enactment that engaged both of us, bringing both of our affective experiences into representational thought. Only later did I consider my disorientation as a kind of swallowing, vicarious reliving, and attempt at metabolizing his confusion while listening to the primal scene. My anxiety about being overheard and seen in the hallway was an enactment of a parent's worry that children might overhear or see parental intercourse. Months later, Greg and I reconstructed his helpless overstimulation as a child, perhaps (re)experienced by me in the enactment under discussion. This returns us to the insight that shame lives in autonomic responses and to the cannibalism in the myth of Philomela, which serves as a concrete representation of the process of visceral affective knowing.

Cannibalistic Engagement

Cannibalism is an apt metaphor for the metabolization of trauma and for psychoanalysis' paradigm shifts, as it has considered trauma, from a focus on repression to dissociation and from cognition, interpretation, and insight to affect, psychoanalytic process, and relational repair (Bromberg, 2011). The therapeutic relationship can be understood unconsciously as cannibalistic: patient and therapist make room internally for the other, each inserting himself into the other, imbibing the other's representational world, and allowing each to chew over, taste, and know what the other has experienced and transmitted. Winnicott (1954–55, p. 263) describes how the baby works through "consequences of instinctual experiences" via use of the mother in a process "comparable to the digestive process" (p. 263), as a result of which "something can be done about something." As prototypical of this process, he describes the actual feeding experience as "a cannibalistic ruthless attack" (p. 267) on the mother, in part because of the infant's "imaginative elaboration of the physical function" (p. 268). The baby experiences nursing as a cannibalistic attack to the extent that he does not distinguish between milk and the mother's body, indeed between milk/breast and mother. The baby experiences himself as eating mother, a fact that mothers intuitively grasp as revealed by their reciprocal, resonating response often expressed, in the ecstasy of adoration, with the words, "I could eat you up!" The mutual wish is to imbibe, take in, devour, and merge as the mother hungers for her baby and attachments are formed by eating each other up.

While these issues, like the fact of sensorimotor experience, are seen by many as characterizing pre-oedipal experiences and hence as relevant to pre-oedipal trauma, they are alive in adult trauma that unravels basic psychic structure, *e.g.,* the relationship to an empathic other. Trauma is unsymbolized, unthought, and recorded in sensorimotor experiences that result in enactments that bring representational thought about trauma into being. The analyst's affective resonance is crucial to the understanding and resolution of enactments as they coalesce into fantasies and emerge in narratives. Traumatic fantasy is a co-construction of patient and analyst after the fact of enactment that describes the enactment and that exists as a representation once it is formulated and "given back" to the patient. An image comes to mind of a parent who first chews a piece of food before inserting it into the mouth of her infant. Returning to the myth of Philomela, we understand the actions of Procne, Philomela and Tereus as reenactments that bring trauma into conscious awareness via mutually responsive actions. The fluidity of primary process helps us grasp that the myth of Philomela is told backwards: First there is enactment, then there is weaving, *i.e.,* symbolic representation. (See Laub and Auerhahn, 2017.)

Bion (1970) posits a beta function that characterizes the senses that take in without meaning, and an alpha or reflective function that processes and digests information from the sensorium and makes sense of it. He proposes that the baby communicates via projective identification with the mother, who performs those psychic mental functions that the baby is not yet able to perform. Similarly, analysts share patients' beta experience and then perform the reverie function for patients. Analysts imagine and think when patients are not yet able to. Eshel (2004), channeling Bion, describes how the patient projects split-off, unbearable parts of experience into the analyst and the analyst—like the mother for the infant —takes in, holds, speaks, and transforms them, allowing the patient to reintroject and contain the hitherto unknown and unthinkable.

This process can be seen in a session with Greg, who furiously rails at me: the mental health profession has misled him, subjected him to treatments that have no demonstrated efficacy. Psychoanalysis has made things worse. Why have none of the professionals who treated him mentioned a blood test that can tell you which psychotropic meds will work? Maybe what he needs is PTSD treatment such as EMDR. On and on he rages. I feel as if I am being torn into and torn apart and feel fear in my chest and stomach. At the end, when he says he refuses to be shamed into thinking this is his fault, I feel sadness, hopelessness and aloneness. I think of rejoinders to particular points, but ultimately feel defeated by the weight of the attacks. When he is about to leave and turns around from the couch, looking at me with a smile, I feel his sadistic pleasure in discharging his rage into me. Over the next sessions, we talk about this experience, with my sharing what it was like for me and his recognizing his own experience in mine. Not only has he felt this way as victim and witness of family members' rage, he admits to having expressed such rage at others. He reveals that the day before that session, his brother had screamed at him, hurling all the accusations Greg had hurled at me, accusing Greg's therapists of having made him worse, demanding to know why they hadn't known what they were doing, *etc*. Greg had felt shamed by the barrage.

I understand then that I have taken in, in visceral form, Greg's experience, chewing it, cogitating on it, naming it, and feeding it back to him, thereby eliciting a calmer process in him during which he becomes reflective about what happened between us and within him. I have taken in, digested, and metabolized his bile. He next shares that after the session during which he had yelled at me, he had yelled at his daughter and then been overcome by guilt the following day. I ask if he felt guilty yelling at me and he said yes. During the next session when my next-door neighbor is noisy, the day after, he can process that he had become frightened by my anger at the disruption and connected it to his fear of his parents' eruptions. In response to my neighbors' noise, I had told him I was going to ask them to lower their voices. He had asked me not to and I didn't. Now he recognizes that my anger had reminded him of the times his father would explode at someone in public. When he had been the target, he would be frightened. When the target was someone else, he would be embarrassed and try to make things right. In my intention to quiet my neighbors, was I protecting him from angry parental voices, reenacting his parents' and at times his attacks on others, or protecting myself from his rage? My action had been an enactment.

A year-and-a-half into Greg's analysis, I am quicker to recognize both Greg's and my enactments. One night I get an email from a colleague in my office telling me that Greg contacted her about seeing her for cognitive therapy to help with his addictive behaviors. She had acquiesced to treating him. I am annoyed that she said yes without first talking to me. My first response, said to myself, is "Hell, no."

I have a visceral, immediate, and negative response, worrying that he will prefer her to me. I feel threatened that his attachment to the other therapist might split the transference, weakening our relationship and compromising the analysis. I think of the numerous triangles Greg has engaged in throughout his life. Only later do I remember why he had terminated with me when we had worked together years ago. It was because he had begun marital therapy and the therapist had told him he could not see both her and me. I think about two recent dreams of his. The first involves being in a seedy bedroom with two women, two beds and a toilet in the middle. He wants to be with the nice woman who is like a soulmate, while the other woman, a colleague's wife with whom he had had a sexualized relationship, wants to be with him although he does not want to sleep with her. The second dream is his first explicit dream about me in which we are dancing erotically and my husband walks in; neither my husband nor I is upset. Greg's association to the second dream is that he is reversing the situation during which he learned about his wife's affair. He did not walk in on her but she told him about the affair. He states that had he walked in on her, he would not have raged but swallowed his anger and been nice as he was when she told him. I then realize that Greg is triangulating my colleague and me and feel strongly that I will not participate in a scene in which he is cheating on me with the therapist down the hall. This leads to my recall of his listening in on my colleague next door and his incestuous relationship with his mother (with whom he shared a bathroom), his relationship with his co-worker's wife, and his affairs with women at work. I decide to tell him that it is against my recommendation that he see a colleague in my office and text him (since he is out of the country on an extended business trip), even while knowing that such a communication is best done in person and second-best by telephone; that texts and emails are easily misunderstood; and there is a good chance he will be furious with me, which he is. Nevertheless, I feel compelled to set a boundary in writing. I am agitated, upset, and anxious. Clearly, I am enacting something but don't know what.

After talking to both my analyst and supervisor, I am able to review my reactions and trace them to my fear that Greg will become emotionally attached to the other therapist, leaving me out. It finally dawns on me, when I reflect on my overwrought state, indeed despair, that my reaction is connected to my traumatized mother always having been elsewhere. My sense as a child was that she had cathected neither myself nor my brother, but her previous family who were all dead and gone, left somewhere in Europe and killed in the past, and that she was lost to me in the present. At first I consider this despair as my personal countertransference response in the traditional sense, one that has no place in my current treatment of Greg or formulation of what is going on with him. But then I ask myself if perhaps his triggering of my deepest despair doesn't tell me something about him—he who has spoken about feelings of loneliness and abandonment throughout his life. The next day I wake up with all this still brewing in my head. What comes to mind is the Zombies' 1964 song "She's Not There" that had run through Greg's mind shortly before my summer vacation and that I had realized at the time fit my state of mind when anticipating my own analyst's vacation. Now it seems like a leitmotif for both of our childhood wounds and jointly held traumatic affect states. I reconsider my insistent text to Greg and realize that I had said to myself in essence "I'll be damned if I'll stay still in a helpless panic in front of an adult who is not there for me but who is deeply connected to someone else." This experience is an enactment of the experience of the flooded child (Greg and myself) whose terror in front of the absent, non-helping other constitutes trauma that is not remembered in language but kept in a dissociated state as procedural memory. This enacted experience of decathexis constitutes an "externalization of an internal catastrophic psychic state which arose in the face of another" (Gurevitch, 2008, p.573). Experiencing and acknowledging my own despair at the loss of connection helped me recognize Greg's, which may well have had its origins in his infancy when he could not hear his mother's presence or feel adequately connected to her, and that an integral part of Greg's organization of the world involves somebody's not being there. In sending him a text, I had recreated this experience by avoiding hearing, listening, and talking to him. This action illustrates the meaning of enactment as a memory in action, and validates Betty Joseph's insights that not only does the patient "live out his early history in ways which are beyond words," but also that the analyst knows this "only through the reactions and feelings the patient unconsciously attempts to arouse in" her (Feldman and Spillius,1985, p.153). I decide to look up the lyrics to the song "She's Not There" which, when it had come to mind in Greg's session, I had remembered as evincing yearning for a loved woman whose voice was "soft and cool" and whose eyes were "clear and bright." I now find instead that it is about betrayal: "No one told me about her, the way she lied…It's too late to say you're sorry. How would I know? Why would I care? Please don't bother trying to find her. She's not there…No one told me about her, though they all knew…"

After sending Greg that email, I present our crisis at a case conference where I feel criticized and think to myself, "I'm quitting if they give me a hard time." I share this thought with my supervisor, who suggests that perhaps Greg is considering quitting the analysis. Sure enough, when I speak to him next, he threatens just that (an enactment of premature ejaculation?). Upset, I bemoan the fact to my analyst and worry about my reduced caseload should he leave. Minutes later, I think of another patient who had expressed interest in analysis; I brighten, realizing that I can fill my hours by seeing him for analysis. "Just as your patient found a substitute for you, you just found a substitute for him," my analyst points out. I realize that enactments may not only precede understanding and interpretations, but may also appear alongside and even intertwined with them in an ongoing and reciprocal manner. I consider that Greg's pursuit of different psychiatrists over the course of our work has been a means of cheating on the analysis itself by trying to rid himself of symptoms without fully exploring their unconscious meanings. I also realize that sexual excitement is being intermingled with anger.

Returning to the myth of Philomela, I now revisit the earlier interpretation, based on the Oedipal paradigm, that Procne murdered her son because she had repressed her love for him. The foregoing analysis suggests instead that Procne's grief swallowed her up so that she forgot her love for her son and her son as her son. She lost her maternal function and maternal self as a result of despair. Her son was not so much repressed as vanished, erased, disappeared. Trauma causes relationships and persons to cease to exist. This void and absent object are at the heart of trauma and responsible for subsequent enactments. Indeed, the onslaught of Greg's and my enactments began when he was out of the country on a business trip and we lost our connection to one another. That is when he contacted my colleague. My despair at not being cathected by my mother told me about his despair at being unimportant and decathected as a child and now with me.

Recruitment of the Body in Metabolizing Trauma

Annihilation anxiety engendered by trauma precludes development of a coherent structure with which to represent it (*cf.* Blank, 2016), infusing cannibalistic experiences with negativity and terror. A powerful example is found in the movie *Alien*, when an egg implanted by the mother alien emerges as a baby alien through the walls of an astronaut's body, tearing him to pieces. Almond (2010) explored how pregnancy often fills mothers with fears of parasitic monsters eating their insides. An analysand, in somewhat less horrific imagery but one equally fueled by profound anxiety, funnels imagery of analysis as a kitchen: "I had a dream in which I was in the kitchen with Frank Underwood from *The House of Cards*. There is a person behind me. I turn around but can't see them. It's a woman, I think. The cook grabs me and stabs me to death. I didn't see them. I wasn't sure they were there. I knew I was going to be stabbed and braced for it. It's not painful. I didn't feel it, but felt myself getting weaker and dying. I am aware I am dreaming. I am freaked out about it." "What about the person behind you?" I ask, sitting behind him. The patient replies, "Being here, being stabbed in the back, in here I'm afraid of letting go of my guard, of talking about things." The analyst as cook is an ominous figure for this patient who associates to the witch in Hansel and Gretel who "shoved the children into the oven" and then corrects himself "I mean Hansel and Gretel shoved the witch into the oven." He recalls a story about "two boys like Dennis the Menace who want to steal cookies from a bakery. They fall into a vat, are cooked and made into big cookies. They eat their way out of the cookies." A baby fears not only that if he eats something, he will destroy it, but also that he will be eaten, an anxiety channeled in the playful exchange between parent and child, "See you later, alligator. In a while, crocodile." Children unconsciously recognize the aggressive and sexual "instinctual roots of the tenderness which adults display towards them" (Devereux, 1953, p.132).

According to Winnicott (1954–5, p. 269), the completion of feeding leaves children with apprehension "about the imagined hole in the body of the mother." He conceptualizes the process of feeding as profoundly relational, and the baby as both giving and receiving. The mother must survive this process for the child to be able to do something about the hole. My survival of Greg's attack on me allowed him to feel guilt over being mean to his daughter and to me. It helped him recover his memory of being attacked by his brother. "It is the analysis of the oral sadism in the transference that economically lessens the persecutory potential in the inner world of the patient" (Winnicott, 1954–5, p.273). After trauma, the absence of the good object is represented by a persecutory object. Therefore, analyzing cannibalistic themes is inherently related to working through persecution and restituting an empathic other. It is mother as a good object who is reestablished after having been eaten.

> "Externally a good breast is one that having been eaten waits to be reconstructed…it turns out to be…the mother holding the situation in time…We [analysts] want to be eaten, not magically introjected…To be eaten is the wish and…need of a mother at a very early stage in the care of an infant. This means that whoever is not cannibalistically attacked tends to feel outside the range of people's reparative and restitutive activities. . .only if we have been eaten, worn down, stolen from, can we stand…being also magically introjected, and being placed in the preserve department in someone's inner world" (Winnicott, 1954, p. 276).

The analyst, like the mother, appreciates the child's need to eat her, wear her down, steal from her, and make her part of himself, and only if this has happened can healing occur.

The mother/analyst makes a place in the child's/patient's mind for herself just as the child/patient makes a place for himself in the mother's/analyst's mind. Just as a mother gets into her baby imaginatively, suffering what he suffers, an analyst gets into the skin of her patient. This is where the equivalency of "therapist" as "the rapist" (Tereus) can feel apt. Kristeva (2000, p. 85) writes that the analyst identifies "with the flesh of the patient." An analysand recalls with horror a Native American story he read as a child about an Indian chief who wants to be as strong as a horse and so has his skin roasted and a horse skinned, and then has the horse's skin wrapped around him so that it melts and merges with his. Unconsciously the patient intuits that invasion, violation, and skinning are part of the therapeutic enterprise. By the end of Shaffer's play *Equus*, the treating psychiatrist Dysart wears the horse's head and has the sharp chain, or bit, in his own mouth. He has become symptomatic by "eating" what the patient offered. Just as a child may contain the disavowed experiences of the parent, so too may a therapist become a receptacle for the patient's unmetabolized introjects. Dysart dreams of slicing children "down to their navel," then parting the flaps, severing the inner tubes, yanking them out, and throwing them "hot and steaming on the floor" (Shaffer, 1974, p. 24). He grasps that patient and therapist, like mother and child, not only put things into the other but also take things out.

Intrusion and extraction go hand in hand, just as ingestion/digestion is inevitably linked with elimination. An analysand walking down a hallway to my office conjures images and motifs from the fourth and fifth movements of Berlioz's *Symphonie Fantastique*, specifically images from "The March to the Scaffold" from the fourth movement and the somber "Dies Irae" from the fifth. He later explains that the former association was more theatrical while the latter was purely musical, and that in both cases the theme of justice's—divine or temporal—being served was foremost in the association of music and action. Images and music conjure a grasp of the analytic situation as a beheading that allow us to look inside his mind to simultaneously indoctrinate (put thoughts in and take thoughts out) and punish him. To prevent me from tinkering with his brain, he keeps me at a distance by slow abstract speech drained of affect, so that I have trouble remembering what he says. There is nothing to chew on, digest, or metabolize. His terror of my pouring myself into him is communicated and defended against by his manner of speech. By the time trauma emerges beyond silence into symptoms, we have the survivor's attempted solution to the difficulties of inscribing trauma.

A second analysand associates to a news story she heard about a Chinese surgeon who plans to do a body transplant. I connect this to her terror at the possibility of my putting my head on her body and her putting her head on mine. Until recently, she, like the above patient, used intellectualization extensively and viewed affects as an intellectual process—something in her head only. More recently, she has begun to connect affect with sensorimotor sensations and to realize that her feelings are like limbs, blood, and guts—parts of her body—a realization that excites, terrifies, and disturbs her.

The equation between feelings and the body was brought home to me in a parallel process. Greg worried that I was becoming sad by the burden of his emotions. "Do you know how you can recognize an experienced Afghan warrior?" he asks. "By the fact that he pees and then goes into battle. I often feel like peeing. I do now." My next patient of the day talks about his anger, then becomes sleepy and can't remember what he was talking about. He says it is like having a slippery fish that he can't hold on to. "Maybe what I need is some chewing gum put onto the end of a stick with which to grab hold of the fish." A piece of gum chewed on by the therapist, I think, to make it pliable and suitable for sticking to a stick. My thoughts go to a nursery song that had gone through my head that morning: "I know an old lady who swallowed a fly. I don't know why she swallowed a fly. Perhaps she'll die." I had connected the song to the parts of this paper that I had written the night before on the role of the analyst in swallowing, working over, and re-presenting the patient's material. I had worried: Was my analyst going to die from all that I was putting into her? Who was putting what into whom? What had I taken from her and what was she taking from me? Later that day, yet another patient tells me of her reaction to our session the day before: After helping her see that, despite her upset at the discovery of her niece's abuse, it was not her this time who was being abused, she had had a sensation in her chest of something opening up, and then had had diarrhea. Was she expelling her identification with her niece? Discharging her own retriggered trauma?

In reflecting on these moments, all in the same day, I was struck by the muck of one person's unconscious paralleling that of another, underlined for me by my own analytic hour, which had begun the day before with patient and analyst being late because both (like the Afghan warrior?) had to go to the bathroom at what was supposed to have been the start of the hour. Great anxiety accompanies both intrusion and extraction and can be embodied in a nonlinear process, coursing through two people in a mutually held somatic experience (Veronica Csillag, personal communication).

Mother's mind must be available for a baby to project into, or the child cannot wall off his anxieties and suffers from persecutory anxiety. The absent object cannot be directly represented, but instead is transformed into a bad, persecutory object that screens over the absence. The breast is experienced as offering only poison. The child tries to not take the persecutor in and becomes flooded with feelings of death, persecution, and falling apart which are expressed symptomatically by, for example, difficulty sleeping and obsessive mechanisms (Ungar, 2016). The traumatized adult is without a good empathic other. Like the traumatized child, he will be haunted by persecutory anxiety and will empty his mind out so as to expel anxiety. What cannot be kept inside, borne in mind, is expelled into the body and is evident in somatic symptoms and masturbatory fantasies. The body will be recruited to metabolize, process, and fantasize about trauma (Ungar, 2016). One patient admits, "I'm interested in violence and pornography. I started masturbating to porn around age 13. My interest in violence started earlier. I grew up reading the Brothers Grimm. There were horrible stories with beautiful pictures of violence. I remember a story about a man who cuts off the thumbs of kids who suck their thumbs; if the kid sucks other fingers, those too are chopped off. So there was a picture of a man with big scissors and kids crying not because they lost fingers, but because now they couldn't suck their thumbs." The patient was telling me that the children cried because they could no longer soothe themselves, intuitively grasping the link between trauma and self-soothing via masturbation, while less aware of the dilemma of the infant who aggressively eats (attacks) thumb (mother), while also trying to obtain nurturance, maintain a relationship, and avoid retaliation.

An individual will recruit not only his body but also the other's mind to help process trauma. He will want to know the analyst's state of mind to ascertain if it is available for him to use in facing trauma and to ascertain if the analyst keeps him in mind as a good object, just as he struggles to keep the analyst in his own mind as a good object. He wants to know if each has swallowed the other so that he is no longer alone internally. On the most primitive level, the patient, like the child, does not distinguish between the therapist's body and his mind and seeks clues about the therapist's mind in his body. An example comes from Dana, an adult child of Holocaust survivors, whose implicit knowledge of the Holocaust is enacted by her daily scrutiny of my office, my appearance, and my tone of voice for signs of irritation or preoccupation. We have come to reconstruct her childhood environment as permeated by her parents' unspoken, horrific, implicit memories that she read as one reads the body language of citizens in a foreign country whose language one does not know. As an adult, she tends not to listen to people's words and instead drinks them in with her eyes and senses. In my office, we suspect that she is enacting fantasies about her mother's body and the terror she experienced in relationship to mother's C-section which she, as a child, had assumed was the result of a sterilization experiment. She re-experiences me as the unpredictably unavailable, traumatized and traumatizing, mother. The interior of my office is an arena for reenacting her terror of the interior of her mother's body and ultimately of her own, while my state of mind is searched for signs that I am present to help or if, alternatively, by finding a place inside myself for her and inside her for me, I will pour my depression into her. As a child, Dana had been equally attuned to the nuances of her mother's tone of voice and body language as the only reliable clues to her availability and state of mind. Mother appeared too devastated to have any internal space for Dana and too traumatized to have been able to verbalize her own traumatic history, which was instead imbibed by Dana and evinced in Dana's inability to see my vitality, as well as in her periodic silent crying, for which she has neither words nor explanation. As we note her enactments, an associational network begins to emerge. She recalls as a child hearing whispered stories of torture of children in the Holocaust and later in school learning about centuries of Jewish persecution and martyrdom. She remembers being told about a relative whose skin was flayed and then learning about Rabbi Akiva who was flayed and burned alive by the Romans. Later the childhood fantasy of not only mother's sterilization but also her own is shared, as well as her hearing years later her mother discuss being given medication in the camps that she feared would prevent bearing children. I comment that it is no wonder that she feels that it is dangerous for her to put things into me and me into her, that perhaps she fears that anything she gives me could be poisonous while what I put into her could burn her skin. She recognizes her determination not to take in what she perceives as my own sadness, which she experiences as poisonous just as she experienced her mother's body, mine, and her own as dangerous and frightening—as potential sites of torture, experimentation, and castration. The body that soothes is the body that can be tormented.

Themes of intrusion and poison are overdetermined in Dana's fantasies. During a particularly anxious time, she notes that a colleague at work had brought homegrown tomatoes from her garden to share, or so she assumes when noticing them in the office kitchen. She thinks of taking some for her granddaughter, then panics that the tomatoes have been injected with poison and that eating them would kill the child. She herself has been unable to eat recently, but has no associations to or understanding of her current aversion to food or to her fantasy of poisonous tomatoes. I wonder whether swallowing is difficult because as a child she could not easily take her parents in, as their feelings were too unbearable. She saw mother's depression as eating mother up and feared swallowing it or being swallowed up whole by it in an act of soul murder (Shengold, 1989). I think of Winnicott's poisonous breast, which covers over the absent object at the core of trauma. In this case the poisonous breast may represent the real executioners in the parental history, the real traumatized dissociative and unavailable mother, mother's real experience of being poisoned in concentration camps, the negative transference, and the universal early "phantasy" of the bad breast. Dana's eating disorder may be a defense against being a receptacle for mother's unmetabolized introjects—those disavowed experiences transmitted across generations—as well as a way to evacuate a frightening, controlling, narcissistically damaged parental *imago* that represents the final common pathway of real intergenerational trauma, early universal phantasy of the bad breast, and current transference enactments.

The terror associated with knowing and telling both about one's own mind and that of another, when those minds contain trauma, is captured by another analysand who recognizes that she is walling off her husband even as he needs her support to deal with fears of cancer. She worries that her affect is not bright enough to motivate her students. It is as if her husband's affect could contaminate her and hers in turn could be transferred to students. She then talks about a book she is reading about parasites. There is one in particular that fascinates her. It can reproduce only in the intestines of cats and then is pooped out where it can grow only in the brain of a rat if "lucky enough" to be eaten by one. When time to reproduce recurs, the parasite must find a way back into a cat's intestines; it changes a rat's brain to disinhibit its fear of cats, causing it to approach a cat and perhaps be eaten, thereby returning the parasite to a cat's intestines where the cycle repeats itself. The patient notes that a parasite that can control the brains of humans has yet to be found but may exist. She then talks about difficulties in sharing her feelings with her husband, who invalidates them with his questions. I wonder if she experiences him like a parasite in her head who questions her actions and takes away her autonomy, recalling her frequent lament that if someone tells her "you will like this," she can't. She answers that she is becoming increasingly quiet with her husband and children, that she is more playful with the kids when he is not around. When he is, he will comment approvingly on her playfulness with them. "I hate that," she recognizes. "It becomes not yours," I note. "He takes over. That is why you put up barriers against his moods, opinions, and influence." This was her situation as a child with a narcissistic, critical, and suicidally depressed mother whose presence in her mind felt parasitic and controlling, precluding the development of a separate identity. It became the template for her relationships with others, who are kept at bay lest she lose her sense of self. She protects herself by trying not to take people in because of her confusion when she does: What is hers? What is others'? For her, swallowing is an aggressive act rather than one involving love or mutuality, implicating the analysis as a parasitic act as well.

The foregoing examples are taken from neurotics who wove together symbolic tapestries comprising enactments, fantasies, and narratives to bridge the gap between their minds and those of others as they strove to create and destroy an "other" to whom to address their trauma. Access to, interaction with, and defenses against the analyst's mind were sought in efforts at self-regulation and co-creation of a holding environment (*cf.* Weil, 1984). The analyst's mind, mood, body and space are but four of the cues available in every analytic exchange that guide patients' associations and transferences; "attending to the patient's search for and use of perceptual cues can lead to essential aspects of the patient's intrapsychic life" (Smith, 1990, p.227). The desire to know the therapist is an enactment of this search, which can emerge in embodied ways that run the gamut from the neurotic to the psychotic. Rashkin (2016) describes a patient who arrives at his first session with a manila envelope containing biographical information about the therapist that he downloaded from the Internet. This patient confused biographical facts with knowledge about the therapist's psychic life. Curiosity about the other's interiority was concretized on a psychotic level by two sisters studied by Lacan. In 1933, Christine and Lea Papin murdered their employer and her daughter, tearing their victims' eyes from their sockets, crushing their faces, stomping on their bodies, and carving up their thighs and buttocks. According to Lacan, they searched in the women's gaping wounds for the mystery of life to decipher their employers' otherness (Clement, 1983) and to vanquish otherness itself. In trauma, the gap between self and other appears insurmountable, leaving the victim alone and the persecutor inaccessible, lending urgency to the need to grasp the interiority of the other.

Rereading Oedipus as Reenactment of Intergenerational Trauma

If we return to the myths of Oedipus and Philomela and use the latter to reread the former, we are alerted to a backstory: Euripides, in *Chrysippus*, tells the story of how Laius, father of Oedipus, kidnapped Chrysippus, son of a royal family in which he was guest and tutor, in order to violate him, causing the gods' revenge on Laius' family. Thus, the myth of Oedipus may be read not only as referring to triadic relationships and the nuclear family, but also to the vicissitudes of intergenerational trauma. Indeed, the tragedy of Oedipus may be less about the child's universal wish to displace his father than about fathers' universal hostility toward their sons as seen in Laius' rape of his charge and attempted murder of his son, which is a paradigm for the seductive behavior of adults toward their children, as well as the universal and longstanding practices of child sacrifice and cannibalism (Devereux, 1953, and Bergmann, 2007). If so, this would make Oedipus closer to Philomela than first thought. In any case, Laius, within a family setting, violated a son, setting the stage for the reenactment by Oedipus of violation of the incest taboo. Oedipus' sons, Eteocles and Polynices, killed each other in a battle for power after which Oedipus' uncle, Creon, took the throne and refused Polynices burial rites. When Polynices' sister Antigone defied this edict, Creon buried her in a rock cavern where she hanged herself, whereupon her fiancé, Creon's son, stabbed himself to death. What had started as a sexual boundary violation in one generation became murder, incest, and suicide in subsequent generations. What we had first posited as contrast—Oedipus as metaphor for the acquisition of forbidden knowledge, Philomela as metaphor for the acquisition of traumatic knowledge—might be more illusion than reality. Perhaps the family romance, penis envy, and the Oedipal complex, all so vitally connected to the Oedipal myth in psychoanalysis, may be more screen memory than bedrock—screen for trauma, that is. The blinding and self-mutilation of Oedipus, for example, representing in psychoanalysis castration anxiety, may symbolize the parasympathetic (vagal) state of detachment that characterizes the dissociative response of the traumatized individual who shuts down metabolically and "strives to avoid attention to become 'unseen'," like the traumatized child who "disengages from stimuli in the external world" and is "observed to be 'staring off into space with a glazed look'" (Schore, 2007, p. 757). Both myths may be mined for what they tell us about intergenerational trauma. In the myth of Oedipus, the third generation, his daughter and Laius' granddaughter Antigone, tries to end the cycle of violence by burying the dead, i.e. giving them their due and reinstating processes of mourning, something that usually requires three generations for resolution. The price exacted by the intergenerational transmission of trauma is that Antigone, in choosing a heroic death in order to reinstate the moral order (in identification with her mother, who killed herself upon learning of her incestuous relationship with her son), forgoes her future as a wife and mother, forfeiting her right to a life of her own and to generational continuity. Trauma's unraveling of the links by which one generation nurtures and gives life to another is sounded even earlier in the myth of Oedipus, when Oedipus' maternal grandfather is orphaned close to his birth by a father, Pentheus, who is killed by, among others, his own mother when she fails to recognize him. Pentheus means "Man of Sorrows" and derives from πένθος, pénthos, sorrow or grief, especially the grief caused by the death of a loved one. Trauma's unraveling of intergenerational links is central to the myth of Philomela in that a mother, Procne, out of grief and terror, forgets her son and her mothering function, highlighting the manner in which a mother's deepest melancholy can destroy her child. It is apropos that Philomela's rapist, Tereus, is the son of Ares, god of war.

Perhaps parallel process in therapy may be considered a form of synchronic enactment, while intergenerational transmission of trauma may be understood as a form of diachronic reenactment.

Conclusion

Rereading Oedipus, the paradigm for repression and linguistic structure, revealed reenacted intergenerational trauma, while rereading Philomela uncovered, beneath an ode to language and artistic creation, the centrality of dissociation and enactment in the vicissitudes of trauma. Both stories highlight a mother swallowed up by depression whose grief robs her of her maternal function, illustrating that trauma makes relationships disappear and intergenerational links unravel. Cannibalism was explored as a heinous, terrifying, murderous, desired, and necessary act of bonding with mother and analyst.

In ending this chapter, we turn to the closing of the myth of Philomela, to the characters' transformations that have been taken by previous writers to signify emergence into voice. Noting the paradoxical voicelessness of the swallow and female nightingale has directed us away from language as trauma's preferred mode of communication toward sensorimotor experience and enactment. If Oedipal fantasy, when put into words, may be likened to a scene or sentence with a subject, object, and action, unconscious traumatic enactment, as a shard or fragment of sensorimotor or affective experience, when sounded out, emerges as a scream or cry. It is apropos then, to end with Tereus' transformation into a hoopoe, so named onomatopoetically because of its sound "oop oop oop." Onomatopoeia connotes not language but a sensory element, gesturing toward the sensorimotor inscription of trauma. Onomatopoeia is often the first step in symbolic representation, imitating the sound associated with what it names by a word that often looks like the sound that it makes; we hear the sound when we read the word. Onomatopoeia thus embodies a performative act, constituting an enactment that returns us to the insight encoded in the myth of Philomela: the centrality of enactment and shared sensorimotor and affective experience in taking possession of traumatic knowledge.

References

Almond, B. (2010). *The Monster Within: The Hidden Side of Motherhood.* Berkeley: University of California Press. Aristotle. Poetics (16.4).

Bergmann, M.S. (2007). "The Taming of God's Aggression and the Need for a Loving God." *Annual of Psychoanalysis*, 35: 111–119.

Bion, W.R. (1970). *Attention and Interpretation.* London: Tavistock.

Blank, A. (2016). Bion's Reverie and Meditation in Psychoanalytic Therapy for Trauma. Plenary at *Listening to Trauma: Insights and Actions: The Second Washington Conference on Trauma*, George Washington University, Washington, DC, October, 2016.

Bromberg, P.M. (2011). *The Shadow of the Tsunami and the Growth of the Relational Mind.* London: Taylor and Francis, Ltd.

Chused, J.F. (1991). The Evocative Power of Enactments. *Journal of the American Psychoanalytic Association*, 39: 615–639.

Clement, C. (1983). *The Lives and Legends of Jacques Lacan.* Trans. A. Goldhammer. New York: Columbia University Press.

Devereux, G. (1953). Why Oedipus Killed Laius—A Note on the Complementary Oedipus Complex in Greek Drama. *International Journal of Psychoanalysis*, 34: 132–141.

Eshel, O. (2004). Let It Be and Become Me: Notes on Containing, Identification, and the Possibility of Being. *Contemporary Psychoanalysis,* 40: 323–351.

Feldman, M. & Spillius, E. B. (Eds.) (1985). *Psychic Equilibrium & Psychic Change: Selected Papers of Betty Joseph.* London: Routledge.

Gurevitch, H. (2008). The Language of Absence. *International Journal of Psychoanalysis,* 89: 561–578.

Isaacs, S. (1948). Nature and Function of Phantasy. *International Journal of Psychoanalysis*, 29: 73–97.

Katz, G. (2014). *The Play Within the Play: The Enacted Dimension of Psychoanalytic Process.* London: Routledge.

Kristeva, J. (1980). *Desire in Language: A Semiotic Approach to Literature and Art.* Trans. T. Goran, A. Jardine, & L. Roudiez. New York: Columbia University Press.

Kristeva, J. (2000). From Symbols to Flesh: The Polymorphous Destiny of Narration. *International Journal of Psychoanalysis,* 81: 771–787.

Lacan, J. (1977). *Ecrits: A Selection.* Trans. A. Sheridan. New York: W.W. Norton & Co.

Laplanche, J. and Pontalis, J.B. (1973). *The Language of Psycho-Analysis.* Trans. D. Nicholson-Smith. New York: W. W. Norton & Co.

Laub, D. and Auerhahn, N. C. (2017). Traumatic Unconscious Fantasies. In N. Goodman & P. Ellman (Eds.), *Finding Unconscious Fantasy: A Clinical Guide to Working with Narrative, Body Pain, and Trauma.* London: Routledge.

McLaughlin, J.T. (1987). The Play of Transference: Some Reflections on Enactment in the Psychoanalytic Situation. *Journal of the American Psychoanalytic Situation*, 35, 557–582.

Ovid (1955). *Metamorphoses*. Trans. R. Humphries. Bloomington: Indiana University Press.

Rashkin, E. (2016). Do You Google Your Shrink? Trauma, Transference, and the Challenge of Analytic Treatment. Paper read at "Listening to Trauma: Insights and Actions: The Second Washington Conference on Trauma," George Washington University, Washington, DC, October, 2016.

Schore, A.N. (2007). Review of Awakening the Dreamer: Clinical Journeys by Philip M. Bromberg. *Psychoanalytic Dialogues,* 17: 753–767.

Shaffer, P. (1974). *Equus and Shrivings: Two Plays by Peter Shaffer.* West Hanover, MA: Atheneum.

Shengold, L. (1989). *Soul Murder: The Effects of Childhood Abuse and Deprivation*. New Haven, CT: Yale University Press.

Smith, H.F. (1990). Cues: The Perceptual Edge of the Transference. *International Journal of Psychoanalysis*, 71: 219–228.

Ungar, V. (2015). Antonio Ferro and Child Analysis. *Psychoanalytic Inquiry*: 35, 478–493.

――― (2016). Eighteenth Annual June Isquick Visiting Scholar Program, Cleveland Psychoanalytic Center, Cleveland, OH, May, 2016.

Weil, N. (1984). The Role of Facial Expressions in the Holding

Environment. *International Journal of Psychoanalysis,* 10: 76–89.

Winnicott, D.W. (1954–5). The Depressive Position in Normal Emotional Development. Paper read before the British Psychological Society, February, 1954. *British Journal of Medical Psychology,* 28, 1955. In *Through Paediatrics to Psycho-Analysis.* New York: Basic Books, 1958, 1975.

Bion's Reverie and Meditation in Psychoanalytic Therapy of Trauma

Arthur S. Blank, Jr.

Washington Baltimore Center for Psychoanalysis, and
Department of Psychiatry,

George Washington University

Author Note:

Presentation at a conference, "Listening to Trauma," The George
Washington University, Washington, DC, October 21, 2016
Correspondence concerning this article should be sent to: 5454
Wisconsin Ave, Suite 1435,
Chevy Chase, MD 20817

Arthur S. Blank, Jr.

Abstract

If psychopathology produced by extreme trauma can be thought of as an inability to fully process and symbolize experience, then recovery may consist of the growth of new capacities to process and symbolize. Freud announced that the psychoanalytic method involved the communication of the unconscious minds of two persons, and in recent years the work of Bion and various observations of early child and caregiver interactions have clarified the constituents of unconscious communication. The work of D. Laub and N. Auerhahn (1993), J. Cohen (1980,1985), F. Davoine and J-M. Gaudillière (2004) and others has helped to understand how a psychic hole, or gap, or absence, is present in persons afflicted by posttraumatic states. The questions remain as to how psychoanalytic therapy facilitates growth in the patient, of that which has not been present, to enable processing and symbolization, and what developments within the analyst promote this. We here offer thoughts about the effects of free association, and the use of concepts of container/contained, reverie, and the practice of meditation, to promote new capacities in analyst and patient.

Bion's Reverie and Meditation in Psychoanalytic Therapy of Trauma

I. Bion

The following addresses the relevance of Bion's theory of thinking, regarding beta elements, alpha elements, and the alpha function (conceptualizing levels of mental activity preliminary to or deeper than what we see in dreams) with reference to the treatment of post-traumatic stress disorder (PTSD), dissociative disorders, and other difficulties caused by severe trauma.

The British psychoanalyst Wilfred Bion was an Army tank commander in World War I when, in 1917 and 1918, he was exposed to intense combat in northern France. He experienced death and gruesomeness all around (over 100,000 fellow soldiers were killed in one battle at Amiens). At one point, his tank was blown up and he had to lead a group ahead on foot against the enemy. At another moment, it appears that Bion was the sole survivor of his tank crew. He received a Distinguished Service Order and the Legion of Honor for his combat performance. (Bion, 1982, 1985, 1997)

His wife has written that "Bion's remarkable physical survival against heavy odds concealed the emotional injury which left scars for many years to come" (Bion, 1997). Various sources (Sofer-Dudek, 2015) (Szykierski, 2010) (Symington and Symington, 1996) (Brown, 2005, 2006, 2012, 2016) (Souter, 2009) write that Bion was personally quite traumatized, and had recurrent nightmares, notwithstanding his life-long high-functioning career as an analyst and extraordinary creativity as an analytic writer. In his war memoirs (1997) he wrote (p. 202) "I never recovered from the survival of the Battle of Amiens."

He did not initially publish anything about his war experiences, but wrote about them after more than 40 years had passed, between 1958 and 1960. Another 37 years went by before these writings were published, in 1997. However, during the 1960s—in the years that immediately followed writing about his war experiences—he laid out in three books the concept of the capacity for maternal reverie in child care and psychoanalysis, as well as a general theory of thinking (Bion, 1962, 1963, 1965). In addition, he applied his concepts of containment, beta elements, alpha function, alpha elements, and reverie to normal relationships between infants and caregivers, to psychosis, and to analyses of persons with psychotic and neurotic problems.

Notably, he did *not* apply his new analytic ideas to the specific psychopathology of severe trauma. But in recent years, various writers (for example, L. Brown, J. and N. Symington, D. Szykierski, K. Souter, F. Davoine, J-M. Gaudillière) have begun to show how Bion's war experiences and their effects on him contributed to his theories and clinical work. Although military and war imagery and metaphors are to be found throughout his writings, the links between his basic theories and his war experiences have, until recently, remained hidden.

II. Effects of Trauma

Certain considerations about severe traumatic events (including war and rape) are relevant here: they produce annihilation anxiety sufficient to cause distinctive psychopathology, such as dissociation, fragmentation of mental contents, interference in symbolizing and processing of events, and PSTD symptoms. We can utilize Bion's concepts to understand that in a person with PTSD, a dissociative disorder, or another trauma condition, there are unconscious pre-thought fragments or beta elements (sensory data), which are memory bits of trauma events and the subject's reactions to them.

Regarding *normal* development, Bion suggested that the infant does not have access to a thinking apparatus mature enough to metabolize, integrate, or process experience, and must instead utilize the mind of the caregiver into which to project sensory data, or the pre-thought fragments dubbed beta elements, so that, now within the mind of the Other, they can be re-shaped, detoxified, organized, and transformed into alpha elements, and then once again absorbed within the infant, can progress eventually via dream thought, day and night, into symbolized or verbal thought.

We can hypothesize that the situation with a *part* of the traumatized person's mind is similar to this view of the infant's mind; that is, fragments of experience are present, especially at the non-verbal levels of somatic and visual registration, as suggested in the 1800s by Pierre Janet (Van der Hart, 1989). Because of the intensity of annihilation anxiety and because the traumatic events in various ways lie outside the individual's capacity to integrate and symbolize, these fragments have the status of pre-thought. They are beyond the individual's capacity to think, and thus belong in Bion's category of beta elements. Thus, part of the severely traumatized individual's mind can be thought of as similar to the overall situation of the early infant, and there is a need to project the pre-thought beta elements—fragmented registrations of the traumatic events—into the therapist. One aspect of the therapeutic situation can thus be considered a recreation of the early infant-caretaker situation, from the viewpoint of Bion's theory of thinking.

III. Enter Reverie

Let us now consider reverie, the pre-condition for the therapist's taking in and processing the pre-thought—sensory data— beta elements from the traumatized patient. The term, from the French *rêve* or dream, has connotations of revelry, delirium, and rejoicing, with some similarities to the state of consciousness known as daydreaming. Long understood as part of doing psychoanalysis, reverie is described by Freud as evenly hovering attention. The analyst's capacity for reverie is homologous with the mother's or other caregiver's capacity for reverie with a small child (Brown, 2005, 2006) (Ferro, 2006) (Harrison, 2006) (Ogden, 1997, 2004). While an element of therapeutic psychoanalysis in general, it is a particularly critical ingredient in the therapy or analysis of a person with trauma effects such as PTSD or dissociative disorder. At times, attaining a state of reverie in the therapist, and a similar state in the patient, is the condition which enables the pair to bring about the projection, by the patient into the therapist, of fragmented bits of mental impressions of actual traumatic events, along with projection of the reactions of the patient to the traumatic events. From this, a conscious, secondary-process version of the experiences and reactions thereto can eventually be assembled by patient and therapist.

To begin with, the creation of a state of reverie is promoted by attempting free association in both the therapist and the patient. The patient attempts free association, allowing and speaking whatever comes to mind. The analyst periodically attempts or allows free association, alternating with purposeful secondary-process thinking. Historically, our concern with free association has been that it promotes a flow of ideas in the patient. However, along with promoting the flow of secondary-process thought, free association encourages in the patient an altered state of consciousness, namely reverie, with the result being to soften the boundaries between conscious, pre-conscious, and unconscious, and thus increase access to beta elements. Reverie is promoted by *un*saturated interpretations from the therapist. *Saturated* interpretations are more complete and differentiated secondary-process formulations, usually requiring a few sentences, spelling out, for example, some aspect of a defense in secondary-process terms. *Unsaturated* interpretations are typically only a phrase or sentence fragment stating one or two ideas, implying possible links amongst multiple ideas from the patient. They somewhat depart from secondary process and approach unconscious levels of meaning. This is due to the relatively unstructured quality and lack of explicitness of unsaturated interventions, which allow for greater interpenetration from the unconscious of both parties.

Unsaturated interpretations convey more meanings with fewer words. They are brief and refer to underlying themes detected across multiple fields, including transference. Unsaturated interpretations by the therapist not only directly help the patient (and also the analyst) access unconscious ideas and affects, but they also serve as a model for open-minded self-observation with which the patient can identify. They thereby encourage the patient's attention to deeper levels of meaning and a deeper state of reverie. (Ferro, 2006).

When both therapist and patient achieve reverie states, there is an increase in mental flexibility and an opening to somatic and iconic levels of meaning. There is an increase in negative capability, a skill which Bion drew from the poet John Keats, who wrote in an 1818 letter: "I mean Negative Capability, which is when a man is capable of being in uncertainties, Mysteries, doubts, without any irritable reaching after fact and reason." This type of openness to the unknown from multiple directions is a critical ingredient in therapy for traumatized states.

IV. Meditation

Overall, the state of reverie in analytic therapy is akin to a state of meditation. Currently well-established clinically as helpful between sessions for patients with trauma psychopathology (Talkovsky and Lang, 2017), we note now that meditation can also be useful to the *therapist* in promoting the skill of achieving a reverie state. Meditation practice helps the therapist find a state of reverie while working with patients, through greater comfort about letting go temporarily of purposeful intellectual activity and greater familiarity with alternating between that state and analytical intellectual functioning. The practice of meditation is an exercise in negative capability.[31]

The new literature (Alfano, 2005, Bobrow, 2001, Harrison,2006) on the relation between psychoanalysis and Buddhist meditation makes clear how critical inquiry and synthesis of intellectual pro-

---

31. There are many varieties of meditation practice, producing a variety of states of consciousness. Some meditation states/practices may be more interesting and useful for various therapists. Understanding and sampling this variety can be accessed from a variety of sources. (Talkovsky and Lang 2017)

cesses can easily alternate, or even go on simultaneously, with the beginner's mind of meditation/reverie. This was presumably intuitively understood by Freud when he found that free association and evenly hovering attention, and thus reverie, can go on in alternation with intellectual formulation, in psychoanalysis.

Although Ogden has referred to reverie as involving a feeling of being suspended between sleep and wakefulness (Ogden, 1997), it may be more accurate to understand the reverie produced by free association and unsaturated interpretations (whether only thought or actually said), as a version of a meditation state. Meditation, after all, comes about by letting go of willful intellectual effort, adopting a disinterested attitude toward one's thoughts, and indeed letting go of memory and desire, as specified by Bion—or by Freud in 1923, who recommended that one avoid "reflection," "expectations," and "memory" (quoted in Alfano, 2005). Bion's and Freud's instructions for reverie are similar to traditional instructions for meditation, whether Buddhist or Hindu in origin.

One author (Alfano, 2005) has clarified how reverie connects with several skills, which she refers to as "transcendent attunement." This set of skills includes: (1) mental flexibility, wherein one alternates amongst various somatopsychic self-states; (2) negative capability (openness to new ideas and experiences); (3) unconscious reception, or receptivity to moment-to-moment shifts by self and other; and (4) intuition, direct knowing mediated by pre-conscious or unconscious processes. As Alfano points out, "Training in psychoanalysis implies theoretical foundations that enable us to listen skillfully to our patients and ourselves; yet analytic training does not usually extend to training the mind itself (as embodied psychesoma)." In meditation practice, "the mind is systematically trained to develop the capacity for receptive attentiveness." (Alfano, 2005) One's own personal psychotherapy or analysis and good supervision might contribute to training the mind toward receptive attentiveness and empathic attunement. However, direct meditation practice perhaps sometimes more powerfully deepens one's receptive skill, because it is more intensively devoted to that purpose.

V. What is the Cure?

Finally, I would like to return to the initial observation that psychopathology from severe trauma represents a processing deficiency disorder. When traumatic events occur, the individual does not have certain abilities with which to process, integrate, understand, or symbolize the experiences which have occurred. So, the experiences are held in suspension, perhaps in somatic or iconic (visual but not verbal) registration, with some in the fragmented state of beta elements straining for expression in the absence of the means of expression.

In my view, in analysis or therapy, the patient is persistently searching, consciously or unconsciously, to communicate to the therapist clues about what is missing by way of capacity for processing of traumatic experiences. In addition to being able to empathically contain aspects of the patient's annihilation anxiety, the therapist is therefore called upon to be deeply receptive to signals that may be transmitted about what is lacking, absent from the patient's mental repertoire. This is required to be able to symbolize and thus process the traumatic experiences.

To use Bion's concepts of thinking, we can say that the beta elements are the shards or fragments of sensations deriving from the traumatic events, and that they are projected into the mind of the therapist if both persons are sufficiently in a state of reverie and thus sufficiently in touch with each other's unconscious. The therapist, analogously to the early mother/caregiver, can somehow discern, again however unconsciously, what needs to be added and given back to the patient (alpha elements) that can now be pointed toward dream-processing and symbolized understanding. The general hypothesis here is that beta elements related to traumatic events contain clues to the capacities for mastery (symbolizing) of the traumas which the patient needs to accomplish, as well as records of the traumatic events *per se.*

This, incidentally, gives us a new understanding of traumatic dreams, which may be thought of as an advanced way station, though painfully permeated by annihilation anxiety, on the road to recovery. One bit of evidence for this is my own observation, in many patients, in contrast to that of various writers, of how repetitive traumatic dreams are almost never identical, but usually show changes in detail. These changes usually can be seen to show progress toward symbolic understanding and mastery. Secondly, if the *pre*-dreaming processes (beta to alpha) here reviewed are operating, and treatment is forward-moving, as a regular feature of recovery over time, one may see changes in the dreams, in the form of greater organization and mastery.

While we have understood for some time that traumatic dreams are dreamed in search of mastery, Bion's ideas lead to the hypothesis that traumatic dreams, by being dreamed, show an *achievement* of mastery. That is, they represent the outcome of sensory fragments' (beta elements) having been detoxified and given new co-herence in the interchange with the therapist, transformed into alpha elements and thus subject to being formed into dreams. Therefore, dreams occurring during treatment, however suffused with anxiety, may serve as valuable markers of the progress having occurred in the therapeutic process.

Although Bion did not directly tie his theory of thinking to clin-ical work with persons diagnosed with trauma effects, he did tie the theory to psychotic states, which in certain ways may be the same thing (see Davoine and Gaudillière 2004), even if the links to trauma in his psychotic patients were either not noticed or left unmentioned. (Symington and Symington, 1996, Brown, L, 2005, 2016, Szykier-ski, 2010). Bion did identify *nameless dread* as a major feature in psychosis, and this applies also to the effect of severe trauma.

The therapy of traumatic states requires that the therapist (1) gather the transference, that is, look for and take note of it every-where, (2) gather the history—including the history of the traumatic events, and (3) gather and organize all the relevant psychoneurotic conflicts—in other words, do all what is required in any psychoana-lytic therapy. However, in addition, if the patient has traumatic psy-chopathology, we need to (4) gather the patient's projections of what has been unintegrated (or dislodged) by the traumas, so that we can facilitate the new personality growth needed to integrate and master the traumas.

In treatment, what are especially germane are clues about the missing pieces, which are mysterious in their nature and effects. These pieces of the traumatic events and the subject's reactions, whose traumatic power—for the particular individual—is obscure, because it was an absence of capacities to contain and process expe-rience that led to the trauma symptoms.

It may be that one reason which has impeded understanding the nature and role of fragmented beta elements in traumatic states is that they are immersed in the annihilation anxiety, and therefore the analyst or therapist must tolerate a special intensity of annihilation anxiety (within himself or herself) in order to allow in, even uncon-sciously, these pre-thought sensory impressions.

In therapy or analysis, one identifies with the overwhelmed sub-ject. So along with the facts of the traumatic events and the subject's various reactions to them, the patient also conveys and projects the details of how he or she has not been able to cope, or symbolize the events and the reactions. So the therapist's internalized empathic model includes the gaps or holes in the patient's capacities for processing the traumas.

This way of looking at trauma disorders helps to understand a number of clinical facts. For example, some persons show an extreme walling-off of the critical events and symptoms, maybe for years, with or without recall of dreams of the traumas. Bion himself wrote that his war experiences were "carried over almost unchewed and apparently undigested for 40 years" (Bion, 1997). It seems that only some analytic therapists—though perhaps a currently expanding proportion—are relatively comfortable with victims of extreme trauma. This might be because only some are able to ease into reverie-meditation states, partly due to lack of consideration of such in training programs. Perhaps this suggests yet another way in which attention to Bion's work, applied to treatment of traumatic states, can expand the scope of psychoanalysis.

References

Alfano, C. (2005). Traversing the Caesura: Transcendent Attunement in Buddhist Meditation and Psychoanalysis, *Contemporary Psychoanalysis,* 41:223–247.

Altman, N. (2016). Wilfred Bion: From World War I to Contemporary Psycho- Analysis. *International Journal of Applied Psychoanalytic Studies*, 13:163–178.

Bion, W.R. (1962). *Learning From Experience.* London: Heinemann.

———— (1963). *Elements of Psycho-analysis.* London: Heinemann.

———— (1965). *Transformation.* London: Heinemann.

———— (1982). *The Long Week-End 1897–1919: Part of a Life.* Abingdon: Fleetwood Press.

———— (1985). *All My Sins Remembered: Another Part of a Life and the other Side Of Genius: Family Letters.* London: Karnac.

———— (1997). *War Memoirs:1917–1918* (Bion, F., editor). London: Karnac.

Blank Jr., A.S. (2009). Psychoanalytic Therapy and Meditation in Treatment of Traumatic States, Presentation at conference: *Transforming Trauma Leadership Forum.* Garrison Institute, Garrison NY.

Bobrow, J. (2000). Reverie in Zen and Psychoanalysis: Harvesting the Ordinary, *Journal of Transpersonal Psychology*, 32:165–175.

Brown L.J. (2005). The Cognitive Effects of Trauma: Reversal of Alpha Function and the Formation of a Beta Screen. *Psychoanalytic Quarterly,* 74:397–420.

———— (2006). Julie's Museum: The Evolution of Thinking, Dreams, and Historization the Treatment of Traumatized Patients. *International Journal of Psycho-analysis*, 87:1569–1585.

———— (2012). *Bion's Discovery of the Alpha Function: Thinking Under Fire on the Battlefield and In the Consulting Room.* International Journal of Psycho-Analysis, 93:1191–1214.

———— (2016). Lawrence J. Brown on 'Bion's Ego Psychology: Implications for An Inter Subjective View of Psychic Structure. *PEP/UCL Top Authors Project,* 1:4.

Cohen, J. (1980). Structural Consequences of Psychic Trauma: A New Look at 'Beyond the Pleasure Principle.' *International Journal of Psycho-analysis,* 61:421–432.

——— (1985). Trauma and Repression. *Psychoanalytic Inquiry,* 5:163–189.

Davoine, F., and Gaudillière, J-M. (2004). *History Beyond Trauma.* New York, NY: Other Press.

Ferro, A. (2006). Trauma, Reverie, and the Field. *Psychoanalytic Quarterly,* 75:1045–1056.

Harrison, J. (2006). Bion's O–An Open Gate Between Eastern and Western Psychotherapy: *Tel Aviv University Psychotherapy Program,* accessed at *pweb.netcom.com/~mthorn/vesnotes. htm*

Laub, D. and Auerhahn, N. (1993). Knowing and Not Knowing Massive Psychic Trauma: Forms of Traumatic Memory. *International Journal of Psycho-Analysis,* 74:287–302.

Ogden, T. (1997). Reverie and Interpretation. *Psychoanalytic Quarterly,* 66:567–595.

——— (2004). This Art of Psychoanalysis: Dreaming Undreamt Dreams and Interrupted Cries. *International Journal of Psychoanalysis,* 85:857–877.

Pelled, E. (2007). Learning From Experience: Bion's Concept of Reverie and Buddhist Meditation: A Comparative Study. *International Journal of Psychoanalysis,* 88:1507–1526.

Simo, J. (2000). On Healing Eve's Grief. *Psychoanalytic Review,* 87:251–276.

Sofer-Dudek, N. (2015). Of Losing One's Self: Bion's Traumatic War Experiences as a Foundation for his Outlook on Psychoanalysis. *Journal of the American Psychoanalytic Association,* 63:659–663.

Souter, K. (2009). The War Memoirs: Some Origins of the Thought of W.R. Bion, *International Journal of Psychoanalysis,* 90:795–808.

Symington N. and Symington J. (1996). *The Clinical Thinking of Wilfred Bion.* London: Routledge.

Szykierski, D. (2010). The Traumatic Roots of Containment: The Evolution of Bion's Metapsychology, *Psychoanalytic*

Quarterly, 79:935–968.

Talkovsky, A. and Lang, A. (2017). Meditation-based Approaches in the Treatment of PTSD, *PTSD Research Quarterly*, 28:1–10 (on line at *www.ptsd.va.gov*)

Van der Hart, O., Brown, P., and Van der Kolk, B. Pierre Janet's Treatment of Post-Traumatic Stress. *Journal of Traumatic Stress*, 2: 1–11.

Transference as Interference When Listening to Psychosis and Trauma

Françoise Davoine

École des Hautes Etudes en Sciences Sociales in Paris

Author Note:

Françoise Davoine, Agrégée de lettres classiques and Ph.D. in Sociology, is a psychoanalyst in private practice, a member of ISPS US, and Erikson Scholar at the Austen Riggs Center, Stockbridge, Massachusetts. She is a retired Faculty of the École des Hautes Études en Sciences Sociales, and was a psychoanalyst for 30 years in public psychiatric hospitals and free outdoor consultations, as well as a member of the ex École Freudienne founded by Jacques Lacan.

Françoise Davoine

Abstract

Listening to trauma, transference takes place with a particular analyst, says Bion, and may lead to "an agreed intersection," which I call interference. This intersection takes places in analogous zones of their respective histories. I will focus on a few sessions, which take place in a stoppage of time, and their outcome of putting time into motion, when the analyst agrees to the patient's listening to catastrophic zones on her side. From there, I will address the question of the existence of this transference as old as the wars, still to be invented from scratch at each time as if it had never existed. I contend it is unwelcome, for it breaks the limits, not only of time, but also between private and social life. I contend that listening to trauma, by claiming unclaimed experiences on both sides of psychoanalysis, bears a political dimension.

Transference as Interference When Listening to Psychosis and Trauma

When Listening to Trauma, the Classical Rules of Psychoanalysis, Benevolent Neutrality and Anamnesis, Do Not Work

1. We are Stuck in an Arrested Time

Timequake is the title given by Kurt Vonnegut to one of his last books. Until the end of his life, he relentlessly wrote about the destruction of Dresden while he was held in captivity underground in a slaughterhouse, *Slaughter-House Five*, situated at the limits of the city. This stoppage of time is very difficult to face, for causality does not work. Once we discover traumatic episodes in a patient's life, she usually says: and so, what? Causation, even psychic causality, needs the flow of time, the past tense of the cause, and the future for its effects. Paradoxically, trauma is not the cause of the trouble, but its purpose. Trauma is not about causality, but about an attempt to make an inscription of that which cannot be said.

2. The Purpose of the Repetition of Traumatic Episodes is to Assess Denied Facts and to Inscribe Them

At the end of his life, Bion wrote three books about what he calls, in the second part of *A Memoir of the Future*, "The Past Presented," the past in the present tense. In *All My Sins Remembered* he writes about his return from WWI: "I did not see that peacetime was **no time** for me. I did not know, however many pretty ribbons I put on a wartime uniform, that wartime also was no time for me. I was twenty-four; no good for war, no good for peace, and too old to change. It was truly terrifying. Sometimes it burst out in sleep. Terrified. What about? Nothing, nothing." (p.16) In *The Long Week-end*: "Oh yes, I died, in Amiens, in Cambrai, in Ypres, on August 1918." (p.165)

Recently a patient said to me: "I died in Vichy, there was nothing, I could make no link to anything." Born in 1935, she had lived during WWII in the town of Vichy, the seat of Pétain's government after his alliance with the Nazis. Her father was a collaborationist officer and a very brutal man (a story which fits Jerry Fromm's paper). Now she adds: "Only by writing do I exist." She came to see me after years of unfruitful psychoanalysis, when she discovered I had written about *Don Quixote*.

My book is entitled *Fighting Melancholia: Don Quixote's Teaching*. "Fighting melancholia" is Cervantes' purpose, according to his own words in the Prologue of his first novel, which aims toward the inscription of the author's successive traumas. He does so by inscribing his successive trauma: he lost the use of his left hand while fighting against the Turks in the Battle of Lepanto; then, on his way back to Spain, he was highjacked by pirates and spent five years as a slave in Algiers. Other traumas happened after he returned to Spain, as he was betrayed by his own people. His masterpiece belongs to what Cathy Caruth calls "Literature in the Ashes of History."

Don Quixote appears to Cervantes when, at 50 years old, he is confined again in a prison of Seville, after a false accusation. In "the ashes of history," he decides to write down his knight's successive sallies out of his house to accomplish heroic deeds. His second sally starts after his best friends burn his library. In the Prologue, Cervantes calls Don Quixote his crazy son. He launches him into delusional episodes that show, in the present time, the traumatic revivals of his author's wars and slavery.

Don Quixote claims that his deeds must be reported to Dulcinea, the Lady of his Thoughts, and to be inscribed for generations to come. In order to help him debrief his successive failures, he gives him a therapist, Sancho Panza—*therapon* means in the *Iliad*, the second in combat and the ritual double in charge of funeral duties. When they both lie on the ground after each episode, a talking cure takes place between them. At some point, Don Quixote becomes a psychoanalyst who cures a mad-man, Cardenio, in the wild space of a mountain, the Sierra Morena. Later on, we learn that the mad-man has been betrayed by his best friend, who hijacked his girlfriend against her will.

3. Cervantes' Dulcinea is Literature.

Cervantes' purpose, to inscribe the folly of wars and slavery, is accomplished when *Don Quixote* quickly becomes a worldwide bestseller, until another trauma compels him to write a second novel. His colleagues are jealous of his success and pay a forger to publish a sequel of the novel to vilify the heroes. At the end of the second *Don Quixote*, Cervantes makes him die to prevent such knavery. This time, he launches his son in a fight against perversion.

Bion also complains of having been regularly "sacked." The lady of his thoughts is at first "the Grid" which stands at the beginning and the end of his theoretical books. This schematic diagram of types of thoughts helps him to think about what he calls "thoughts without a thinker, for which words are things and things are words... looking for a thinker to be thought." In the last part of his life, Bion discovers also that his Dulcinea is literature itself. He writes a book of fiction, *A Memoir of the Future*, in which he becomes a character under different names, such as PA, psychoanalyst or Captain Bion.

I just came back from a conference on Bion in Paris where I gave a paper entitled "Bion Quixote." By choosing this title, I wished to point out how Bion's patients compelled him to disclose and write down, in his old age, the timeless experience of WWI, as the background of his listening to psychosis and trauma. He calls this interference "an agreed intersection." The analyst must agree upon an intersection, for both himself and his patient, between their small stories and the larger history.

4. The patient listens to traumas of which the analyst is unaware in his own story

This interchangeability of place is set concretely in a novel of Pat Barker's, *Trilogy*. She wrote it from the clinical notes of William Rivers, a famous neurologist and anthropologist, who became a psychotherapist for returning soldiers from WWI. He listened to them while reading Freud and modifying his technique.

One particularly striking scene takes place in a military hospital in Scotland. One of the soldiers notices that Rivers stutters at times. He asks him about his symptom. Rivers proposes to exchange seats with him. Sitting in his patient's chair, Rivers associates his stuttering with his lack of visual memory, and sincerely investigates the link between the two.

Later on, in the novel, he will discover, thanks to this patient, a transgenerational trauma. His ancestor, another William Rivers, was a sailor who killed the man who killed Admiral Nelson. His leg had been amputated without anesthesia and he is said to have endured the cutting without a word. The scene was represented in a picture displayed in his childhood home. As this visual memory comes back, Rivers realizes that through his efforts to bring traumatized soldiers to speak, he contradicts the order to be silent for himself as well.

This order echoes the last sentence of the *Tractatus*, written by Wittgenstein, another veteran of WWI while he was fighting in the Austrian army on the Eastern front. This last sentence reads: "Whereof one cannot speak, one should stay silent." This is especially true for the analyst who sticks to the neutrality requested by his training. After ten years of suicidal and brutal behavior in Austria, Wittgenstein returned to Cambridge in England, and according to his own words, in his *Philosophical Investigations,* he used "philosophy as a therapy." He then changed this sentence into: whereof what cannot speak, one cannot help showing what cannot be said. Rivers realized that by stuttering he was showing his patient what the patient himself could not tell.

Dori Laub emphasizes the question asked by survivors of the Holocaust and their descendants before they give him their testimony: "Who are you?" This question was regularly asked by patients whom I encounter in psychiatric hospitals and in my office, who force me out of hiding and lead me to discover, even now, unwritten pieces of my history.

5. This Discovery of Transference as Interference Happened at the Very Beginning

When I decided to train as a psychoanalyst, in the seventies, I joined the École Freudienne founded by Jacques Lacan, and decided that a psychiatric hospital was a better place to train. Jean Max Gaudillière joined me in that foolish decision, although our degrees were not in medicine or in psychology but in classic literature and sociology. We met, by chance, in a meeting of the École Freudienne, with a psychoanalyst who was the medical director of a ward in a public psychiatric hospital situated in the North of France. He agreed to take us, for free. For our boss in sociology, Alain Touraine, we launched into a research on "madness and the social link," which became the title of our weekly seminar in the Research Institute of Social Sciences, which continued for forty years until Jean Max's death.

Traveling to that hospital in the North of France, we passed by military cemeteries with white crosses on both sides of the road. Still I did not notice them, for they were normal scenery on a land where so many wars were fought. "Knowing and not knowing," says Dori Laub. Then a dream struck me like thunder, which told me what I was doing there: I had traveled to listen to trauma through a personal "interference" with the history of the place. My very Lacanian analyst did not pay any attention to that fact.

The dream occurred when I returned to Paris after seeing a chronic patient confined in that hospital since the fifties. He had become delusional after the war, and had received ECT in Paris, a treatment that was considered an archaic method when I saw him. Now, no more. This man smoked his pipe while we talked in the common room of the ward. The following night, I dreamt of my grandfather, who had died in the fifties. He also smoked his pipe and looked a little like him. He used to hold my hand when I was a kid, and stay silent. He had been a stretcher-bearer on every battle ground of WWI, and probably in that region. Then I knew that my purpose in coming there was to encounter the folly of wars. (I was born in 1943, in the Alps). Other patients made me discover that psychosis and trauma belong to the same field of research on unsymbolized matters, at the crossroads of our story and history.

In another hospital situated in the suburbs of Paris, where we followed the same medical director, I met a young woman talking quietly with the maddest patient on the ward. "You are an intern psychologist?" I asked her. "No, I am a psychotic," she answered, "And you, what are you doing there?"

"I am a psychoanalyst on the ward." And I added, disclosing my other job for the first time: I work on "madness and the social link" in a research institute in Paris.

She immediately said: "Apropos of madness and the social link, I am Italian, my father was the only survivor of a massacre in the Battle of El Al Ahmein"—a battle which took place in Egypt in 1942 where the Italians, allied with the Germans, were defeated by the English. I was dumbfounded. My father had been a survivor of a massacre of hostages by the Nazis, on a pass leading toward Italy. She happened to be schizophrenic and delusional at times, and had indeed been a Ph.D. psychologist, who had also been abused by her thesis director. We worked regularly every week together, for free, in the outdoor consultation area of the hospital, and then in my office after I retired. Now she is out of psychosis and she often asks me, "By what coincidence did I meet you that day, in the hospital?"

6. When the Symbolic Chain is Broken and Causality Does Not Work, We Rely on Coincidences.

Surrealist objects, such as a pipe or an uncanny encounter, have meanings that need to be grasped and "made to speak." After all, the word "surrealism" was invented during WWI by the French poet Apollinaire while he was fighting and writing poems on the front. The things that speak against all odds when it is impossible to speak may be a book, a dog, a house, an embryo, in other examples I will give you.

I was sitting in the common ward of the same hospital where I used to work, when an African man entered the room, very disturbed, walking to and fro. He stopped by me, staring at me with bloodshot eyes and he said: "What are you doing here?" I told him I was a psychoanalyst on the ward and he shot back: "Don't try to do ethnopsychiatry on me, I want to be Erwin Schrödinger,"—one of the founders of quantum physics. I told him right away that by chance, I was reading Schrödinger's Lectures, given at Cambridge, in 1956, entitled *Mind and Matter.*

His expression changed completely. "Come on," he said, "we have to talk." We went into the little room that I used as an office, and he told me his story. He had been a student in physics in his country in Africa, when a dictator took over. He protested with others, was arrested, put in jail, heavily whipped, and escaped to France, where strange beings besieged him to force him to kill, especially the evil genius of his country. It was very tiring. He was stunned that we both knew the good old genius Schrödinger. Perhaps he could eventually resume his studies in physics. I never met him again, for he never came back to the hospital.

Still it is no miracle, rather, an interference, that allows for the possible genesis of speech between the two people in the room, by linking irrational elements charged with an impressive amount of energy, to somebody who answers to them.

7. Those Elements Have Been Acknowledged Under Different Names, At Different Times, by Authors Who Had the Experience of War.

Bion calls them beta elements. Aby Warburg, the art historian who became mad at the beginning of WWI—believing, like Don Quixote, that he was the chief general of the German army—and who recovered in the twenties, calls them "surviving images." They are taped on what he calls the "seismograph of the soul" and survive the psychic death of trauma.

Schrödinger himself, in the lectures I was reading, advises psychotherapists to abandon neutrality and work on interference with their patients, for in the same way light disturbs subatomic particles called photons, our particles of unsymbolized matter disturb our patients. He knew that from experience, for he was the only non-Jewish scientist to abandon a prestigious position in Berlin and flee from the Nazis to Ireland, where his wife became crazy. She was eventually healed by Wittgenstein's disciple, Maurice O'Drury, in Dublin.

Listening to trauma is as old as the war. Socrates, another veteran of wars between cities in Greece, calls these "beta elements" *stoicheia aloga*, elements without *logos*, without speech and reason. And he adds, "Only by interlacing words do we transform irrational and unknowable elements that we feel into syllables that can be acknowledged and expressed to allow a true judgment."

8. **This "Interlacing" Occurs When the Analyst Decides to Name Uncanny Impressions that Interfere with the Turmoil of the Session, when a Ruthless Agency Enters the Session.**

When time stops and the patient wants to quit, or commit suicide, the therapist has to quickly make up his mind: either fight the evil agency that enters the session and destroys all capacity to think, or fly toward theories diagnosing psychosis as a disease or a structure—and send the patient to a psychiatric hospital.

This ruthless agency is not a metaphor. It is encountered concretely when one is betrayed by his own people, as says Jonathan Shay in *Achilles in Viet Nam*. This can be a betrayal by parents or neighbors in child abuse, by one's own command, during wartime, by the civilian at the rear at the time of homecoming, and by totalitarian systems, when a perverse social link destroys all possibility of trust and truth. Pioneers of the psychoanalysis of psychosis who were trained in military hospitals during the First World War, such as Ferenczi in Hungary and Frieda Fromm Reichman in Germany, knew about that murderous agency, which was at work on both sides.

In her book *I Never Promised you a Rose Garden*, Joanne Greenberg writes about her psychoanalysis just after WWII, when she was a crazy adolescent, and insists from the beginning on the interference between her psychoanalyst, Dr. Fried, and her Jewish grandfathers who had immigrated from Latvia beforehand. Dr. Fried, that is, Frieda Fromm Reichmann, had escaped from the Nazis to Chestnut Lodge in the thirties. She went out of psychosis while a genesis of otherness occurred little by little in the course of interferences triggered along the transference.

9. **In Greek, Trauma Means a Wound. In this Case, it Means a Wound that Severs Otherness.**

Otherness, the Big Symbolic Other, warrant of truth and trust, is a keystone of Lacan's theory. But when the Symbolic Other is destroyed by a ruthless other for whom there is no other, time stops, for it relies on symbolic numbers to go on. Anamnesis does not work either, for memory needs the past. Instead, a strange memory takes place in the present tense, unable to be forgotten.

"You cannot remember when you are three," said a psychiatrist to a former patient of Jean Max who came to see me last month. At that age, he had witnessed the assassination of her mother by her father who had shot himself afterward. This seems outrageous, but still it is true. "One cannot remember what one cannot forget," says Bion. "Each session is a first session."

Each lecture on that topic is a new lecture. In our Conference, I ask again and again, like veterans who tell always the same story: with what apparatus do we listen to trauma? Ears are not sufficient. Sometimes we listen with the soul of things, of animals, the only form of otherness available.

Some years ago, an analyst came to see me who was a wreck. Although she spent ages in analysis, and is now quite well known, she thought she was a nobody and wanted to kill herself. In a session, she mentioned a corpse who had always been in her psychoanalyst's waiting room but remained unknown. I had no clue either. One day, she wished to stop to see me, and I was useless. On that rupture line, this dead body started to speak to me. It spoke of the death of a house, the bankruptcy of her father's business when she was 7. He had started it in France under his own name, after the extermination of Jewish members of his family in Eastern Europe. I told her that her name—and famous Name of the Father, according to Lacan—had been put in jeopardy. "And so, what? She knew that," she said. "What was the big deal?"

The big deal was that this dead house spoke to houses that my father had built during the war in the Alps, for cheese cooperatives. I was born in one of them. While he was in a Resistance network, their huge cellars, where cheese was ripened, were used to hide weapons and food for the underground. He abandoned them after the war and broke his contract with the mountaineers under the pressing urge of my mother to quit the region. She had been imprisoned by the Nazis during the war, pregnant with me, and he could not resist her wish.

Ten years ago, I read in an article about the history of cheese in Savoy, the province where I was born. It said that the cooperatives had been created in the sixties by So-and-So. I asked my father if he knew the name of this man. Of course, he knew him. During the war, he was a member of the French militia, an armed force collaborating with the Nazis. He had taken over the cooperatives and cut out the period of the war from history. I said I would write to the author of the article. My father became furious. "Don't do that, you will be killed." Ten years ago, we were still in wartime.

I did not disclose this story to that analyst. But my conviction that the corpse was a dead house for her and for me triggered a new energy. She could remember the years of dereliction which followed the bankruptcy. They had remained present until now in her invisible loneliness among her success in the media. When they resonated with my own story, time was put into motion again.

10. Those Examples Tell You About my Personal Method

After all, Descartes wrote his *Discourse of the Method* as a personal method to deal with traumatic dreams and hallucinations, which scared him in November 1619 when he was a soldier at war. He had volunteered in the armies of the Thirty Years' War, and was staying at Ulm, in Germany. In his first nightmare, he was falling under the horrific pressure of winds from the Beyond. Then he heard terrible voices, and saw his room filled with spooky lights during the night. It took him 28 years to write his *Discourse*, published in 1637 in French, not in Latin, so that it might be read by women, who make up half of the world. It starts as follows: "My aim here is not to teach a method that everyone ought to follow to conduct his reason, but solely to reveal how I have tried to conduct my own" (p.16). The purpose of his personal method is not to attract groupies named Cartesian disciples, but to face the nameless dread of his nightmares, especially when he falls into the abyss of loneliness. A few pages later, he writes: "But like a man who walks alone and in the shadows, I resolved to go so slowly and to use so much circumspection in all things that if I did not advance, but very little, I would at least, very well guard myself against falling." (p. 33).

Periodically, we analysts fall from our armchair, as happened to Freud in 1897. Apparently, he abandoned his method of listening to trauma: "I renounce my Neurotica," he writes to Fliess in September 1897. From now on, traumas would be considered as fantasies. His avoidance of transference as interference is striking. At a moment of rupture "when patients leave him after a good start," he refuses to incriminate the fathers accused of sex abuse, and especially his own father. In February of the same year, he had indeed written to Fliess: "My father is one of those perverse who abused sexually my little brothers and sisters and is responsible for their hysteria." At the beginning of psychoanalysis, this interference in the transference between his story and his patients' disappeared. Lacan used the same sleight of hand to avoid dealing with transference in psychosis. Hence the slogan: "There is no transference in psychosis, it is a structure once for all."

Still, as Cathy Caruth shows us, the question of trauma continued to haunt him. Freud mentions "an unconscious which is not re-pressed," in different texts about madness and trauma, such as the *Gradiva*—in which a young man becomes delusional on the site of the disaster of Pompei—in *The Uncanny*, and in *Moses*, written while his books were burnt in Berlin by the Nazis. Bion agrees: interference is not counter-transference triggered by some unanalyzed repression, but another kind of unconscious. Jean Max and I call it a cutout un-conscious, without any repressed symbolic inscription. Some speak of dissociation. I prefer to talk about exile. An exile to the land of ghosts and "surviving images."

11. To be Able to Listen to Trauma, a Cutout Language Must be Retrieved from a Land of Exile.

The cutout unconscious manifests itself concretely in the writ-ings of Cervantes and Bion. At the beginning of *Don Quixote*, the narrator loses the manuscript, and finds it by chance written in Ar-abic, among discarded papers. The new narrator will be Cid Hamet Ben Engeli, coming from the land of Cervantes' slavery.

At the beginning of Bion's writing, there is also a lost manu-script. His *War Memoirs* was written as a journal instead of the letters he should have sent to his parents. He wrote them again accurately, with the traumatic memory that does not forget, and lost them again. They would be found and published after his death in 1979.

Ten years before, in 1968, Bion was 71; he had gone West, to Los Angeles, to escape "the cozy domesticity of England." Only then and there did he start to write about his departure from India to England, alone, at 8 years old, and about his war. During his exile in California, I imagine that he heard the American accent that triggered memo-ries of the voices of American soldiers who had fought at his side in France, and brought back the surviving images of his dead comrades.

I, too, had to travel to the battlefields in the North of France. I also traveled to my birthplace in the Alps where I had not returned for a long time, to listen to the ghosts on the slopes of the mountains now occupied by ski resorts. Why do I persist in focusing on history? Is it or is it not psychoanalysis?

For history is rarely mentioned in Bion's theoretical books. I was puzzled when I read his description of some sessions when "cata-strophic change happens" in the course of an analysis that seems to go well. He hardly mentions his patients' story, and does not say any-thing about the source of his "strong emotional reactions," on which he relies to make comments in the here and now of the session. Only in his *Brazilian Conferences*, at the end of his life, did he insist on the analyst's particularity. We listen to trauma and psychosis with our "personality." We register a "withoutness," made up of surviving images without in and out, without past and future, which invade the analyst's dreams or daydreams with surrealistic things: a pipe, an abandoned house, a book, the smell of unburied corpses, or a dog.

I once made a dog speak, by telling a delusional patient about the story of a Saint Bernard dog who had died while saving my mother's life in the mountains the year before my conception. This patient's delusion was that he was the White Knight. His psychiatrist had heard about my seminar on *Don Quixote*, and phoned to me say: "Don Quixote is in my office, may I send him to you?" When the Knight arrived in my office, I told him I would be his Sancho Panza, and asked him right away what had happened to him. He immediately told me about the death of his dog, who choked among the luggage aboard the Air France plane which was carrying him for the first time to France from Latin America, when he was five years old, without his parents. His grandfather, whom he had never seen, was a veterinarian. He greeted him at the airport and treated this death as if it were nothing. I showed him the photo of the Saint Bernard dog sitting on my shelf, and told him about her sacrifice so that I would live. He decided to stay, and start what he called our common research.

12. Bion Calls this Common Research a "Commensal Inquiry"

A "commensal" in French, means the companion at a meal table. It is the best place to learn how to listen to trauma, as shown in Plato's *Symposium*, where different commensals give their conception of Love, *Eros*. When it is time to deliver his discourse, Socrates speaks through the mouth of his Dulcinea, the prophetess and medicine woman Diotima, and defines transference in the case of trauma. According to her saying, Eros is the son of *Poros*—which means in Greek "the passage," the etymology of porosity—and of *Penia*, Poverty. In the penury of symbolic resource, in the absence of any reliable other, a passage is possible thanks to the porosity of the therapist. According to Diotima, Eros is neither a god nor a human but a link between the two, an "in-between," *metaxu* (the unconscious), which she calls a *daimôn*, a demon. It intervenes in day and night dreams. Although the word demon has been used to vilify the gods and semi-gods of pagan animism, it tells about the special transference while listening to trauma that gives birth to a new subject of speech, in the middle of reification.

Socrates' craft to deliver the psyche in that case *proceeds* from a strange habit witnessed by his contemporaries, especially at the very beginning and at the end of the *Symposium*. Suddenly he might stop walking and stay still for a long time. When the Banquet starts, his companion tells the others that he will be late, for he is stuck in the middle of the street. At the very end, Alcibiades arrives completely drunk and to speak about Eros, he gives a discourse in praise of Socrates, saying how Socrates refused to go to bed with him.

Then he depicts how he fell madly in love with him, during the wars between Greek cities, when he was a general on a horse, and Socrates a private on foot, practicing the art of psychotherapy, taking care of Alcibiades' wounds and also of his comrades' panic when they were defeated. He convinced them to face the enemy instead of fleeing to an unavoidable death. Alcibiades links Socrates' craft to his strange habit, on the battlefield, of staying still during a whole day, in the middle of the astonished soldiers. I conclude, for our purpose, that when he stops, in the middle of the battlefield, Socrates listens to trauma on his side and can use his porosity to help his comrades in the penury of words. In the same manner, we must stand still and listen to our cutout unconscious, in order not to flee from the ruthless otherness intruding on the session, and to get rid of it by starting a symbolic link from scratch.

13. Starting from Scratch Again and Again, Listening to Trauma is Triggered by an Embryonic Knowledge

I probably listened to traumas since my childhood during the war and even before my birth, in my mother's womb, when she was caught by the Nazis and spent the beginning of our pregnancy in a crowded cell beside the torture chamber.

Bion insists on this embryonic knowledge. In the chapter "The Dawn of Oblivion" of *A Memoir of the Future*, the germ cells dialogue with other critical ages in his life. At each time, he had to start the possibility of speaking all over again. Of course, Bion had read Laurence Sterne's novel *Tristram Shandy*, which starts by making an embryo speak. The book, in which the chronology is constantly muddled—"shandied" in Sterne's terms—is written in a fight with the arrested time of trauma. Laurence Sterne was the son of a military man who fought on the same battlefields as Bion, in the North of France, two centuries before. In his late forties, he decided to write a version of *Don Quixote* set in the middle of the 18th century. He starts his novel by giving the speech to the germ cells of his hero, at the very moment of his almost failed conception, while his parents are at war with each other. The first sentence of the novel reads: "I wish either my father or my mother or indeed both of them, as they were in duty both equally bound to it, had minded what they were about when they begot me."

This "wish," the master word of psychoanalysis, does not express a repressed unconscious, but a cutout experience "of terror, natural to so young a traveler, ... prey to suddenly starts and a series of melancholy dreams and fancies for nine long months together." But right away, Sterne claims "the Homunculus' rights, in this age of levity, to the eye of folly or prejudice—to the eye of reason and scientific research." The research concerns the birth of an otherness when nobody is there to think about you. The only one who speaks to the child in the whole novel is neither his father nor his mother, but his uncle Captain Toby, who has been wounded during the battle of Namur in Flanders and left alone on the ground where Captain Bion's comrades died two centuries later. In between them commences a music, the music of the novel—the music which resonates between patient and analyst—explicitly mentioned by Sterne, which put time into motion.

Conclusion

"You are the music while the music lasts," wrote T.S. Eliot in "The Dry Salvages" while he was in London in 1942, during air raids. The music I try to make you hear is the music which transforms the noise of the wars between countries or families and makes psychoanalysis go the other way around, for it aims toward what Bion calls "The Dawn of Oblivion," which is the beginning of repression. At that point, Wittgenstein says, "When the tool with the name is broken, a nod of the head can take the place of the broken tool." The analyst gives such a nod of the head when he recognizes that he has been "touché"—a French word used in fencing—and is able to answer for an "unclaimed experience," in Cathy Caruth's words.

Françoise Davoine

References

Barker, P. (1992) *Regeneration*. New York: Dutton.

———— (1994) *The Eye in the Door*. New York: Dutton.

———— (1995) *The Ghost Road*. New York: Dutton.

Bion, W. (1975, 1991) *A Memoir of the Future*, London: Karnac Books.

———— (1982). *The Long Week-end, 1897–1919*. London: Karnac Books.

———— (1985) *All my Sins Remembered*. London: Karnac Books.

———— (1920, 1997) *War Memoirs*, ed. Francesca Bion. London: Karnac Books.

———— (1994) *Clinical Seminars and Other Works*. London: Karnac Books.

Caruth, C. (2013). *Literature in the Ashes of History*. Baltimore: Johns Hopkins University Press.

Cervantès, M. de (1603, 2013) *Don Quixote*. J. Ornsby, Trans. Canterbury: Canterbury Classics.

Davoine, F. (2016) *Fighting Melancholia, Don Quixote's Teaching*, A. Jacob, Trans. London: Karnac Books.

Descartes, R. (1637, 1994). *Discourse on the Method,* G. Heffernan, Trans. Notre Dame, IN: University of Notre Dame Press.

Eliot, T.S. (1967). *The Complete Poems and Plays, The Dry Salvages.* New York: Harcourt Brace & Company.

Freud, S. (1985) *The Complete Letters of Sigmund Freud to Wilhelm Fliess, 1887–1904.* J.M. Masson, Trans. Cambridge, MA: Harvard University Press.

Freud, S. (1907) *Delusion and Dreams in Jensen's Gradiva*. Standard Edition 9: 1–95.

———— (1919) *The Uncanny,* Standard Edition 17: 2X17–256.

———— (1939). *Moses and Monotheism*, Standard Edition, 19: 1–137.

Greenberg, J. (1964, 1989). *I Never Promised You a Rose Garden.* New York: Penguin Books.

Homer, *The Iliad,* 16 (1924) A. Lurray, Trans. London: William Heinemann.

Lacan, J. (1958, 1977). *Ecrits à Sélection, On a Question Preliminary to Any Possible Treatment of Psychosis*. A. Sheridan, Trans. New York: Norton.

Laub, D. (1993). Knowing and Not Knowing. *The International Journal of Psychoanalysis* 74.

Plato (1989) *Theaetetus*, R. Waterfield, Trans. New York: Viking.

———— *The Symposium.*

Schrodinger, E. (1956, 1990). *Mind and Matter.* Cambridge: Cambridge University Press.

Shay J. (1994). *Achilles in Viet Nam.* New York: Simon & Schuster Touchstone Books.

Sterne, L. (1759,1980). *The Life and Opinions of Tristram Shandy, Gentleman*. London: Norton.

Vonnegut, K. (1997, 1998) *Timequake*. New York: Berkeley Books.

———— (1969, 1997). *Slaughterhouse-Five*. New York: Random House.

Warburg, A. A Lecture on Serpent Ritual. W. Mainland, Trans. *Journal of the Warburg Institute*, 2, 1928–39.

Wittgenstein, L. (1918, 2001).*Tractatus Philosophicus.* London: Routledge.

———— (1953, 1958).*Philosophical Investigations*. Oxford: Blackwell.

Meta-Witnessing:
A New Perspective on Witnessing Trauma

Marilyn B. Meyers

The Washington School of Psychiatry

Author Note:

Marilyn B. Meyers, Ph.D. is on the faculty of the Washington
School of Psychiatry, where she teaches Attachment Theory and
Object Relations Theory and supervises in the post-graduate
Clinical Program on Psychotherapy Practice. She maintains
a private practice in Bethesda, where she sees couples and
individuals.She is particularly interested in inter-generational
trauma. She is co-author and co-editor of *The Power of Witnessing:
Reflections, Reverberations and Traces of the Holocaust-Trauma,
Psychoanalysis and the Living Mind* (Routledge 2012, eds. Nancy
R. Goodman and Marilyn Meyers). Her publications include
"When the Holocaust Haunts the Couple: Hope, Guilt and Survival
in *Psychoanalytic Perpectives on Couple Work* (2005) and "Am
I My Mother's Keeper?Certain Vicissitudes in the Mother-
Daughter Relationship Concerning Envy" in *The Mother-Daughter
Relationship* (Jason Aronson, 2008).

She is past Chair of the Clinical Program and Chair of Admissions.
She is past President of the Section on Couples and Families of the
Division of Psychoanalysis (39) of the American Psychological
Association.

Correspondence concerning this article should be sent to:
marilynbmeyers@gmail.com
6917 Arlington Rd. #220
Bethesda, Md. 20814

Marilyn B. Meyers

Abstract

In the face of trauma, the experience may be processed in isolation, with no external witness. This leaves the individual with a dual traumatic experience. Is there an "other" who can "know" and bear witness? Is the traumatic memory real? What if the perpetrator is a parent upon whom one is dependent? The very person to whom a child should be able to turn for help and safety is the one doing harm. What if the trauma occurs, as in the Holocaust, as a societal, man-made trauma? What if the perpetrator is a priest or a teacher? How is the trauma embodied? These experiences, of trauma without witness, lead to a psychic retreat and a deadening of the mind. In effect, the person cannot bear witness to his own experience in isolation. Laub, D. and Auerhahn, N.C. delineated various levels of knowing that result from trauma. With the opening of space that a witnessing other provides, the level of knowing can evolve from not knowing to metaphor. The level of meta-witnessing that I am introducing is seen as a broader, more layered level, in which the witnessing can be witnessed. Memorials, museums, writing, and visual art are all forms of witnessing and meta-witnessing. The *Listening to Trauma* Conference reflects a form of meta-witnessing.

Meta-Witnessing:
A New Perspective on Witnessing Trauma

Meta: a higher or second order, pertaining to an abstract, high-level analysis. (e.g., meta-language: a language to talk about language)

In this paper, I am attempting to develop a concept of meta-witnessing, a form of witnessing that goes beyond the witnessing of trauma and beyond the honoring of the act of witnessing. Felman and Laub (1992) wrote about three levels of witnessing in relation to the Holocaust experience: "(1) the level of being a witness to oneself within the experience; (2) the level of being a witness to the testimonies of others; and (3) the level of being a witness to the process of witnessing itself." I would like to add a fourth level of witnessing: meta-witnessing.

In developing this concept, I deeply appreciate and respect the levels of witnessing described by Felman and Laub. Their three levels of witnessing are essential to our understanding of the essence of witnessing trauma. I honor these levels of witnessing; however, I want to expand our perspective to a more abstract meta-level.

What do I mean by this? I think of a hall of mirrors. We can view the witnessing of trauma from multiple perspectives; up, down, and around, internal, and external. We are likely to become disoriented in this hall of mirrors. What are we looking at? Are we seeing reflections? Are the reflections of our own experiences, or those of others? How do we maintain a sense of balance while engaging in this complex process?

Effects of Time Passing

It has now been more than 70 years since the end of World War II. In our book, *The Power of Witnessing: Reflections, Reverberations and Traces of the Holocaust* (Goodman and Meyers, 2012), I developed the concept of the Historic and Psychic Timeline (Meyers, 2012). I explored the ways in which witnessing the Holocaust both opened and closed space over time. It is painful to acknowledge, but it is a reality that at this point in time there remain diminishing numbers of survivors of the Holocaust to communicate their experiences, to give testimony, and to bear witness directly. *"As we enter the 21st century, we are faced with new challenges to witnessing. This remains a process without an end point..."* (Meyers, 2012, p.42).

The Conference *Listening to Trauma: Insight and Actions* represents a form of meta-witnessing. At the conference, participants who both needed and wanted witnesses were able to witness one another. We value witnessing as a necessary and essential part of being human. We collectively recognize the importance of witnessing and serving as witnesses to one another.

The Role of the Clinician as Witness: Being "With," Containing, and Holding

The role with which we, as clinicians, are most familiar is to be willing to be with, and listen to, the person who has suffered trauma and take testimony and bear witness. The person giving testimony is being witnessed and held in mind. This can, and I think must, serve as an experience of a relational bond with a willing other. In that experience, the patient's feeling is: "I am in a trauma state (or have suffered trauma) and I am not alone." This state can mirror the experience of a child who is in distress and receives comforting and care-giving help. Help may take the form of "being with," not necessarily of "doing." This act is in keeping with Winnicott's concept of the environmental mother, wherein he describes the ordinary mother in her ordinary care of her baby (Winnicott, 1973).

Felman and Laub (1992, p.71) state that "the task of the listener is to be *unobtrusively present*...the interviewer has to be both unobtrusive, nondirective and yet imminently present, in the lead." The therapist is faced with the challenge of staying still and being receptive to the patient's experience in the face of intense affect and pain. In "Opening the Mind to Trauma through Oscillations of Focus" (p.247), Nancy Goodman writes about the film *Schindler's List* and the movement in and out of trauma. This movement in the film titrates the traumatic material, thus enabling the audience to bear witness to this heartbreaking story without feeling overwhelmed and consequently retreating to a dissociated state. She suggests that this same process is necessary in the treatment setting, wherein the therapist must be attuned to the patient's need to modulate the traumatic state. So, the acts of witnessing have complex layerings. The film *Schindler's List*, created by Steven Spielberg (1993), was based on the book by Thomas Keneally (1982). Both the book and the film were forms of witnessing based on true stories. People who read the book and saw the movie were witnesses to the work of both Spielberg and Keneally. The viewers of the movie had the opportunity to talk about and process their experience of seeing that difficult story portrayed in the film. Goodman's study of the oscillations of trauma in the film introduced a way of thinking about witnessing. Both the film and Goodman's work represent a form of meta-witnessing: that is, seeing something from above, below, and within as both an observer and a participant.

Trauma Without Witness

Stolorow and Atwood (1992) state that trauma lies in the experience of unbearable affect, and that painful or frightening affect becomes traumatic when the requisite attuned responsiveness that the child needs to assist in its tolerance, containment, modulation, and alleviation is absent. These authors emphasize the relational context for tolerating a traumatic experience. They posit that the experience of trauma is made more unbearable and intolerable without the presence of a witness to perhaps modulate the trauma, and thus help with affect regulation. Not having a witness is a secondary trauma (p.52).

Meta-Witnessing: An Example of Witnessing the Creative Act of Witnessing

Clem Loew's chapter entitled "My Lost Father" describes his experience that captures the concept of meta-witnessing:

> *"Several years ago, I sculpted from clay the full body of my father. In making my father's sculpture, I could not have anticipated the experiences that would evolve from that creation.*
>
> *Since I have no memory of my father—he was killed when I was about 4. In June 1941, , my family and other Jews were rounded up at gunpoint and corralled into the ghetto. My father was caught up in a roundup and herded into a train to Belzec concentration camp. I never saw him again.*
>
> *In the sculpture, I used the wedding picture of my mother and father taken in 1936 as the model for his head, and my son, then 23 years old, as the model for his body, purposely trying to establish a continuity from grandfather to grandson.*
>
> *I carved his torso and put on a double-breasted suit that he might have been wearing in 1941—the last time I had any contact with him. But sculpting his head was what engrossed me. That is when the depth and intensity of emotion emerged.*
>
> *With my fingers, I carved my father's eyes, nose cheek and ears. I looked closely at the photo to see the shape of his*

mouth. His lips were thin, but the cheeks were high, with eyes set open [...] with my forefinger I pressed a hole for his inner ear. I felt a sensation stirring in my fingers. Touching his mouth aroused images of my children when they were babies in bed with me, poking their fingers in my mouth, ears or nose [...] I remembered those times as warm and loving experiences...now sculpting my father I began to experience myself as a child exploring his face for the very first time.

I stayed long after my class and into the evening to be alone with my father. I was by myself in the empty studio that smelled of clay, glue and dust, surrounded by sculptures draped with white cloth.

When I left the studio [...] I was saddened, but I also felt a sense of security and stability as if my center of gravity dropped below my knees, making me more physically and psychologically stable and more difficult to tip over.

An artist, knowing my history looked at the statue and asked me 'You know. I wonder what was behind his eyes when he knew he might not see you again?' I was thinking what were his thoughts? I felt jarred. The question surprised me. He was encouraging me to fill out my father's emotional presence, something I had not thought of before.

[...] for the first time, I was able to empathize with my father about the loss of his son and the ending of his own life, a compassion that strengthened my closeness to him, despite the fact that I have almost no personal memory of him."

In this story, his artist friend serves as a meta-witness to Loew's experience of creative witnessing. His friend knew his story, and when he reacted to the sculpture, he added a perspective previously concealed from view for the artist. The friend stood both above and within Clem's experience. Both the artist and his friend had space in which to absorb this meta-perspective.

The Meta-Witnessing of Writing the Holocaust

By focusing on various forms and levels of witnessing, writing the book *The Power of Witnessing* was an act of meta-witnessing. (Goodman and Meyers, 2012) Nancy Goodman and I entered the hall of mirrors without fully realizing what we were getting into. Friends of mine expressed concern for me that I would have nightmares. I dismissed their concerns. Yet when we first met to begin writing, I inadvertently left the keys in my car with the engine running. I was already in an unconscous state of disorientation and dissociation. Perhaps I should have recognized that we were entering into a process that would lead to our feeling disoriented and overwhelmed. At times, the process of bearing witness, of knowing such deep trauma, was unbearable. At other times, we experienced the secondary vicarious trauma that is common to the witnessing process. The creative process was often both satisfying and illuminating as we opened space for creativity. Occasionally, we were able, or rather needed to, laugh, and experience some of the relief that dark humor provided. We particularly appreciated the outrageous humor of Larry David in the TV show, *Curb Your Enthusiasm*. As predicted by my friends, I had many nightmares during this journey, some of which we documented.

As a form of meta-witnessing, the dream is a process of consolidating the workings of the psyche.

One of my Dreams:

> *I am lying in bed with someone who comes in with medical tape. I am not sure if it is me in the dream or someone else. Someone comes in with medical adhesive tape, putting the tape on my skin, looking for evidence, like I am being accused of something...like finding something subtle on my skin. The person who is doing it ([is] I think a Nazi). Something bad is going to happen if they find whatever they are looking for. (Power of Witnessing, p. xv)*

I have made many associations to this dream, including: Medical tape; a procedure for finding something bad. We are finding something bad in the work. What is the injury? Am I doing damage to myself or others with this work? What am I being accused of? Have I done something bad? Must I feel shame or guilt? I continue to have new associations to this dream as I write this.

Intergenerational Transmission of Trauma: Knowing and Not Knowing

A form of not witnessing one's own trauma may lead to intergenerational transmission of trauma. Without the survivor's capacity to construct a somewhat coherent narrative and thus achieve some symbolization of the trauma, the child of a traumatized parent may become an unknowing witness through the enactment of the unmetabolized/unsymbolized acting out of the trauma. One form that this enactment can take is that the child of Holocaust survivors can be viewed as a "memorial candle" child (Wardi,1992). This can be seen as a form of hijacking the selfhood of the child in the service of what was lost to the parent.

Laub and Auerhahn (1993) have delineated eight levels of knowing and not knowing. Here I will briefly summarize the essential aspects of these different levels of knowing.

1. *Not knowing*: at this level, massive psychic trauma overwhelms the capacity to contain the experience. One form is that of the experience of a "me/not me" state of self.

2. *Fugue states:* there is an intrusion of traumatic memory with varying degrees of awareness.

3. *Fragments:* in this form of memory there is a retention of parts of a lived experience but they are decontextualized and are no longer meaningful.

4. *Transference phenomena:* unintegrated fragments of the trauma are enacted on the level of object relations. For example, a traumatized person believes no one can be truly trusted.

5. *Overpowering narratives:* the memories can be described and narrated, but in the telling, the person may lose perspective and be re-experiencing the trauma.

6. *Life themes:* there is a degree of distance from the experience and there is less immersion in the concrete details of the trauma. This level tends to become an organizing principle for the person's personality.

7. *Witnessed narratives:* the observing ego remains present as a witness so that true memory is established.

8. *Metaphor:* creative expression in the form of art is possible.

These "levels" are neither distinct nor linear. There is overlap and fluidity among these levels of knowing. It is beyond the scope of this paper to explore each of these levels in detail. One effect of the not-knowing can lead to intergenerational transmission of the trauma. The parent who survived the Holocaust and continues to live with annihilation terror may place an undue burden on the child which, in a way, can be thought of as a form of meta-witnessing. It is witnessing without knowing. What lies underneath remains not known. The child becomes an unwilling witness to unprocessed, unmetabolized traumatic affects, experiences, and anxieties. The traumatized parent can sometimes be both frightened and frightening. These oscillations are unpredictable and not readily understood. Separations may be fraught and filled with fears of catastrophic loss. In such instances, the child may carry the unmourned losses of the parent.

Each of these levels of knowing and not knowing roughly corresponds to whether or not there is a witness to trauma.

Clinical Manifestations of Levels of Knowing and Not Knowing

It is beyond the scope of this paper to fully explore the levels of knowing described by Laub and Auerhahn. I will briefly summarize some of the levels and provide some of the clinical manifestations.

Level of Life Themes

A patient of mine, a child of Holocaust survivors, always had an exit plan. His immediate family had escaped four concentration camps and had managed to survive, while several members of his extended family had been murdered. He always had a suitcase packed. Pictures did not get hung on the wall. He had an obsession with maps and never traveled without obtaining and studying maps. There was always a sense of an urgent readiness to leave. Attachments in relationship were fraught with the terror of loss. Life was devoid of pleasure and suffering was inevitable. All of this manifested in the transference, where he always had an "exit plan" and did not allow himself to form an ongoing attachment to me or to our work together.

Trauma as Metaphor

In this level of knowing, the use of imagery and language are present.

> *"The element of play is possible and achievable. Free association and playfulness and, in fact, pleasure become available. The traumatic imagery is not without impact. Inner reality both shapes the ultimate imagery of trauma becomes more conscious, colorful, plastic and variable than that found in other levels of knowing. [...T]he motive for this form of traumatic memory comes more from a need to organize internal experience than, as with other forms, from*

a need to organize the external historical reality" (Laub and Auerhahn, 1993, p.297).

In the clinical work, my patient began to open creative space and create collages that incorporated and represented his traumatic memories. This creativity both resulted from and represented the opening of space that the witnessing relationship provided.

Interview of the Interviewer as an Act of Meta-Witnessing

I now want to present a portion of the interview that Nancy Goodman and I conducted with Dori Laub in preparation for our book (Goodman and Meyers, 2012, p.17). We saw him as a resource for comprehending the experience of witnessing witnesses. He had been taking testimony for many years for the Yale Fortunoff Archives and we wanted to understand his subjective experience of that. How had he absorbed and internalized the act of taking testimony for more than 40 years? This act is representative of the image of peeling away layers. He took testimony and we were bearing witness to his process and memory of that experience. The first testimony taken for this project was Eva. B. In our interview, Dr. Laub recalls that first interview.

DL:

"I could sense that we had set something in motion. It was a beginning. We started with life at home, with growing up. We suggested to imagine like you are sitting in your living room and there is a photo album with those old photographs that are brown, before photos were black and white" (Note the visual power, the evocativeness of this suggestion). Laub continued: *"Open the photo album and tell me what you see, and what comes to your mind. It was a visual invitation, run this in your mental movie house, and watch the movie and tell me what you see."* (By utilizing this imagery, Dr. Laub provides a way of modulating the trauma). *"Not what you read in books, but what you watch in your own movie."* (He is helping her to make it real but tolerable.) We talk about the changeover. At that time, videotapes lasted 20 minutes. The videotape had to be changed during the interview.

NG

"What happened during the changeover? Was it quiet?"

DL:

"No, no, no. The interviewer would say. 'My God, how can you remember all that?' We were allowing ourselves to speak about the wonderment and awe that we felt and would say 'please say more.' The crew members were crying. From where they were in the background they could not do anything, they couldn't say anything. But they zoomed in and out. Their emotions, their experience, informed the zooming, when they wanted to zoom out, when they wanted to zoom in."

Meta-Witnessing as a 21st Century Phenomenon: Technology Enters

A recent article in *Smithsonian Magazine* (2012) highlights the use of technology to expand how we view witnessing. This article describes in detail many of the horrific events that took place in the Ponary Forest outside of Vilnius. The massacres of thousands of Jews are beyond comprehension. I found myself overwhelmed as I read this article. The barbaric actions of the Nazis against the Jewish population remain incomprehensible.

My attention, however, was drawn to the innovative use of technology to bear witness to these horrors. The article describes the work of Richard Freund, an American archeologist. Freund uses ground-penetrating radar as well as other computerized electronic technology to uncover the killing fields of the Ponary forest. One aspect of the story of the massacres in the forest was that of prisoners who managed to secretly dig a tunnel in order to escape. Paul Bauman and Alistair McClymont, both geophysicists, used electrical resistivity technology to explore the site. "We were able to get a readout not in real time, but close to it... ...we'd pull the data off the control box...run the data through software...and then we could see it." They saw the tunnel that until their discovery had not been physically identified. The determination to bear witness remains, and the use of technology serves to provide more evidence of the horrors.

I am telling this story with a twofold purpose. One purpose is to highlight the determination to "know" and how the use of technology can be seen as a form of meta-witnessing. The second purpose is my close personal relationship with the events that took place in the Ponary forest. Despite great effort on the part of my father and his sister, we were never able to learn directly of the tragic endings of members of our family. The family lived in Vilnius and it is my belief that they were murdered in the forest. It remains unknown. I am deeply touched by the ongoing efforts to know.

Conclusion

In this chapter, I explore the concept of meta-witnessing, employing the image of a hall of mirrors in which the experience is that of viewing witnessing from multiple perspectives. The viewer is both in and out, both a part of and outside of. The viewer may feel dazed, confused, and disoriented. It may feel like too much. I have turned to numerous examples that I hope will illustrate the phenomenon. As clinicians and members of our broader society we have the potential to employ our capacities as willing witnesses on many levels. My experience is that this potential can be both deeply gratifying and deeply disturbing. The title of this conference, *Listening to Trauma: Insights and Actions*, implies this active stance. It has been my honor to participate.

References

Felman, S. and Laub, D. (1992) *Testimony: Crisis of Witnessing in Literature, Psychoanalysis and History*. New York: Routledge.

Goodman, N.R. and Meyers, M (2012). *The Power of Witnessing: Reflections, Reverberations and Traces of the Holocaust.* New York: Routledge.

Keneally, T. (1982). *Schindler's List.* London: Hodden and Stoughton.

Laub, D. and Auerhahn, N. (1993) Knowing and Not Knowing Massive Psychic Trauma: Forms of Traumatic Memory. *International Journal of Psychoanalysis* 74: 287–302.

Loew, C. (2012) My Lost Father. In N.R. Goodman and M. B. Meyers (Eds.) *The Power Of Witnessing: Reflections, Reverberations and Traces of the Holocaust,* (pp. 209–210). New York: Routledge.

Shaer, M. (March, 2017) The Holocaust's Great Escape. *Smithsonian Magazine*, p.54.

Spielberg, S. (director) (1993) *Schindler's List* (Motion Picture) United States: Universal Pictures.

Stolorow, R.D. and Atwood, G. (1992) *The Intersubjective Foundations of Psychological Life*, Contexts of Being. New York: Psychology Press.

Wardi, D. (1992) *Memorial Candles: Children of the Holocaust,* New York: Routledge.

Winnicott, D.W. (1964,1973). *The Child, The Family and the Outside World.* New York: Penguin Pelican.

Finding Metaphor and Symbol for the Unbearable: A Trauma Museum of the "Terrible Real" and "Creative Representation"

Nancy R. Goodman
The Contemporary Freudian Society, Washington, DC
Program and The International Psychoanalytic Association

Author Note:

Nancy R. Goodman, Ph.D. is a training and supervising analyst with the Contemporary Freudian Society, Washington DC, and the IPA. She maintains a psychoanalytic practice in Bethesda, Maryland. She is Museum Director of the online Virtual Psychoanalytic Museum: www.virtualpsychoanalyticmuseum.org with IPBooks.

Recent publications include *Finding Unconscious Fantasy in Narrative, Trauma, and Body Pain: A Clinical Guide, The Courage to Fight Violence against Women: Psychoanalytic and Multi-Disciplinary Perspectives,* (both edited with Paula Ellman) and T*he Power of Witnessing: Reflections, Reverberations, and Traces of the Holocaust* (edited with Marilyn Meyers).

Correspondence concerning this article should be sent to:
nrgoodmanphd@gmail.com
6917 Arlington Rd. #220
Bethesda, Md. 20814

Nancy R. Goodman

Abstract

The psychic helplessness of severe and cumulative trauma creates eerie silence and cacophonous screams. Oscillations between despair and hope awaken a vertiginous vortex that threatens to drown. Entering the world of the unbearable is painful and excruciating. It is important through the writings in this book, as it was at the *Listening to Trauma Conference*, that we have others to be with—people who want to know about trauma—people who essentially hold each other. In psychoanalytic therapies, patients bring their traumas and therapists offer help to absorb and contain in order to find the capacity for knowing and speaking the unbearable. The truth of the most terrible appears and eventually metaphor, the symbolic, can be created to both remove us from the center of terror and to bring affect and communication out of the nothingness.

Finding Metaphor and Symbol for the Unbearable: A Trauma Museum of the "Terrible Real" and "Creative Representation"

The process of finding metaphor and healing begins through the "Power of Witnessing"; that is, when someone, the witness, claims a passionate desire to know the truth, to be willing to receive invasions of trauma, even genocide, upon the conscious and unconscious mind. Symbolization through metaphor offers the possibility for birthing an alive mind, discovered in the intimate reciprocity of analyst and patient and between victim and witness. Making metaphor is the building of a monument to the horror and an assertion of survival and connection to others. The development of raw narrative, poetic verse, and visual imagery takes place with witnessing and constructs a type of "museum" in the mind, a museum that therapist and patient agree both to create and to enter for posterity. This holds true as well for society when witnessing brings about monuments to historic atrocities and traumas. The presence of witnessing begins a process described by Dori Laub (1992) in regards to the receiving of Holocaust testimonies.

> For the testimonial process to take place, there needs to be a bonding, the intimate and total presence of an *other*—in the position of one who hears . . . the witnesses are talking to *somebody*: to somebody they have been waiting for a long time." (pp. 70–71, Laub, 1992, emphasis in the original).

With the construction of a sacred place for the trauma story, within the space of a relationship, narrative and symbol take on enough form to be lasting.

The Laying Down in My Mind of the Duality of "Death" and "Life"

I am so fortunate to carry within me the feel of an event I attended with Dori Laub in New Haven, Connecticut. It was 1979 and I was invited to the home of a Holocaust survivor where many survivors and their families were gathered. Dori and Laurel Vlock, co-creators of the Yale Archives of Testimonies of Holocaust Survivors, were showing the first tapes of their interviews. I was anxious. Would I find damaged people who were weeping, traumatized, and in despair? Would I be overwhelmed and inadequate to the task of being a witness? What I saw and felt was unexpected and remains a deep presence in my mind. There was celebrating, eating good food, hugging, and seeing grown children amazed at their parents' happiness at knowing they could speak of their history. Horrific journeys through the hours, days, weeks, months, and years of the Holocaust were capable of being known and shared. A curtain of silence was lifted by the knowledge that an archive was valued and would be preserved. I wanted to be able to provide a picture of this event for this book, so I emailed Dori to see if photos had been taken that night. He wrote that he would ask the archivist but that he thought no photos were taken because "no one thought it would be so important." Now, we understand that a process was begun that night that has influenced the witnessing of trauma for individuals and for society. Psychoanalytic treatment has been profoundly affected by the discovery of the ways that testimony, receiving of the trauma story, evolves.

In the book *The Power of Witnessing: Reflections, Reverberations, and Traces of the Holocaust—Trauma, Psychoanalysis, and the Living Mind* (Goodman and Meyers, 2012), I express the duality of death and life as follows;

> The Holocaust places a dead place in the individual and in humanity. This traumatic place is so dark and dense. It has no pulsation, no breathing, no flexibility. Sometimes, it is solid like cement, separate from all else that is alive in the mind, sometimes it oozes out and invades other places in the mind. [. . .] the horrific known and the too much unknown are present [. . .] In turn I have come to think of the power of witnessing as the force providing a clearing away and lighting for a living surround near the dead space where an opening, a new space, develops and takes hold. [. . .] My favored imagining is of a circular surround first narrow and over time widening, [. . .] penetrating, mining, and refining the dead space. There can now be communication between the trauma and the living mind. (p. 5–6)

In psychoanalytic treatments, the living surround often appears through enactment processes; that is, a playing out of the traumas in transference and countertransference occur most often with the analyst's first identifying and feeling the trauma and understanding interactions carrying the past into the present where narrative develops. Through this process the symbolic and metaphor often begin to take form. In *Finding Unconscious Fantasy in Narrative, Trauma, and Body Pain: A Clinical Guide* (2017), Ellman and Goodman, with their psychoanalytic contributors to the volume, highlight enactments as a singular "royal road" to the trauma and to the unconscious. That which could not be known and spoken appears in multiple ways in the process between therapist and patient, bringing horrific traumas into the "here and now" of treatments to be traced to centrality in the unconscious mind. It is the evolving creativity of psychoanalytic treatments that enables the "finding" of the traumatic mind, the unconscious mind, and their intermingling in psychic realities.

Invitation to a Psychoanalytic Museum of Trauma and Metaphor

I invite you to a museum, a virtual museum in which various levels of witnessing are presented. As trauma becomes known, it can move from the unknown dead place in the mind through iterations of form into a symbolized living place. There is the "too real," the historic fact with time and place, which is then followed by the more representational and metaphorical. Psychoanalysts refer to trauma in the mind as "the abyss," a "black hole," a "dead place," or "negative space"—each name attempting to communicate the nothingness of the "too-muchness" of psychic helplessness that cannot be known when the mind is overwhelmed and shut down and therefore unsymbolized. When enough form has taken place, an internal museum in the mind collects the images, both the specifically raw traumatic and the iterations of more symbolic and impressionistic versions.[32]

In this imagined museum, "The Trauma and Metaphor Museum," I place many exhibits from material deriving from the "too real" of mass trauma and of metaphoric representations when "life" enters the mind through being witnessed. There are certain features of museums that help define the internal place of museums in the mind. A museum has structure and space, containment and creativity. Here in Washington, D.C. a new museum opened on September 24, 2016— The Museum of African American History and Culture. It is a magnificent archive immediately selling out of tickets for hourly attendance. John Lewis, congressman and Freedom Fighter with Martin Luther King, with emotion stated in an interview: "Now don't make me cry." He spoke about the museum with pride: "Having a museum is so important." In Washington, DC, visitors to the Holocaust Museum have similar experiences. Both museums provide honor and remembrance with their recognition of terror, atrocity, and resilience. People are drawn to museums of remembrance throughout the world because it is meaningful to have a place to visit, a valued place. When trauma invades and takes over the mind, memorialization helps heal

---

32. (A virtual psychoanalytic museum by IPBooks, director Nancy R. Goodman, 2015, can be found at www.thevirtualpsychoanalyticmuseum.org for other exhibits of imagery and psychoanalytic subjects.)

the destruction and the wound. The capacity to experience mourning increases when the trauma attains the structure of a monument that now has a place contained in a form, a symbol. Then the geography of the traumatic mind seems more anchored and can be visited again and again.

Museum of Trauma and Metaphor

In this imagined museum, I contrast paired images, dreams/ nightmares, and examples of monuments to demonstrate how the "too real"—the overwhelming trauma—and the symbolic, the metaphorical, can co-exist. In other words, I am representing what is close to the "dead space" of catastrophic trauma and what is developing in the "living surround" where light appears. It is within witnessing, with external and internal witnesses, that the layers of knowing develop: what Dori Laub and Nanette Auerhahn (1993) refer to as forms of "Knowing and Not Knowing".

Entering the "Trauma Museum"

At the entrance to the museum I place a plaque, a quote from Primo Levi from *If This is a Man* (1958, in Italian; 1969 in English):

> I recognize and ask indulgence for the structural defects of the book. Its origins go back, not indeed in practice, but as an idea, an intention, to the days in the Lager. The need to tell our story to "the rest," to make "the rest" participate in it, had taken on for us, before liberation and after, the character of an immediate and violent impulse, to the point of competing with our other elementary needs. (p. 15)

The "violent impulse" identified by Levi is a violent impulse of life force that faces the trauma and creates forms of remembrance. Each of the images and narratives in the Trauma Museum is a representation of what Saul Friedlander (1992) calls the "limits of representation."

A Pair of Images: The "Too Real" Nazi Train and the imagined "Anti-Train"

The first pair of images is about trains—the Nazi trains and what I call the force of the Anti-Train. I have had many patients refer to Nazi trains when they are in deep distress and trying to find a way to communicate their terror and psychic helplessness. The Nazi trains taking Jewish men, women, and children to their deaths in concentration camps, including death camps, form images related to psychic terror, helplessness, and "annihilation fears."

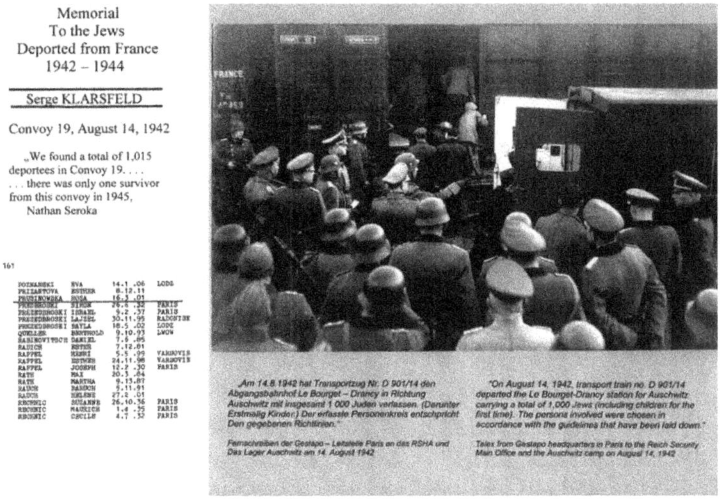

Image 1. Convoy 19: August 14, 1942

The Transport of Henri Parens' mother, from *Renewal of Life—Healing from the Holocaust*, Henri Parens, (2004)

Henri Parens, a psychoanalyst, researcher, and child survivor, granted me permission to use a photograph that was sent to him of his mother's transport to Auschwitz on August 14, 1942. On the anniversary of that date in 2002, Henri started to write his Holocaust memoir, *Renewal of Life: Healing from the Holocaust* (2004). In "A Holocaust Survivor's Bearing Witness," (in Goodman and Meyers, 2012) he reflects on the writing of his memoir. He informs us that only one person survived the transport; it was not Henri's mother. This photograph is a record of the "too real," the traumatic actual. Looking at the photograph and knowing that Henri Parens' mother is right there and is about to be on her "final journey" brings us face to face with the truth of Nazi annihilation and a feeling of connection with her son, who is now in possession of the photo.

Henri Parens survived because of his mother's determination to send him to a labor camp, even though it meant his leaving her. He was 12 years old when he last saw his mother. I borrow the term "final journey" from the book title by the historian Sir Martin Gilbert (*Final Journey: The Fate of the Jews in Nazi Europe* (1979), who chronicled details with narrative and photos about the Nazi transports that took place throughout Europe, taking Jews to their death. In his

Holocaust books, Sir Martin Gilbert takes names from records with dates and times of the transports and murders, knowing that there are unlikely any family members or communities alive to remember and grieve.

Image 2. The Anti-Train

I link the transport Nazi train photo to a different and opposing image of a witnessing train, an idea I developed in "Anti-Train: A Metaphor for Witnessing" (Goodman, 2012). The anti-train is a place where one is with a community of witnesses and thus more able to witness traumatic horrors that I place outside of the train. I describe the "Anti-Train" as "a force, an anti-trauma force . . . to counter the overwhelming impact felt when facing absolutely horrifying events" (p.45). I elaborate the interior of my imagined anti-train and invite all who witness annihilating trauma to construct their own internal "anti-train" images as well. "My fantasy Anti-Train has dark wood, shiny brass, velvet, and thick carpet. The sound of the train moving along the tracks is rhythmic and soothing with an occasional low whistle being emitted. This is an idealized train for sure, probably inspired by 1940s films and perhaps from picking up a relative at the Chicago Union Station and hearing trains from the windows of my childhood bedroom" (p.49). This space within the anti-train is an imagined interior, offering a place to be with others and to feel the sense of trauma. It is a place where the horror of intense trauma can at least be minimally recognized and absorbed. Here are additional descriptions of the space of the Anti-Train that are so essential for absorbing the "too-muchness" of atrocity and providing enough absorption to allow creative representation to evolve.

> The details of the structure of the Anti-Train metaphor bring about space and maintain a barrier between the events of the Holocaust and the viewing of the Holocaust. From the interior of the train, there is a choice about when and for how long to look out of the window at the landscape of the Nazi death machine. The windows and the movement of the train provide framing of what is being seen so that a sense of seeing and not seeing and seeing again is established. This alteration of focus is an essential aspect of being able to perceive and process overwhelming anxiety [...] The capacity to believe that narration, making a story with words and symbols that are bound in a sense of time, is strengthened in the feeling of being with others who want to hear perceptions and emotional responses. (p.46)

By including the rhythm of the movement of the train in my Anti-Train, it is my intent to place features of early mothering (soothing, absorbing, and containing) into the functioning of the force of anti-trauma.

Three Dreams: Symbolizing Depth

For a perfect museum display these dreams would be on video in a small space where the viewer experiences the dreams. Each of these dreams creates imagery that conveys the full affect and resonance with unconscious meaning about the deepest feeling of being human. There is also the truth that the dreamer of the nightmare wakes to be a witness to oneself and to others. Each of these dreams/nightmares[33] is a personal and inspiring revelation. I place the three dreams/nightmares here to exemplify the way metaphor is the result of psychic work, during the night, in which the "too real," the overwhelming trauma, is psychically translated into identifiable fear and grief and acceptance that one is alive to have the presence of the trauma in mind. Dreams are very personal and meaningful, and dreams/nightmares stirred when facing trauma contain intense imagery and affects that awaken one to fear and grief. These intimate internal experiences, from myself, Katalin Roth, and Myra Sklarew, arose when each of us was immersed in writing about the Holocaust for *The Power of Witnessing* book when these dreams interrupted sleep. Each of us is a passionate witness in our work and willing to let our minds feel and dream/nightmare.

Dream Series: Nancy Goodman's Dreams/Nightmares while Witnessing and Writing About the Holocaust and Atrocity

Marilyn Meyers and I immersed ourselves in the world of the Holocaust for a year before we began writing individual chapters about our human and psychoanalytic approach to understanding annihilation trauma and witnessing. We read widely in the field of memoirs, beginning with Primo Levi and Elie Wiesel, along with the more recent memoirs of Henri Parens, Margit Meissner, and Geoffrey Hartman. We used the Holocaust Archives at the United States Holocaust Museum in Washington, DC, discovering both the past and the contemporary witnessing of atrocities in Rwanda and Bosnia.

Actual early interviews of concentration camp survivors and film

---

33. These dreams/nightmares appear in the book The Power of Witnessing: Reflections, Reverberations, and Traces of the Holocaust—Trauma, Psychoanalysis, and the Living Mind (Goodman and Meyers, 2012).

clips from the liberating armies under Dwight Eisenhower were all available online. Psychoanalytic writings about trauma and therapeutic work with survivors and the children of survivors had expanded over time and we consumed all that we could find. We have read almost all of the tome of work by Dori Laub, who developed the Yale Video Archives of Holocaust Survivors with Laurel Vlock in New Haven, Connecticut (beginning in 1979) and has written over 100 psychoanalytic articles about clinical work with Holocaust survivors, their children, and survivors of other horrific traumas. We watched documentaries, read and watched testimonies from the Yale Archives of Holocaust Testimonies. We read a wide range of literature, including *The Lost: a search for six of six million* by Daniel Mendelsohn (2006) and *The Hare with the Amber Eyes* by Edmund de Waal (2010), and watched DVDs of Holocaust films including Spielberg's *Schindler's List* and the docudrama *Conspiracy*. We followed the work of scholars of the Holocaust, Jan Gross, Christopher Browning, Sir Martin Gilbert, and Erwin Staub, integrating our psychoanalytic thinking with their observations. We were each focusing in on topics we would write about; we were living in the world of the Holocaust and could do this together by being each other's witness.

Eventually, at one of our twice-weekly meetings, Marilyn said it was time to start bringing in our own writing. We had gathered together psychoanalysts and artists and scholars who were now working on their chapters. Beginning writing meant imagining the book as complete; in our minds, the book would live while so many people had been murdered and forgotten. I described our focus: "We are involved in a special project capturing the reciprocity that occurs when there is witnessing between people. To me this reciprocity seems as close as attuned breathing between mother and infant" (Goodman and Meyers, 2012, p.xiii). And, in proceeding with the book, we were allowing breathing with the core of the catastrophe of the Holocaust.

Nancy Goodman's Dream Series

These dreams occurred as my writing began to take shape. I was so deep in my affects—as if feelings were fueling the words and images I developed. Many individuals have asked how I could write about the Holocaust. Others have told me about their writing blocks when approaching their writing of memoir about severe trauma, including intergenerational Holocaust trauma. Marilyn Meyers was there to receive my dreams/nightmares. Writing arose from the same place in me as did the nightmares I report here.

Dream One

I dream I am going outside of my house on a walk and that I am naked and do not know I am naked; and when I realize it I know I have Alzheimer's and will have to stop working; and I do not want to stop working, and I feel so bad for my kids and husband and patients, knowing how sad they will be to see me disappear. (Goodman and Meyers, 2012, p. xii)

Marilyn and I associated together. Associating with another is a form of witnessing and it is helpful to know one's conscious and unconscious mind with another. Thinking about what Alzheimer's means is terrifying—there is no memory and I have this nightmare just as I am formulating how to remember trauma. I recognize that I may wish to lose my mind and that I am recognizing the private guilt of surviving when others have not. There are so many reasons to be terrified in my knowing and ability to symbolize extreme trauma. Marilyn and I both thought of the scenes from Holocaust films of naked women in concentration camps. It is as if I wanted permission from them to remember for them and to write.

Dream Two

I dream that I am with my grandchildren, feeling the absolute gratitude that they are in my life. We are near water. One of them falls into the water and I jump in to grab this baby and I cannot. The baby slips through my hands and the water is too dark to see into. I am beyond horrified and want to die. This is impossible. I cannot bring this pain to others. (Goodman and Meyers, 2012, p.xiv)

This dream was extremely horrifying and terrifying. I was not sure I could contain the feeling of it at all. How would I tell it to anyone—I knew I would tell Marilyn and we both realized how deeply I was living out in my psyche the terror of the Holocaust, and all the individual stories that there were, and how loss and helplessness had to be felt and faced. Once again, awareness of being separate from those actually murdered meant I could wake up from a nightmare and grieve the trauma and the deep personal levels of terror I was awakened to feeling. Being able to dream was a way of being pulled out of water and knowing I was alive.

Each of the nightmares I had while writing produced intense affect in me that stayed with me for days. I recognized the emotions and traumas I was attempting to represent through the symbols and terror-felt activity taking place in my nightmares. The dreams carried within them aspects of my own personal history and the traumatic secondary trauma of being a witness to the Holocaust through writing what could never be "right." I felt grief for those who suffered and rage at my helplessness to change anything. I also came to think of having nightmares as the presence of life forces meeting death forces, a way to try to defy the traumas by proclaiming, "I am here to dream so I can formulate ways to reveal psychic truths of trauma to others." I felt resonance with the resilience of so many who continued dreaming and having nightmares after the Holocaust.

Katalin Roth's Dream when Writing About Her Father's Holocaust Experience

Katalin Roth wrote about her father in the Power of Witnessing book, memorializing his life and his Holocaust experience, "Miklos: A Memoir of My Father" (2012). She follows many strands of her father's Holocaust experience, his love and guidance of his three children, and of the way Holocaust transmissions have taken place across generations. One of her father's tragedies was the death of his first wife and child, aged four, in Auschwitz. Katalin did not learn about this loss until well into her teens. She witnessed her father through a dream. She was writing as a witness to her father and to her mother and to herself and her brother and sister and her own children, the third generation. She watched the testimony her father gave to the Fortunoff Video Archives at Yale University. She wanted to make clear how her father was resilient and passed on to his family a sense of strength, fortitude, and ability to love. Her witnessing led to a dream about her brother.

Dream About her Brother

Last week I dreamed I was at my niece's wedding, and there met a relation of the groom, a man about my age, a Jew from South Africa. We felt a strange and strong attraction to each other, and talked for a long time. Slowly we told each other our life stories. He told of being a blond toddler, rescued from the gas chambers at Auschwitz by a German officer's wife who longed for a blond baby. Later he came to know that he was Jewish but he never learned who his parents were. In my dream, I recognized him from old photographs, and knew that he was my brother Paul. I awoke in tears. (Roth, 2012, p.176)

Her capacity to create this dream with such true feeling is impressive and illustrates how such terrible trauma, even over generations, can enter a symbolic and deeply meaningful form. Katalin's father was full of love for his children and represented resilience and hope. In other words, life forces accompanied the knowledge of death forces, helping to allow space for dreaming and grief.

Myra Sklarew Dreams as She Witnesses her Cousin Leiser

Myra Sklarew tells us about her remarkable relationship with her cousin Leiser, who survived the atrocities in Lithuania perpetrated by the Nazis. In "Leiser's Song" (2012), she poetically tells of how she and Leiser maintained a connection through phone calls for 9 years (1999—2008) until his death. They sometimes spoke as often as nine times a day. Myra was in Washington, DC; Leiser was in Zurich, Switzerland. She was his very passionately present witness, and he became able to speak to her about layers and layers of horrendous events he suffered as a boy in the Holocaust. The stories are terrible and tormenting, but Myra listened and listened. In her writing, she uses a style of free association from fragment to fragment. When she is grieving the death of Leiser her witnessing turns to a dream:

> Since Leiser died, I cannot sleep. I have taken his habit. No more than an hour or two at a time. I am become him. That shall be my way of mourning this time. Each death is different. So, will I dream of his mother? Or his brother enveloped in flames? Or the small infant wrapped in a man's undershirt, and buried? I do dream. Of a purse. With identity papers. A missing purse. Perhaps it is to death we go. Without identity. No need then. (Sklarew, 2012, p. 126).

Myra Sklarew finds words for her grief and for universal grief. She is a poet and a researcher about the murder of the Jewish population of Lithuania. Her forthcoming book is entitled: *A Survivor Named Trauma: Holocaust and the Construction of Memory,* SUNY Press.

All of these dreams enter the arena of metaphor, symbolic expressions of the pain and remembrance related to tremendous trauma. Each is in essence a work of art by the individual dreamer and a testimony to deep understanding of human experience. In the "Museum of Trauma and Metaphor" I imagine small rooms with depictions of the living dreamers surrounding those attending the museum. There is a reaching across, from soul to soul, of both the horror of the traumatic history and the living mind bringing light to the darkness. The dreaming/nightmaring of all of these witnesses, including myself, often appears when creative action is taking place—when one knows that one is alive and different from those who were murdered. Having these dreams and nightmares is a building of monuments to those who cannot speak for themselves. This is what witnessing is—dreaming and nightmaring the trauma story into existence.

Monuments—symbolizing and representing

Monuments create a place to remember, grieve, and join with others. Monuments provide witnessing in the very fact of their existence—a place marking the traumatic events. Monuments indicate that the society is ready to recognize the truth of the trauma. The form of the monument provides a symbolic representation once removed from the actual trauma—the intermediary location that is somewhat more tolerable to hold in one's mind. The abyss lies behind what is able to be represented but does not swallow up our minds. The symbol of the monument functions, as does metaphor, in relation to the psychic hole of trauma that impacts severely. For example, the Vietnam Memorial in Washington, DC provides a place for remembering and for even touching the name of someone known. The blue light monument to 9/11 is an abstract memorial to where the Twin Towers were and where there is now communication and symbolization. There are many catastrophes that are not yet memorialized, such as famines and terror in the Soviet Union and in China.

Perhaps the most impressive monument to the Holocaust is in Berlin, where the governance of the Nazi Party was located. The Memorial, called "Monument to the Six Million Murdered Jews of Europe," was designed by Peter Eisenman and completed in 2005. It is in the center of Berlin and near the Reichstag and the Brandenburg Gate. The memorial museum, under the monument, is one of the best I have ever seen in its simplicity and presentation of historic truth. Elsa Blum, a psychotherapist and photographer, knew that when in Berlin she would search out the monument and take photos. In her writing about her experience in "A Photographic Commentary on the Memorial to the Murdered Jews of Europe" (2012), she states the following:

> Being behind the lens had an effect on my perceived emotions, both intensifying and diluting my experience. The ultimate goal of my photos is to communicate and perhaps intensify, to capture what was for me the essence of the memorial. (p.239)

I use two of Elsa's photos here to illustrate the feel of this memorial. Photo One shows the monument in its placement beside new buildings, residents, and shops.

Space was made for the monument's representation of death and genocide in the midst of the ongoing life in central Berlin.

Photo Two brings the viewer of the photo into the reality of the monument. This monument takes up 2 square blocks and the area between the various sizes of the stelae make walking paths where one can be contained, move, and feel anxious as the high columns hide the outside world and begin to encase. There is a sense of infinity that takes over, memorializing six million murdered individuals.

Concluding Remarks

In this paper, I have addressed the relation between the unknowable trauma, the psychic black hole, and the creation of symbolism that develops with secure witnessing. When there is a feeling that someone else will not abandon you because of the enormity of having a direct or indirect experience of trauma, there is capacity to feel deeply, to dream and nightmare; and from this human bond there arises a form of monument to the trauma, now able to appear in various forms of creative representation. There is an Anti-Trauma force, an Anti-Train, that makes it possible to accompany the traumatic "too real" with the symbolic. I have used the idea of a museum, the trauma museum, to show how witnessing brings about imagery for the terrible real and metaphoric images and imaginings including dreams and nightmares. I conclude with a quote from the historian Saul Friedlander (1992):

> The extermination of the Jews of Europe is as accessible to both representation and interpretation as any other historical event. But we are dealing with an event which tests our traditional conceptual and representational categories, an "event at the limits." (*Probing Limits of Representation: Nazism and the Final Solution* (Saul Friedlander, Harvard Press, 1992, pp.2–3).

*In this chapter I refer to experiences writing a book *The Power of Witnessing: Reflections, Reverberations, and Traces of the Holocaust—Trauma, Psychoanalysis, and the Living Mind* (Routledge, 2012) with my co-editor and friend, Marilyn B. Meyers. I use the work of Elsa Blum, Dori Laub, Katalin Roth and Myra Sklarew who wrote for the *Power of Witnessing* book. At times I refer to the book with the abbreviated title: *The Power of Witnessing.*

References

Blum, E. (2012). A Photographic Commentary on the Memorial to the Murdered Jews of Europe. In Goodman and Meyers (Eds.), *The Power of Witnessing: Reflections, Reverberations, and Traces of the Holocaust—Trauma, Psychoanalysis, and the Living Mind* (239–245). New York: Routledge.

Boder, D.P. (1949) *I did not interview the dead*. Urbana: University of Illinois Press.

de Waal, Edmund. (2010) *The Hare with the Amber Eyes*. New York: Farrar, Straus and Giroux.

Ellman, P.L. and Goodman, N.R. (2017) *Finding Unconscious Fantasy in Narrative, Trauma, and Body Pain: A Clinical Guide.* London: Routledge.

Friedlander, S. (1992). *Probing Limits of Representation: Nazism and the Final Solution.* Cambridge: Harvard Press.

Gilbert, M. (1979). *Final Journey: The Fate of the Jews in Nazi Europe.* London: Allen and Unwin.

Goodman, N.R. and Meyers, M.B. (2012). *The Power of Witnessing: Reflections, Reverberations, and Traces of the Holocaust—Trauma, Psychoanalysis, and the Living Mind.* New York: Routledge.

——— (2012b). Preface: An Invitation. In N.R. Goodman and M.B. Meyers (Eds.), *The Power of Witnessing: Reflections, Reverberations, and Traces of the Holocaust—Trauma, Psychoanalysis, and the Living Mind* (xi–xxiii). New York: Routledge.

Goodman, N.R. (2012). The "Anti-Train": A metaphor for witnessing. In N. R. Goodman and M. B. Meyers (Eds.), *The Power of Witnessing: Reflections, Reverberations, and Traces of the Holocaust—Trauma, Psychoanalysis, and the Living Mind* (45–56). New York: Routledge.

——— (2015). *The Virtual Psychoanalytic Museum.* New York: IPBooks. (thevirtualpsychoanalyticmuseum.org).

Laub, D. (1992). Bearing witness or the vicissitudes of listening. In S. Felman and D. Laub, *Crises of witnessing in literature, psychoanalysis, and history* (pp. 57–74). New York: Routledge.

Nancy R. Goodman

Trauma Manifested in Social Spaces

Trauma Made Manifest: Its Persistent Forms

Myra Sklarew

American University

Author Note

Myra Sklarew is a Professor Emerita of American University. This article is an excerpt (Chapter VII) from the book, *A Survivor Named Trauma: Holocaust and the Construction of Memory*, forthcoming from SUNY Press.

Correspondence concerning this article should be addressed to: Myra Sklarew, 6521 Marywood Road, Bethesda, MD 20817.

Contact: msklarew@gmail.com

Myra Sklarew

Abstract

As part of a book-length project on the effects of trauma on memory, particularly focused on the Holocaust in Lithuania, this chapter will explore three areas: the erasure of language; the alteration of a familiar landscape; and symbolic condensation. Some who were fluent in numerous languages that remained intact, could, at the war's end, no longer retain the ability to speak and understand Lithuanian. "Not only do you have to rid yourself of the images, but of the language which might contain the images," according to one survivor. Perception of a familiar and welcome landscape—for a man who has endured multiple traumas—was altered, so that during his first visit to the sea after the Holocaust, he had the sensation that the sea waters had turned to blood. Trauma resurfaces with the encounter of a diagonal line or with the sounds of multiple footsteps in completely harmless situations after the initial experience in childhood of witnessing the emptying of the Kovno Ghetto, as some 9,200 inhabitants are made to walk up a diagonal hill to the Ninth Fort, where they will be killed.

Trauma Made Manifest: Its Persistent Forms

1) The Erasure of Language: Lithuanian language vanished, though all other languages are retained.

2) The Alteration of a Familiar Landscape: The first visit to the sea after the Holocaust—the sea waters have turned to blood.

3) Symbolic Condensation: A diagonal line represents the emptying of the Kovno Ghetto as some 9,200 inhabitants are made to walk up a diagonal hill to the Ninth Fort, where they will be killed.

Introduction

Although trauma can take many forms, three that are explored here had their origins during the German Occupation of Lithuania from 1941–1944: the erasure of language, the alteration of a familiar landscape, and symbolic condensation. For a number of people who were fluent in Lithuanian and who knew many other languages, Lithuanian seemed to vanish, though all other languages are retained. In terms of the alteration of a familiar landscape, one survivor described his first visit to the sea after the Liberation. The sea waters appear to have turned to blood. Finally, many have described how a condensed image can evoke a major *Aktion*: a diagonal line in a painting brings the survivor not only to the memory of 9,200 being marched up a diagonal hill to their deaths, but also to the experience of being back there at the present moment.

The Erasure of Language

Sam Schalkowsky (2014) never lost the ability to speak and understand the many languages he knew; he lost only Lithuanian, a language he had once spoken with ease:

I have been puzzled by the fact that of all the languages that I knew before the war, only Lithuanian was—selectively and completely—wiped from my memory: after the war I could no longer understand any written or spoken Lithuanian, and I certainly could not speak it. What was it in my wartime experience that brought this about?

Visual images and words tend to run together in my memory. For example, to remember someone's name, it helps me to associate an image with it. To effectively repress—to block out—memories of traumatic experiences, it seems necessary to remove the

Myra Sklarew

associated words, in order to contain the emotions of fear, extreme anxiety, and the sense of impending doom connected to them. But if this is so, then why did I not only retain, but even increase, my knowledge of the German language as a result of my ghetto and concentration camp experiences? The memories of many of these experiences were also repressed, but the German language associated with them was not. What is the difference? (pp. ix–xi)

One explanation, he tells us, "is that being able to communicate with the Germans in concentration camps was essential to my survival. But knowing Lithuanian was, at least for me, not relevant to my survival efforts." Essentially, as Schalkowsky points out, his survival depended on avoidance of Lithuanians.

Schalkowsky, when he retired from his work in engineering, volunteered at the United States Holocaust Memorial Museum and was given the assignment to create a finding aid, inventory, and description for researchers of a document written in Yiddish by members of the Kovno Ghetto Jewish police in the Kovno Ghetto from 1941–1943. This history was part of some 30,000 pages assembled by the Jewish ghetto police that had been buried and not discovered until the Sixties. Despite the fact that the Kovno Ghetto was burned to the ground by the retreating Nazis, these documents and others survived. As Schalkowsky had been in the Kovno Ghetto, what he read in these documents was extremely personal. It would be years before they would become available. A copy was finally obtained by the USHMM in 1998.

As he read through these documents, Schalkowsky was reminded of the outbursts on the street and his "fear of being dragged out" and killed:

"Hiding in the house, I didn't see them—there are no visual memories, only the shouting in Lithuanian. The trauma of this seven-week period preceding the establishment of the ghetto is therefore predominantly connected to words spoken in Lithuanian [. . .] The abruptness of this stark change from a normal existence to being engulfed by the Lithuanian orgy of brutality, humiliation, and the slaughter [. . .] makes my complete repression of the Lithuanian language seem understandable." (p. xi)

"What did I learn about memory?" Schalkowsky asks. "Memory is adjustable." He speaks of traumatic affect without a specific memory attached to it, and the converse, a specific memory without the accompanying emotional affect.

A man with a meticulous memory, Schalkowsky, when comparing his experience of a specific event involving the fate of a small child with that of his companions, remembers the event and its outcome differently. He describes what he calls the "modification of the gate," not only for the past and past memory, but for what is actually permitted to be taken in now, today—a kind of vigilance which does not permit certain kinds of information to be experienced or even to gain entry. "Not only do you have to rid yourself of the images, but of the language which might contain the images."

Masha Wolpe Baras, who is fluent in eleven languages and who has an intact memory of *Aktions*, selections, forced marches, completely lost her Lithuanian language skills by the end of the War. Another survivor who has lost his knowledge of Lithuanian speaks of having heard Lithuanian spoken—but not being able to see the Lithuanian collaborator—as Jewish neighbors in an adjoining room were taken away. He describes the language on the other side of the wall as the "agent of death."

Zev Birger (1999) writes in *No Time for Patience: My Road from Kaunas to Jerusalem* that during the period following the Children's *Aktion* in Kaunas, he would secretly leave the Ghetto and observe:

> the reaction of the Lithuanians when they saw the columns of Jewish workers moving through the streets [....] I was shocked not only by their conduct after the invasion of the Germans, but also by the fact that the Lithuanian and Ukrainian units did the dirty work for the SS. I was so deeply and lastingly shocked by the inhumane, almost animalistic conduct of the Lithuanians that a short time after the war I discovered I was no longer fluent in Lithuanian. Suddenly I could no longer utter sentences in the language that I had spoken as well as my mother tongue. Worried that there was something very wrong with my brain, I went to a doctor who determined that I had suffered such a shock from my observations outside the ghetto, that a mental block now paralyzed my memory, preventing me from recalling this language. I have never since tried to master Lithuanian again. (p. 58–59)

The Alteration of a Familiar Landscape

Here is a boy, a teenager who, in the middle of the night, is ordered along with his father to the basement of their apartment building on Laisves Aleja (Freedom Way) in Kovno. All the men and boys are shot. The boy, Leiser Wolpe, is also shot, but lies still, and when the bedlam is over, he rises up and seeks help. A short time later, all survivors are forced to leave their homes and go to the ghetto. After helping his mother deliver his infant brother in the ghetto, he must then bury the infant a few days later. He witnesses the burning to death of his younger brother in a hospital where all the doctors, nurses, and patients are killed in this way. He survives the ghetto, and is taken to Dachau Concentration Camp. He somehow manages to survive Dachau, but spends over a year in a hospital due to contracting tuberculosis. When he finally is released, he describes his first experience of going to the sea after the war:

> When I went into the sea, I saw a sea of blood. In Spain, I wanted to paint. I would paint only blood. Is something wrong with me? No. I was in Spain. In Palanga. In school. I was with the school in Palanga. An excursion. A few days, I was never to the seaside. Only Palanga. Then to Spain. I was so dirty. I have a feeling I have to wash myself 300 times. It was not normal. In the first flat, no warm water, no shower, no real bed, a camping bed. First time I had a feeling, a sea of blood with dead people. Then it went away. Then I enjoyed it. A holiday in Spain and Italy. Mostly, I kept everything in order. (L. Wolpe, personal communication, 2003)

Symbolic Condensation—A Trigger that Elicits the Original Trauma in the Present

On October 28, 1941, a selection was made in the Kovno Ghetto, and over the next day 9,200 Jews were forced to walk to the 9th Fort where they were all killed. Shalom Eilati (2008), a child in the Ghetto, witnessed the solemn march and heard gunfire:

> It surprised me to realize that this road, which was visible to all as it rose diagonally from left to right, was already mostly full of people. Had I not looked up to find the source of the gunfire, their march would have been completely unheard and undetected. And then, only then, did the data from my sight and hearing come together in my mind. [. . .] I suppose that my childhood ended right then—its innocence, the privilege of being unafraid. (p. 46)

This became known as the Great *Aktion*. Afterwards, whenever Eilati saw a diagonal line—in a painting or in his line of vision—or heard the sounds of multiple footsteps, he was taken back to that moment in the Ghetto, not as a distant memory but as if he were there. Many years later, Shalom Eilati (2008) was in Washington, D.C.

pursuing his studies, when he decided to visit the White House. As one group would wind its way to the entrance, another would exit the building. They moved quietly. "Surprised, I found I was choking anew, after so many years, at the scene of the big *Aktion* in Democrats' Square. Shocked and upset, I left the place immediately, in turmoil." (p.50)

In November 1995 in Jerusalem, after the assassination of Yitzhak Rabin, Eilati joined thousands who had come to say farewell. "As for me," Eilati (2008) tells us, "as soon as I began waiting in the silent crowd, a feeling of suffocation fell upon me, of deep oppression, that grew as I moved forward in line, as though fifty-four years and one week had not gone by since the big Aktion. I turned around and went home. Sometimes it seems as if a part of me is still unsure that I was saved, as if it is ready for the bubble of time allotted to me to burst." (pp. 50–51)

In a talk that he gave at Yad Vashem in recent years, Eilati tells about a fictional movie in which a baby from outer space lands on earth inside a capsule made of a special metal. A farmer takes him home and raises him as his own child, but the child still holds a piece of that metal from out of this world. It is forever in his pocket, marking his unique identity:

> And so we, too, the child survivors who have been returned, parachuted into the existential world in which we now live. There is this piece imprinted in us, which sets us forever apart from those around us, and even seems to be bequeathed—to our sorrow— unto our children. Even if you try—try very hard—to be "like everyone else"—you will never again be "like them," despite all your efforts. For the effort is great and the attempts are many but in fact, each of us is at any given moment a kind of secret agent, living a double life in the full sense of the word. There is the outward "normal" life, reflected in the office, on the street, in the family; and the other, hidden deep under seven seals, which you endeavor to peer at only in the dark of night, associate with as little as possible, for the sake of your sanity and functioning.

Eilati (2008) notes that "Of the approximately 5,000 Jewish children under the age of 14 in the city of Kaunas (Kovno) before the war, 150 children survived" (p. 132). The *Kinder Aktion* took place in 1944 (though the killing of children and adults in over 200 villages occurred at the beginning of the German occupation in 1941). His mother decided that on her way to forced labor, she would arrange for him to go into hiding with a Lithuanian family. They crossed the river

Myra Sklarew

on a boat with others; his mother removed his two Jewish stars and
instructed him without stopping or looking back: once they reached
the opposite bank, he was to cross the road and go up a path into the
hill beyond. He would be met by a woman who would give him instructions. All went well, except no one met him on the path. He continued walking. Then suddenly, a woman whispered that he should
continue up the path and she would advise him. Eventually, he found
himself in the house of an elderly Lithuanian woman named Julija.[34]
"Like Moses," Eilati (2008) writes, "in the bulrushes I was cast by
Mother onto the shore of life, my mother, who gave me life twice,
but was unable to save her own even once." (p. ix–x). Eilati, now in
Israel, describes his role:

> On urgent reserve duty, gliding like an albatross, gazing like a
> hawk from an immense height….For years I have been decipher-
> ing military aerial photographs. Like ancient diviners examining
> the liver of a young calf, I bend over the stereoscope, examining
> the minute clues sketched in the emulsion of the film before me.
> Like those haruspices, I look for signs and portents, trying to
> prognosticate events before they materialize. Thus I can be on
> constant lookout, observing the horizon for events still beyond
> it, know in advance things that may happen before too long. As I
> have said, I no longer like surprises. (pp. 32–33)

In this way, he gains a degree of mastery over danger.

In the writing of his book, *Crossing the River*—over a period of
20 years—Eilati is able to find a means to confront what has lived
in him since childhood. Eilati describes his early attempts at telling
this story, and eventually discovering a method to do so: "find the
place where there were fewer land mines, and there try placing the
foot. Not in chronological order [. . .] not by topic. Not by force, but
by association only, while listening constantly for signals from the
soul—did it want, or did it not want, the next subject." The soul, he
tells us, "had no end of hesitations and resistance." The strategy involved "patient circling while persistently reducing the 'no trespass-
ing' areas. As if manufacturing dynamite. Piece by piece, patch after
patch, in order to avoid creating an explosion you cannot withstand."
The advantage, he notes, is that "things could become ripe in you, ter-
rors that you brought out yesterday, to tame them and introduce them

---

34. Julija Grinceviciene. Eilati was saved by others as well, whom he later
nominated to be honored at Yad Vashem. The willingness of some to hide Jews,
putting their families and communities in mortal danger, is a vital part of this
period and deserves its own place in this history.

gradually into your conscious world." (M. Sklarew, Letter to Norton)

Judith Herman (1992), in Trauma and Recovery, writes that:
Traumatic reactions occur when action is of no avail. When neither resistance nor escape is possible, the human system of self-defense becomes overwhelmed and disorganized. Each component of the ordinary response to danger, having lost its utility, tends to persist in an altered and exaggerated state long after the actual danger is over. Traumatic events produce profound and lasting changes in physiological arousal, emotion, cognition, and memory. Moreover, traumatic events may sever these normally integrated functions from one another. The traumatized person may experience intense emotion but without clear memory of the event, or may remember everything in detail but without emotion. [As noted earlier in the words of Sam Schalkowsky] She may find herself in a constant state of vigilance and irritability without knowing why. Traumatic symptoms have a tendency to become disconnected from their source and to take on a life of their own. (pp. 34–35)

Dr. Herman goes on to characterize posttraumatic stress disorder in three main categories: hyperarousal—the persistent expectation of danger; intrusion—the indelible imprint of the traumatic moment; and constriction—the numbing response of surrender. We see this response today in our returning veterans. We can barely imagine the effects on Syrians living under the constant siege of life-threatening bombing and war, and for the children transported during their most formative years into this nightmare of constant and insidious danger.

Neuropsychological View of the Formation of Trauma

How would neuroscientists, people like Joseph LeDoux, Bessel van der Kolk, Antonio Damasio, or Mark Solms, look at these effects of trauma and their formations? How might we explore the integration of the neurobiological, psychological, sociocultural perspectives with material drawn from oral histories?

In 1890, Sigmund Freud completed work on the "Project," a neuroscientific view of mind/consciousness/memory. At the time, the tools in the neurosciences were not sufficient to probe deeply enough to produce observations and results that included subjective observation, made available through psychoanalysis and the related approaches. The Project was abandoned, and was never published during Freud's lifetime. Alexander Luria, the Russian psychologist, picked up this thread in the early 20th century, but it is only today that we have the remarkable tools in neuroscience—functional MRIs and other methods of imaging—to really begin to bridge the fields of subjective and objective mental activity. In the work of Mark Solms, who is expertly trained in both psychoanalysis and neuroscience, we find a pathway toward the synthesis of these fields.

Antonio R. Damasio, professor and director of the Brain and Creativity Institute at the University of Southern California, said in an interview with the *Harvard Brain* (Liston, 2001):

> What we really want to understand, the relation between brain systems and complex cognition and behavior, can only be explained satisfactorily by a comprehensive blend of theories and facts related to all the levels of organization of the nervous system, from molecules, and cells and circuits to large-scale systems and physical and social environments. For almost any problem that is worth one's interest, theory and evidence from all of these levels are, in one way or another, relevant to the understanding of physiology or pathology. Since none of us can possibly practice or dominate knowledge across all of those levels, it follows that one must practice one or two very well, and be very humble about considering the rest, that is, evidence from those other levels that you do not practice. In other words, beware of explanations that rely on data from one single level, whatever the level may be. (p. 2)

In the area of memory—how we have come to think about the formation, encoding, and retrieval of memory and the unique character of traumatic memory—scientists from many areas, using their distinct knowledge, have come together to explore this powerful subject. We are tempted to think of memory as that which we experience entering the brain's library, as it were, and coming whole-cloth onto the appropriate shelf or location, like a book to be reached for when needed later on, ready and willing and still completely intact. Such a view loses sight of the remarkable plasticity of the brain and complexity beyond our imagining.

Borges' "Library at Babel" (1964) gets at this idea in his narrator's declaration that the Library contained all books, "the minutely detailed history of the future, the archangels' autobiographies, the faithful catalogue of the Library, [...] false catalogues [...] the true story of your death, the translation of every book in all languages [...]" (p. 54–55). Extravagant happiness about this eventually gives way to depression concerning the "books" that are inaccessible. His narrator resolves the problem by suggesting that letters and symbols—like DNA—should be juggled until by chance they construct themselves into canonical works, a kind of newly created world brought into being by chance. This enormous library is neither efficient nor flexible enough to be useful. On the other hand, perhaps he was forecasting the remarkable simplicity of the DNA molecule, four nucleotides' repeating in certain specific patterns. The basic building blocks are streamlined, yet their use is infinitely complex.

Perhaps we have held to the "library" version of brain function because it is comforting to think that we might point to a certain area of the brain and declare it the precise location of memory or emotion. Yet to examine the "cellular architecture" of the brain—to use Regina Pally's (2000) term—we must consider the brain's 100 billion neurons; each neuron with its axon and dendrites making "a synaptic connection with approximately 60,000 to 100,000 other neurons; the number of possible combinations of synaptic connections more than the number of positively charged particles in the known universe!" (pp. 8–9). Thus, we observe the brain's ability to process essentially an infinite amount of information, and a clue to the enormous plasticity of brain function. We have not yet mentioned the dramatically changed role that is now apparent regarding the deeply important role of glial cells in particular astrocytes. Once thought to be no more than support tissues, they are now key to understanding brain function.

Here, we will explore the neurobiological and corresponding psychological bases of trauma, and their effects upon memory formation and retrieval. These effects include issues of encoding during hyperarousal; dissociation; fragmentation; repetition; repression; the limiting of consciousness and focus on central perceptual details; and the limits of language to convey traumatic experience. An important note here is the difference in interview techniques that can strongly shape the nature of responses. The most directed interviews—the Lithuanian Documentation Project where the purpose was informational rather than focused on psychological exploration, for instance—leave very little room for examining individual responses. However, much can be learned from bystanders and witnesses to trauma in the way that experience is remembered and told. In some cases the witnesses, following the interviews, are asked to visit the places where the actual trauma occurred, and during these visits, the affect of the interviewee quite often radically differs from that during the prior interview situation.

Trauma: Issues of Hyperarousal and Dissociation: The Role of the Amygdala and Hippocampus—Emotional Memory

One day recently, I walked out of the front door of my house to the mailbox, crossing the garden, and as I returned I heard an ominous sound—a crunching of wood breaking. Without determining its source—apart from the sure knowledge that it was above my head—I simply ran as fast as I could toward the house. It might have been wiser to look up and to determine at what angle the huge branches, torn off by the wind, would fall. Had I done so, however, and taken the time to ascertain the full situation, it might have been too late to get out of the way of the falling branches.

Joseph LeDoux (1996), professor at the Center of Neural Science at New York University, describes putting his:

> [. . .]face close to the thick glass plate in front of a puff adder in the Zoological Gardens, with the firm determination of not starting back if the snake struck at me; but as soon as the blow was struck, my resolution went for nothing, and I jumped a yard or two backwards with astonishing rapidity. My will and reason were powerless against the imagination of a danger that had never been experienced. (p. 112)

What brain functions had been called into play in these moments of potential threat? Why had his determination beforehand not prevailed when the puff adder struck, though the recipient of the attack was safely behind a plate-glass barrier?

During the mid-fifties, I worked as a research assistant at Yale University School of Medicine, studying prefrontal lobe function and delayed-response memory. Paul MacLean's work in that same lab involved the limbic system. Its importance was considered a revolutionary hypothesis at that time—a system charged with maintaining the balance between the internal world and external reality, containing both innate circuitry and circuitry modifiable by experience, a system charged and concerned with emotion and instinct. It was MacLean who first coined the term "limbic" and who posited the notion of the triune brain: the primitive or reptilian brain, the intermediate or limbic brain, and the rational brain or neocortex.

Originally, this was considered a hierarchical system—brainstem and hypothalamus (regulation of internal homeostasis), limbic system (mediation between internal function and external reality) and neocortex (analysis and interaction with the external world). Later, it became clear that these systems operate in highly complex interactions. As Bessel van der Kolk (1996) notes, a "well-functioning neo-cortex is necessary for reasoning strategies to attain personal goals, for weighing a range of options for action, for predicting the outcome of one's actions, and for deciding which sensory stimuli are relevant and which are not. In these discriminatory functions, it is assisted by a well-functioning septo-hippocampal system." (pp. 216–217)

LeDoux (1997) posits the importance of the amygdala, the almond-shaped organ in the brain which appears to be the "link between all sensory systems and all fear response systems." The amygdala is most clearly implicated in the evaluation of the emotional meaning of incoming stimuli. LeDoux (1997) makes a distinction between emotional and cognitive processing: "[E]motional processing often leads to bodily response, whereas cognitive processing leads to more cognitive responses." The biology of these two systems differs, and in evolutionary terms, for good reason. "Emotional reactions are really reactions that are important in survival situations. The advantage is that by allowing evolution to do the thinking for you first, you basically buy the time that you need to think about the situation and do the most reasonable things." LeDoux (1997) points out that when danger appears, animals and people generally freeze first. Yet if we had time to think about it, we might move about or run, which might cause further harm. When the bomb detonated during the Olympics in Atlanta in 1996, people hunched "over in a freezing position for a couple of seconds," and then took off running.

Another point of interest is that the "connectivity of the amygdala with the neocortex is not symmetrical. The amygdala projects back to the neocortex in a much stronger sense than the neo-cortex projects to the amygdala" (LeDoux, 1996). Thus, the earlier incidents—falling tree branch and puff adder—likely induced a response from the amygdala first, getting the body into play before cognitive function had a chance to weigh the pros and cons of a proper course of action. According to LeDoux (1996), the "amygdala's ability to control the cortex is greater than the ability of the cortex to control the amygdala," which may explain "why it's so hard for us to will away anxiety; emotions, once they're set into play, are very difficult to turn off. Hormones and other long-acting substances are released in the body during emotions. These return to the brain and tend to lock you into the state you're in at the time. Once you're in that state it's very difficult for the cortex to find a way of working its way down to the amygdala and shutting it off." This, says LeDoux (1996), is the difficulty of therapy. The role of the neocortex in controlling the

Myra Sklarew

amygdala is like "trying to find your way from New York to Boston by way of country roads rather than super highways." On the other hand, the amygdala is able to control the neocortex by arousing a number of areas in a non-specific way.

Another way to think of this is as follows (Edwards, 2005):

The amygdala is essential for decoding emotions, particularly threatening stimuli. External stimuli reach the amygdala via two different pathways, which complement each other. A short, imprecise route comes from the thalamus, which receives sensory stimuli and allows us to prepare for potential danger before knowing exactly what the danger is. A longer, more precise route comes from the medial prefrontal cortex, the area of the brain that is involved in the final phase of fear, in which the brain reacts to danger and chooses a course of action.

Thus, extreme trauma and the response to it may be more deeply embedded and less under the control of cognitive processes, and may surface in memory in powerful and unbidden forms. What would have been appropriate responses to danger initially are no longer warranted when the danger has subsided; yet it is not possible to close off the response. At a later point, the occurrence of anything suggestive of the original experience is capable of eliciting "profound fear responses by reactivating these powerfully potentiated amygdala circuits." (p. 3)

Some contemporary examples might serve to illustrate this phenomenon. In 1970, when I started teaching at the university, my first students were men returning from the war in Vietnam. They were, in general, unrehabilitated: some were heavily addicted to drugs; some appeared to be in shock, still dazed by the world they had recently left. One veteran always stood at the back of the hallway, nearest the stairway, while we waited for the preceding class to leave the classroom. It was as if he needed to be sure he had a clear escape route. I had not known the details of his experience in Vietnam, until after an assignment reading Dante's Inferno. He dropped by my office one afternoon and handed me a packet, telling me that he had not been able to talk about his experience in Vietnam, nor to write about it until now, and that Dante and the descent into the Inferno had given him a route for his expression. He asked that I read his writing, and I told him that I would as soon as I had time to do so. Of course, I took the pages home that same evening and read every word. What I learned was that he had been part of a special reconnaissance group that took the forward positions, putting him and his men in grave danger. That he was, at a certain point, airlifted into a helicopter from a ring of fire. That all of the men in his unit had been killed. That he could identify a tripwire fine as a hair that might be attached to explosives. That when he saw the film Platoon, and came to the part where the American soldiers in Vietnam found a metal box and began to open it, he screamed in the movie theater for them to stop; he knew it would contain explosives. He described the terrible longing they felt to find signs of the enemy, to touch something the enemy had used. He was attuned to danger, at the ready to read whatever environment he was in for the least sign that might require sudden action for survival. This hypervigilance endured, even though he was now safe in America and its necessity was no longer required.

During the Iraq War, a young man on a brief army leave comes home to America and goes to a shopping mall with his family. He describes his terrible unease that he is without his machine gun, that no one is guarding the entrances and exits of the mall, that people are moving about in large numbers and that no one seems concerned. In Iraq, every face and motion must be interpreted. His life depended on this knowledge. He speaks of being afraid that he will feel this terror and the need for vigilance for the rest of his life.

A woman who survived as a child during WWII by hiding in the sewers beneath Lviv, Poland lived for fourteen months in a tube five feet high by four feet wide amid sewage and sewer rats. When asked how that experience manifests itself in her present-day life, she describes visiting a new house and feeling fearful about going down to the basement. But then, when exploring the attic, she thinks immediately that this might be a good place to hide. She points out how hard it is, after living on instinct during those years, to feel free of the need to do so. Cognitive function assures her that she is safe and the earlier need to fear for her life is no longer necessary; yet, the ingrained emotional response says otherwise. (K. Kristin, Interview, May 18, 1995)

Shalom Eilati (2008) describes a memory from his childhood in the Kovno Ghetto. The morning after a selection that took 9,200 people to their deaths, he is walking in the square where the selection had taken place when he comes upon "strangely shaped lumps among the mound of rubbish." When he draws near, he realizes that these are dead bodies. Ever after, he is transported back there by a series of triggers, including music:

Mahler's First Symphony, for instance, the second and third

movements: first a slow funeral march, accompanied by deep rhythmic drumbeats against a background of a meandering Jewish tune—and I cringe, accompanying the marchers' slow progress up the hill. Then suddenly, after a brief silence a paralyzing scream bursts out from dozens of instruments, and I choke in tears, hold my head in desperation and cannot be consoled. I am there. (p. 75)

Here we can observe a number of aspects of traumatic memory: the triggers that enable us to gain access to memory; the ways that memory is encoded in multiple sites and is constructed and retrieved through a series of operations—hormonal, neuronal, the action of neurotransmitters. And as Bessel van der Kolk has observed, we begin to see how the body remembers.

When he visited the Dachau concentration camp and walked into the barracks that had been reconstructed, Sam Schalkowsky (in conversation) describes "seeing the wooden planks that made me itch." Walking by the Dachau crematorium "brought back the smell," brought back the experience in Stutthof concentration camp where he was forced to clean up after the killings in the crematorium there.

Prior to being interviewed by the Shoah Foundation, Masha Wolpe Baras began to hunger for bread, as she had hungered in the concentration camp for the small ration of bread prisoners were allotted, insufficient for survival. For several weeks, she ate little else but bread, a literal repetition of the earlier situation in extremis.

Conclusion

Perhaps my uncle David Wolpe's description of a nightmare teaches us about the endurance and the power of trauma. "During a restless night in one of my nightmares I saw my childhood. It was an image suspended on a leafless branch hanging over the grave of the disembodied community of Keidan. How was it that I knew it was me and my own childhood? It was from the vision of a child's withered hand stretched across the strings of a shattered brown fiddle that once belonged to my uncle."

References

Birger, Z. (1999). *No Time for Patience: My Road from Kaunas to Jerusalem*. New York: William Morrow.

Borges, J. L. (1964) *Labyrinths*. New York: New Directions.

Edwards, Scott P. (2005). "The Amygdala: the Body's Alarm Circuit." *Brain Work: The Neuroscience Newsletter*, 15(3).

Eilati, S. (2008). *Crossing the River.* Tuscaloosa: University of Alabama Press.

Liston, C. (2001). "An Interview with Antonio R. Damasio." *The Harvard Brain,* 8(Spring).

Herman, J. L. (1992). *Trauma and Recovery.* New York: Basic Books.

LeDoux, J. (1996). *The Emotional Brain: The Mysterious Underpinnings of Emotional Life*. New York: Simon and Schuster.

———— (1997, Feb. 17) "Parallel Memories: Putting Emotions Back into the Brain: A Talk with Joseph LeDoux." Edge. Retrieved from: *https://www.edge.org/conversation/joseph_ledoux-parallel-memories-putting-emotions-back-into-the-brain*

Palley, R. (2000). *The Mind Brain Relationship*. New York: Other Press.

Schalkowsky, S.(2014) *The Clandestine History of the Kovno Jewish Ghetto Police*. Bloomington and Indianapolis: Indiana University Press.

van der Kolk, B., McFarlane, A. & Weisaeth, L, eds. (1996). *Traumatic Stress: The Effects of Overwhelming Experience on Mind, Body, and Society*. New York: The Guilford Press.

Wolpe, David E. (1997) *Ich un Main Welt* (I and My World), Johannesburg-Jerusalem, pp III–IV.

National Nightmare: The Legacy of Perpetrator Trauma

M. Gerard Fromm

Erikson Institute, Austen Riggs Center

Author Note:

M. Gerard Fromm, Ph.D., is Distinguished Faculty in the Erikson Institute of the Austen Riggs Center and Assistant Clinical Professor, Yale Child Study Center.

A version of this paper was originally published in the Summer 2017 issue of *Organisational and Social Dynamics*, Vol. 17 (1), pp. 111–126, 2017.

It is reprinted here with permission of the OSD editors.

Gerard Fromm

Abstract

This chapter reports on the themes and process of a conference organized by Thomas Kohut and the author through the Erikson Institute of the Austen Riggs Center. The title of the conference was *The Legacy of Perpetrator Trauma in Groups and Families* as experienced by descendants of Nazis, generations not guilty in deed but inevitably caught up in powerful feelings of guilt, shame, and horror by association. In this chapter, I examine the nature of the transmission of this trauma, the forms it takes, and some of the group dynamics that play out in relation to it.

Key Words: Trauma, Nazi Perpetrators, Intergenerational Transmission, Family Dynamics

National Nightmare: The Legacy of Perpetrator Trauma

In the last footnote to the Introduction of his magnificent *A German Generation* (2012), Thomas Kohut quotes his psychoanalyst father: "If the depth psychologist (or the historian, for that matter) is to make a contribution to the understanding of man's role in history and his control over his destiny, then he must try to extend his empathic observation not only to the victims but also to the persecutors, not only to the martyrs but also to the torturers. He must discover the human, the all-too-human, whether in the normal [...] or in the psychopathological, in the good and in the evil" (H. Kohut, 1969–70, p. 119).

Thomas Kohut is not only a psychoanalytically-trained historian, but he is also a son who learned deeply from his father. Taking up the latter's encouragement to find the all-too-human within the horrific, Kohut proposed that the Austen Riggs Center's Erikson Institute—of which I was the director and he was a Board member—convene an interdisciplinary conference, which came to be called *The Legacy of Perpetrator Trauma in Groups and Families.* With the help of a number of German colleagues, especially the scholar Hanna Schissler, Kohut invited the key participants from Germany and Austria, and I directed what turned out to be a profound, intellectually stimulating, and emotionally intense two days. This chapter is one outcome of that conference; it was initially written as a contribution to a volume called *History Flows through Us*, edited by Roger Frie and meant to honor Thomas Kohut's work. It was also written just as current societal dynamics were turning toward the populism and authoritarianism we have since seen develop more fully.

There was a history to the conference theme. For two consecutive years, the Erikson Institute's Fall Conference had studied the transmission of trauma, the clinical relevance of which was becoming increasingly clear. Papers from these conferences were published under the title *Lost in Transmission: Studies of Trauma across Generations* (Fromm, 2012). They joined a literature that began with Selma Fraiberg's classic paper, "Ghosts in the Nursery" (1975) and expanded enormously as the suffering of second-generation Holocaust survivors became known and treated. In succeeding years, we have learned that, as the French psychoanalysts Françoise Davoine and Jean-Max Gaudillière argue in *History Beyond Trauma* (2004), paraphrasing Wittgenstein, "Whereof one cannot speak, thereof one cannot stay silent." What human beings cannot contain of their experience—what has been traumatically overwhelming, unbearable, unthinkable—falls out of social discourse, but onto and into the next generation, as an affective sensitivity, a strange symptom, a chaotic urgency. In the words of one of our presenters, Gerhard Wilke, this manifests as "an encapsulated presence," and sometimes as an unconscious mission. Phillipe Sands (2016) begins his recent book—part legal treatise, part Holocaust history, part family study—with a similar point, based on a quote from the Hungarian psychoanalyst Nicholas Abraham: "What haunts are not the dead, but the gaps left within us by the secrets of others."

The Challenge of Empathy

This new conference was radically different from the earlier two in the subjects of its focus. As Wilke pointed out in the conference brochure, "Psychoanalytic understanding of the working through of such traumatic material is largely based on work done with survivors, émigrés, refugees and their children. What we know less well are the transgenerational phenomena of 'children of perpetrators'—a generation not guilty by deed, but so often caught up in feeling ashamed, guilty, responsible and horrified by association." In this conference—that Kohut, and, in some ways, his father proposed—we hoped to learn about the configuration and dynamics of this particular traumatic history.

In a clinical case conference some time ago, a young male patient, unknowingly echoing Abraham, told the staff that the hospital "is haunted by the forces of the dead." "They are here as much as there are helping people here," he said. To the degree that a person is unconsciously preoccupied with what may well be a haunting family history—who even at times may represent this hauntedness to and for his family—to that degree, the person's subjectivity is "lost in transmission," sometimes with tragic consequences: the German patient whose grandfather worked in the V-2 program at the beginning of World War II and who, years later, hurled himself from his dormitory balcony, thereby becoming a human missile. The Austrian patient whose suicide attempts always involved the products of his grandfather's pharmaceutical company, itself implicated in a horrific Holocaust history. Erikson scholar and psychoanalyst Vamik Volkan has discussed this kind of uncanny but stunning intergenerational enactment in a remarkable case history published recently under the title *A Nazi Legacy* (2015).

The task of the *Legacy of Perpetrator Trauma* conference was to explore this phenomenon through the stories of post-war German and Austrian generations. We hoped to help clinicians and scholars revisit and understand more deeply the psychological aftermath of the Third Reich through a consideration of the inner conflicts of those who may carry this psychic burden, on behalf of their families, their society and, in fact, for the rest of us. What might we learn about individual, family, and group dynamics associated with the offspring of perpetrators, and what are the implications of this learning for society?

True to Erikson's conviction that learning occurs in the boundary areas between fields of study, the conference represented a range of disciplines: history, psychoanalysis, psychology, sociology, and others. The tradition of the Erikson Institute is to hold *working conferences,* by which we mean that the presenters do not have the answers to the questions of the conference, except perhaps for themselves. Learning occurs through active dialogue among presenters and members. Sometimes how we talk about something—the process dimension of the conversation—illuminates more deeply what we are talking about. In this conference, that process dimension was inescapable. We were dealing with an extremely serious subject and highly charged material. Members joining this conference represented an act of courage, because it inevitably meant encountering genuinely disturbing feelings and challenging us to think more deeply, more discerningly, and, as Heinz Kohut suggested, more empathically about those feelings.

Freud spoke about every family's "archaic heritage" (1939a, p. 38), and one task of transmission turns out to be the generational struggle to resist the dissociation of that heritage, to recognize, in Davoine's and Gaudillière's phrase, the "cut-out unconscious" (personal communication)—cut out, that is, from the official narrative, whether that narrative is the family's or the society's—and to bring its full, tragic story into social discourse. How the unconscious gets "cut out"—and an astonishing 1930's dream journal kept by a woman named Charlotte Beradt (1968) may open a window onto that process—leads to one set of questions. How it gets re-inscribed, if you will—the profound task of telling the story—is where the conference began.

The Danger of Love

The conference was structured around three presentations, with considerable time for general discussion. The first theme to emerge was a simple but powerful one: how to love when the object of that love is implicated in horrific crimes. Alexandra Senfft, a freelance journalist whose personal story, *Silence Hurts: A German Family History* was published in 2008, put it in hypothetical form: "What if my grandfather had taken me onto his lap and I had begun to love him?" (This and other quotations come from the presentations and discussions at the conference.) Other similar, yet not at all hypothetical, statements spoke to the visceral experience of trying to contain the good and the bad at the same time, of vomiting out at the moment of taking in, of genuine love and horror at the feeling of loving.

It was as though it fell to the next generation to at least attempt to integrate what they experienced with their parents and what they also knew about them, an integration that the parents themselves seemed not to make at all. Rather, the perpetrator generation, the generation of "knowing and not knowing," seemed essentially to be living out that old definition of schizophrenia, that is, the split personality, and living permanently in what Melanie Klein (1946) called the paranoid-schizoid position, the place where good and bad must be kept separate at all costs. The maturational effort toward what Klein called the depressive position, that is, the task of holding the good and bad in the same space toward some sort of integration, fell to the next generation. It was a profoundly difficult emotional assignment.

Part of the integrative task that fell to the children of perpetrators included feeling the guilt and shame of their parents' actions, which the parents themselves had warded off. Their children's responses took more than one form. We heard examples of essentially manic efforts at reparation, not necessarily directed to the victims of the Nazis, but to other suffering people in far-off countries. By "manic" I mean not only frenetically active and obsessively preoccupied; I also mean what is termed a "manic defense," that is, manic reparation in the service of keeping at bay the very feelings of guilt motivating it. We noted, as well, friction between this generation and their children when the latter did not want to continue the reparation project, but rather hoped to go on with their own lives. That latter wish, understandable as it is, is of course not at all easy to accomplish, not only because of their parents' pressure to continue the reparative mission, but because of the larger task of individuating from the chaos of such immense family disaster.

In the second and third generations, another form this effort to process parental perpetration took was identification with the victims, sometimes very literally and to a quasi-psychotic degree. In his recent book *A Nazi Legacy* (2015), Vamik Volkan tells the story of a man who leaves his bed to frantically open windows night after night in his sleep. Though this man's troubles were many and complex, this particular stubborn and mysterious symptom was eventually understood in relation to his Nazi grandfather, who murdered Jews by gassing them inside a school bus. His victims—*like his grandson years later*—frantically tried to open windows.

Alexandra Senfft structured her presentation around two questions: her mother's question, "Why did they kill my father?", and her own, "Why did my mother die?" In the story, Ms. Senfft's mother loved her own father and was devastated when he was hanged for war crimes when she was 14. Over time, as she learned about his Nazi career and his role in deporting 65,000 Jews, she became increasingly depressed and alcoholic. In a family context where her own mother refused to believe or to speak about what had happened, and admitted no guilt or shame at all, Ms. Senfft's mother spiraled into madness.

Perhaps she spiraled instead into a mad sanity. In her alcoholic state, she would panic about being closed in and scream for help. Davoine and Gaudillière, in *History Beyond Trauma* (2004) report clinical work in which psychosis and trauma go hand-in-hand. They are convinced that the psychotic patient is madly conducting a research into the rupture between his family and the social fabric, a rupture brought about through trauma and betrayal. Beyond her screaming about the suffocating silence of her family, was Ms. Senfft's mother also living out her fragmented imagining of what her father's victims might have experienced? And was that part of her tragic death, self-inflicted while drunk, in scalding water?

One more thing Ms. Senfft's mother did while drunk was much more in the direction of an active transmission. She talked to her oldest child, and as Ms. Senfft said, "I let her." Frightened of "becoming" her, Ms. Senfft needed to know why her mother died one year after her grandmother did, and the boxes of letters that were left to her became a way into that terrible story. Like another presenter, Marcus Carney, whose award-winning documentary, *The End of the Neubacher Project*, tells the story of his mother's family and its involvement in Austrian National Socialism, Ms. Senfft took up the task of inscription of a cut-out history, the task of "how to give my mother a voice."

After this revelation, she encountered the same terror her mother felt: the terrifying dilemma of exploding the silence or sinking into it. In a sense, by taking the risk of learning and then speaking the truth of her family history, she found herself in another transmission role: destroying the family myth, *she became the perpetrator*: the one who inflicts on her family, *for the first time*, the horrific images and feelings that have been so strenuously split off and kept at bay. In a paper called "Fear of Breakdown," the psychoanalyst Donald Winnicott came to a remarkable intuition: "The patient needs to 'remember'[. . .] but it is not possible to remember something that has not yet happened, and this thing of the past has not happened yet because the patient was not there for it to happen to" (1974, p. 105). It's as though Ms. Senfft's family had dissociated themselves so thoroughly from their own lives that, in a very powerful sense, they were at risk of experiencing *in the future, at her hands*, the trauma of what they had already done.

Ms. Senfft experienced enormous and sustained family resistance to her writing her book. She was criticized and shunned, and seen as having something terribly wrong with her. "Drive carefully," spoken to her after one such family meeting, had a menacing ring to it. Ultimately, she lost her family when her book came out, though, crucially, not her whole family: her father supported her throughout the project. As she said, "I don't know what I would have done if he had turned against me." And, in a sense, her mother was there too, as the "open wound" of her family that "nobody treated," until her daughter did so by writing her story.

The word "therapist" has an ancient Greek root in the word "therapon," the second-in-combat, the one who *attends to the burial ritual of the warrior* (Davoine and Gaudillière, 2004). In a sense, this is the role that Ms. Senfft served for her mother. In his enigmatic statement that the symbol is "the murder of the thing" (1977, p.104), the psychoanalyst Jacques Lacan evokes the varying levels at which inscription—and the witnessing embedded in it—destroys something. He also refers to inscription's role in a person's ability to fundamentally separate from the traumatic context: the way that inscription on a tombstone allows leaving the dead—and the trauma leading to the death—because now one knows where to truly find them.

A Delegated Life

Another presenter, Gerhard Wilke, a sociologist and organizational consultant, referred to present-day Germany as a "posttraumatic society." Today's understanding of PTSD includes three major elements: overwhelming exposure to horror manifested in the symptom triad of flashbacks, dissociation, and hyperarousal; the experience of sudden serious loss; and what has come to be called "moral injury."

Coined by the Veterans Administration psychiatrist Jonathan Shay (2014), and broadened by Brett Litz (2014), moral injury refers to a deep sense of betrayal of "what's right," committed by someone in legitimate authority or by oneself, in a high-stakes situation: the devastating emotional legacy of witnessing or participating in something that fundamentally violates one's most basic sense of moral order. All three elements occur simultaneously and with extraordinary intensity in perpetrator families.

Wilke captures one aspect of the second and third generations' sense of themselves in the statement that "We live a delegated life." From his point of view, his generation is always representing someone to someone else, and is implicated constantly in working out something for someone else, one way or the other. This is part of the perhaps naïve but nonetheless urgent longing for "one's own life." Wilke personally attempted to get some grasp on this phenomenon for himself by leaving Germany for London, from which vantage point two things happened. First, he was constantly seen as a Nazi, which he actually found useful. In the safer, more playful context of London, he could dare to face the Nazi in himself. His former countrymen, however, did not have the luxury of this perspective from a distance, so the second thing that happened was Dr. Wilke's dedication to helping them achieve it, as best he and they could. He does this through consulting on their work lives and helping them see the playing out of war trauma in their daily relation to authority, to ordinary assertiveness, to their need for order, and so on—not an easy task, to be sure.

Following Wilke's presentation, we had set aside a considerable length of time for conference discussion. The first half of that time was to be a space for volunteer members to express freely what they had experienced in the conference—and where those experiences had led them in their associations—on which Wilke consulted. The second half was to be a more reflective and integrative conversation for everyone, on which both he and I were to consult. But first, the opportunity was to simply bring out whatever members were carrying emotionally from the presentations and discussions so far. This was obviously not an easy task, even if it promised some degree of relief, learning, and even intimacy. As I had done from the very beginning of the conference, I told myself once again to try to "hold the whole thing," meaning that I was keenly aware of how critical it was for the staff to contain this process, to manage boundaries, and to be present as sensible authority.

In the first discussion, members were very attentive to the presence of two Holocaust survivors in their midst. Nevertheless—or perhaps because of this—the unfolding conversation was extraordinary in its emotional scope and detail. Stories about members' families came out, many of which were associated with wartime experiences. References to the conference material included very personal reactions, sometimes of feeling things from both sides. Anxiety ebbed and flowed, and at one point in the midst of the unstructured opening up of experiences, one of the Holocaust survivors spoke with feeling about "needing a framework" for what was happening. Not long thereafter, a second Holocaust survivor began to speak rather theoretically at some length about trauma. As interesting as his comments were, the effect was to interrupt the expression of what members were carrying and how it linked to their personal experiences.

Wilke consulted on what might be the group's need, via this member's discourse, to protect itself from the intensity of feeling that had been emerging. Despite this intervention, members seemed to defer to the Holocaust survivor who had been speaking, and his comments, which were again very astute but conveyed almost as a lecture, continued at some length, thus limiting the opportunity for other members to speak about their experiences. Eventually, one German member and Wilke again intervened with the speaker in ways that some members felt to be too confrontational. And suddenly, just as this part of the group discussion was coming to an end, we were back to the old roles of German perpetrator and Jewish victim. Sadly, a framework of sorts had fallen into place, and the flow of conversation—if not of history, to pick up on one of Kohut's concepts—had stopped.

In the broader reflective discussion that followed, the group tried to process what had happened with only partial success. Feelings were still running high, and tended toward polarized positions. The group did its best to reflect on the events of the first discussion, and at least allowed members' different perspectives to be articulated. The hypothesis I found myself with, and offered to the group, was that as this powerful conversation was coming to a close—and therefore as we were all about *to be silenced permanently,* this discussion group being the last conference event—there was something unbearable about, in Heinz Kohut's terms, the effort to "extend (our) empathic observation" such that we might end up on the wrong moral side of history, not to mention stuck with unbearable identifications. The old roles—and the sense of being back to square one—disappointing as they were, were nevertheless reassuring. We knew where, in a projective sense, to leave the good and the bad. Although it was hard to know what members did with my intervention and indeed how they actually understood what had happened, it seemed to me that the potential learning from and about the group's process was invaluable.

In the Name of the Father

The title of the volume for which this paper was written, *History Flows Through Us*, comes from the final chapter of Thomas Kohut's *A German Generation* (2012). In my contribution, I have tried to illuminate some of the intergenerational and group processes by which this flow works to shape individual feelings, attitudes, and behaviors. The title of Kohut's concluding chapter is "The Authority of Historical Experience," with the word "authority" connoting to my mind not only the power historical experience unconsciously exercises over people, but also the set of rights or claims one generation makes on the other. It seems to me, as I have argued elsewhere (Fromm, 2012), that the transmission of trauma from one generation to the next reflects a complex authority issue. To some degree, the experience of the next generation has been "authored," if you will, by the unspoken, and indeed unspeakable, traumas in their parents' histories, to use Christopher Bollas' apt phrase (1987), or one of these children—Ms. Senfft's mother perhaps—are lost in this transmission.

Others, like Ms. Senfft herself, may have been especially, if unconsciously, "authorized" to carry the parent's trauma into the future. "She talked to me, and I let her." This may take the form of a symptom, of an "unthought known," of an urgent question: for example, "Why did my mother die?" One way or the other, such transgenerational experience "must come into being as emotional understanding if the (person) is ultimately to take authority for his or her own life as distinct from that of the traumatized parent" (Fromm, 2012, p. 113). Ms. Senfft's story suggests that the authority of one generation's historical experience, and its raw, if unconscious power over the next, can be mitigated by that next generation's finding the authority—and to be sure, the courage—to become its author, and to somehow inscribe this "archaic heritage" (Freud, 1939a, p. 38) into the larger human discourse.

Ms. Senfft needed her father to find this authority, and fathers are a major part of the story Kohut tells in *A German Generation*. He argues that the defeated, humiliated fathers of World War I—who from the PTSD perspective, experienced a set of profound losses, horrific shocks and moral injuries—set the experiential stage for the next generation's profoundly powerful peer relationships—indeed their driven merger with the collective. In turn, this made them vulnerable to, and indeed hungry for, the return of a powerful, idealized father. Charlotte Beradt, in an amazing dream journal from 1930s Germany (1968), reports a dream in which the phrase "In the Name of..." is proclaimed over the radio repeatedly, but its last word is "Führer" (p. 40). In this dream, Hitler supplants all fathers, including the Heavenly One.

Beradt's journal suggests the ways that the perpetrator generation—a generation led by vengeful fathers—attempted to keep secrets from itself, leading to profound, collective dissociation and the licensing of horrific destructiveness, in the context of terror and destructive group processes. A natural experiment in what Gordon Lawrence (1991) called "social dreaming," the journal illuminates the steady assault on a person's inner life, and the way that massive social trauma and malignant authoritarianism turn a dreamer's privacy into dangerous secrecy, even from the self. As I noted elsewhere, "(r)elentlessly, we see the ethno-syntonic but ego-dystonic conflict resolved in favor of membership rather than identity or conscience. The totalitarian outcome is the self-alienated subject rather than the citizen, and the destruction of dream life—one space for self-other confrontation—is at the heart of the totalitarian method" (Fromm, 2000, p. 293).

In the Preface to *Young Man Luther* (1958), Erikson—the son of a German Jewish woman and a Danish Gentile father whom, to his great pain, he never knew—concludes with

> "...a memory which had been utterly covered by the rubble of the cities and by the bleached bones of men of my kind in Europe. In my youth, as a wandering artist, I stayed one night with a friend in a small village by the upper Rhine. His father was a Protestant Pastor; and in the morning, as the family sat down to breakfast, the old man said the Lord's Prayer in Luther's German. Never having 'knowingly' heard it, I had the experience, as seldom before or after, of a wholeness captured in a few simple words, of poetry fusing the aesthetic and the moral. . ."(1958, p. 10).

Erikson's longing for wholeness is found, however temporarily, through a father.

Thomas Kohut concludes his introductory chapter with a memory, too: "My own interest in history can be traced back to fishing trips with my father in rural Wisconsin when I was very little. I do not recall us ever catching anything, but I vividly remember listening with rapt attention as my father told me stories of the Persian and Peloponnesian wars as we sat in a little rowboat in the hot sun on a lake…"(2012, p. 18). Barely fifteen years after his escape from Vienna, Heinz Kohut and his son were together, alone on a boat, safely separate from other people, warmed by the sun, waiting for nature to offer something special from its depths, telling and listening to stories of long ago and far away wars. From this comes a life's vocation, a story of too close a war, and our gratitude that some transmissions are more profoundly generative than others.

References

Beradt, C. (1968). *The Third Reich of Dreams*. Chicago: Quadrangle Books.

Bollas, C. (1987). *The Shadow of the Object: Psychoanalysis of the Unthought Known*. London: Free Association Books.

Carney, M. (2007). *The End of the Neubacher Project*. A documentary film written and directed by Marcus J. Carney.

Davoine, F. and Gaudillière, J-M. (2004). *History Beyond Trauma*. New York: Other Press.

Erikson, E. (1958). *Young Man Luther.* New York: W.W.Norton and Company.

Fraiberg, S., Adelson, E. & Shapiro, V. (1975). Ghosts in the nursery. *Journal of the American Academy of Child Psychiatry, 14:* 387–421.

Freud, S. (1939a). *Moses and Monotheism*. S.E. 23. London: Hogarth Press.

Frie, R. (Ed.) (2017). *History Flows through Us. London*: Routledge.

Fromm, M.G. (2000). The other in dreams. *Journal of Applied Psychoanalytic Studies*, 2: 287–298.

Fromm, M.G. (2012). *Lost in Transmission: Studies of Trauma Across Generations.* London: Karnac.

Klein, M. (1946). Notes on Some Schizoid Mechanisms. *International Journal of Psycho-Analysis.* 27: 99–110.

Kohut, H. (1969–70). On leadership. In P. Ornstein (Ed.), *The Search for the Self: Selected Writings of Heinz Kohut*, Vol. 3 (pp. 103–128). New York: International Universities Press, 1991.

Kohut, T. (2012). *A German Generation*. New Haven: Yale University Press.

Lawrence, W.G. (1991). Won from the void and formless infinite: experiences of social dreaming. *Free Associations,* 2: 259–294.

Litz, B. (2014). Clinical heuristics and strategies for service members and veterans with war-related PTSD. *Psychoanalytic Psychology* 31(2): 192–205.

Sands, P. (2016). *East West Street: On the Origins of "Genocide" and "Crimes against Humanity."* New York: Knopf.

Senfft, A. (2008). *Silence Hurts: A German Family Story*. Deutscher Biographiepreis.

Shay, J. (2014). Moral injury. *Psychoanalytic Psychology* 31(2): 182–191.

Volkan, V. (2015). *A Nazi Legacy*. London: Karnac.

Wilke, G. (with Binney, G. and Williams, C.) (2005). *Living Leadership*. Harlow: Pearson Education Limited.

Winnicott, D.W. (1974). Fear of breakdown. *International Review of Psycho-Analysis,* 1:103–107.

Trauma and Identity: The Challenge of Becoming Oneself

Marilyn Charles
Austen Riggs Center

Marilyn Charles is a staff psychologist at the Austen Riggs Center and a psychoanalyst in private practice in Stockbridge, MA. She is also a Training and Supervising Analyst at the Chicago Center for Psychoanalysis, and on faculty at Harvard Medical School, Boston Graduate School of Psychoanalysis, and Universidad de Monterrey.

Marilyn Charles

Abstract

Most individuals seek psychoanalytic treatment because there was insufficient interest in their *becoming* to effectively negotiate developmental tasks. Such deficits leave the individual jumping past developmental milestones in ways that provide them with no firm foundation on which to stand. The analyst who can recognize that dilemma is in a good position to take a stand for the importance of beginning where one is, rather than further subverting development through a focus on where one would like to be. That stand can be seen as the type of ethical imperative Lacan points to in his discussions of the primacy of the subject as the focus of the work. The analyst's interest helps invite the patient's interest in a process of self-discovery that includes a willingness to be laid bare in a moment of empathic connection, moments that the analyst uses to fuel and refine his or her ability to attend meaningfully to the patient. In this chapter, I will discuss some of the theory that has been helpful to me in finding my way through such difficult territory. Each new patient poses new challenges. A human life, singular in its importance, is in our hands. To the extent that we can try the various theories on for size and become intimately familiar with the metaphors they offer, we can be better prepared for the particular challenges posed in a given moment by a given patient. To illustrate the importance of relying heavily on our metaphors while treading lightly with our theories, I will offer a case where the negotiations regarding where the trouble lay became essential to the eventual work.

Trauma and Identity: The Challenge of Becoming Oneself

We are living in a time of too much: too much pressure and too much data. Current life encourages us to press forward rather than taking the time to integrate and make sense of our experience, ourselves and our relations with one another. Trauma is everywhere and tales of human suffering inundate us, leaving us too often either in despair or numb, uncertain as to how to relieve the ongoing cries of human suffering that come to us from all corners of the globe as well as from our own backyards. Unacknowledged oppressive sociocultural forces leave shame seemingly lodged in the individual in ways that further impede constructive resolutions. The rage of abjected voices erupts in acts of violence that leave us further unsettled. How our humanity can survive in such a world is an ongoing challenge, exacerbated as claims of righteousness are used to excuse turning a blind eye on the suffering of others.

The too-much of daily living is exacerbated by the press to move ever more quickly, and to accumulate data rather than assimilate it. Schools test "competencies" rather than developing reflective functions in our children and, with these, the capacity to learn that is so essential to civil discourse and democratic process. At a time when we desperately need to be able to think together about the complicated issues facing us, we are undermining the ability of future generations to engage in those essential reflective processes. Around the globe, we see an increasing and alarming turn towards accumulating data about performance rather than encouraging the type of reflective capacity that might ensure quality performance. Even our news media tends towards managing opinions and profit shares rather than ensuring an informed public. Our minds, our hearts, and our children are increasingly at risk. In such a world, *becoming* a viable self is made problematic, not only by the extent of suffering, but also by the inundation of facts, figures, and feelings, without sufficient provisions to help us adaptively digest the data.

The press towards moving on rather than coming to terms with difficult experiences leaves parents less available to be resources for their children in the crucial function of identity development. Identity is built upon early interactions with caretakers, through which we learn to make sense of self and experience, augmented by the process of creating a narrative through which a life story is built (Charles, 2014a). If early engagements build sufficient self-regulatory capacities, then the child is free to learn. If not, then *that* fundamental instability conditions all later learning and experience. Disruptions become traumatic *because* they derail. The literature on disorganized attachment shows that it is precisely those parents who are otherwise "good enough," but who become derailed by unresolved mourning, who are most confusing to their children (Liotti, 1999; Main & Hesse, 1990). Not knowing whether one will encounter the receptive human face or the preoccupied absent one sends development awry.

Under these conditions, the transition from child to adult is impeded, and people look for the authority on whom they may rely to show them the way. In such a world, suffering individuals look for the diagnosis that will tell them how to understand whatever impasse they have come to in their lives. Often, however, along with the growing emphasis on appearance over substance, rather than seeking greater clarity in order to better navigate, there is a desire to break through the impasse, and to jump past developmental challenges in the hope of arriving at the "right" place. Our medical systems are similarly upended, as our standards become increasingly narrow and codified in ways that offer answers that do not solve the more complicated problems at hand (Charles, 2011; Charles & O'Loughlin, 2013). Increasingly, I find it hard to make sense of the troubles my patients encounter in relation to the lexicon offered by modern psychiatry. The most recent DSM even does away with my old reliable "identity problem," leaving me turning with even greater assurance toward the language of development rather than psychopathology to mark the deficits that underlie the struggle of so many people.

This is a deliberate stand I take, in a world in which multiple stressors push towards finding simple solutions to complex problems, and in which constricting, pragmatic "standards" press towards actions that may, in effect, be further dehumanizing to people seeking assistance. In such a world, how do we stand by an ethic grounded in both principle and a method we can count on? As simplistic solutions fail, many young people turn towards psychoanalysis as a means for grappling with complexity. Psychoanalytic therapy is not for the faint of heart. It demands every bit of fortitude we can muster, as we struggle to remain present in the face of profound human suffering and the very real limits we come to in our ability to ameliorate that distress. Psychoanalysis provides a framework within which we may take on precisely those challenges that are not resolved through direct routes, dilemmas that are intransigent precisely because there are multiple determinants, some of which are not consciously known.

In our consulting rooms, we see people who bear the marks of trauma that they may not be able to articulate in any coherent form.

That difficulty marks not only signs of unresolved trauma, but also a history that has taught the person not to engage or even to hope, lest he be once again disappointed. As failures build upon failures, it is easy to get lost in a maze of funhouse mirrors where the human face marks not hope, warmth, and safety but rather pain, disappointment, and the shame of being rejected and left feeling needy. Such abjection is itself traumatic, in part because we find ourselves implicated in and haunted by a shameful history that can neither be resolved nor worked through, because it is not our story but rather our legacy (Abraham, 1975). Shame imposes an alienated cut through which we become isolated in our pain, thereby further attenuating the possibility of redemption, through which we might reclaim an identity disentangled from the traumatic past (Apprey, 1993).

One legacy of unresolved trauma is that individual groups can become caught within the confines of their own chosen trauma (Volkan, 2001). That type of generalized, structural trauma resists mourning, in part because it becomes perversely gratifying, bearing the stigmata of privileged pain (LaCapra, 1999). The result of accumulating such unresolved collective traumas across the globe leaves us living in an *era of trauma*, an era of fear that is being exacerbated by individuals for their own ends. As pressures push towards doing over being, we are lost, not only in relation to one another, but also in relation to ourselves, as groups become further isolated from one another and parents become caught up in living in ways that undermine their children's efforts to be. The attachment literature shows us how unresolved mourning and preoccupied parents inhibit identity development in their children, leaving those children with little resilience with which to withstand and work through the traumatic events that assail us in our daily lives.

Clinical Context

Because of my awareness of the contextual factors that impede identity development in today's world, I find myself increasingly thinking in developmental terms rather than in the language of psychopathology, illness and cure. Although most people come to my consulting room seeking *solutions to problems*, I consider the real work of therapy as providing a place in which the subject can develop beyond whatever impasses have occurred. I use the word *subject* advisedly, to stress that part of the move towards adulthood is to move from the object position, from learning who we are through how we are treated, to taking up the *subject* position, willing to take a stand for our own values, needs, goals and desires. That transformation process is complicated by the ways in which experience forms—and de-forms—the self over time. From a psychoanalytic framework, we can think of the consulting room as providing a place in which the subject can develop beyond whatever impasses have occurred.

In this age of diagnostic criteria linked to specific treatment demands, it is easy to think in terms of discrete problems rather than human dilemmas; but when a person enters the consulting room, ideas of diagnoses and disease can present one more impediment to actual engagement. From a psychoanalytic perspective, the problem *itself* has exchange value. It is a way of beginning a negotiation over what might be possible to know and to accomplish, and the conditions under which this work might be done. We hope that our empathic concern and curiosity may invite the patient's interest in a process of self-discovery that includes a willingness to be laid bare in a moment of empathic connection, moments the analyst uses to refine his/her ability to attend meaningfully to the patient, as we negotiate a deepening engagement with one another. Part of this process entails developing sufficient safety in the relationship to be able to move beyond the more facile "truths" we hide behind in order to more fully encounter the pockets of distress that have not received useful attention.

Most people seek treatment because there was insufficient interest in their ability to effectively negotiate developmental milestones. The literature on disorganized attachment reveals the devastating impact of unresolved mourning on successive generations and some of the mechanisms by which identity development is impeded, even in families that seem to be functioning well (Liotti, 1999; Main & Hesse, 1990). When an otherwise loving and devoted parent is absolutely unavailable, that discrepancy itself is confusing to the child. Reflective capacity is built on the ability to know oneself in relation to others who may be both similar and different, built upon the moments of disruption and repair so crucial to the development of identity and resilience (Beebe & Lachmann, 1994). These encounters with otherness allow translations to occur so that one can make the transition from the concrete realm of the *symbolic equation* to symbol-formation proper. Kleinians note the developmental progression from the use of symbols in more concrete form—the language of child's play—to the ability to manipulate symbols in ways that make use of their more varied possibilities (Segal, 1957), to move from metonymy to metaphor. Trauma tends to make meanings concrete, hence making it difficult to make use of words in creative ways. One challenge for the clinician, then, is to make offerings that further the reflective capacity of the patient rather than taking its place—to keep the interchange in the arena of a playful exchange through which meanings can be tried on for size, shaped, discarded and reconsidered (Winnicott, 1971).

Winnicott distinguishes between a type of play that is ruminative and obsessive, that destroys reality, versus play that is creative and fruitful. This distinction is particularly useful in our work with individuals whose language may appear thoughtful but, on closer scrutiny, is locked into routines of speech and activity that are deadening. The potential space afforded by psychoanalysis can represent an impossible demand for those who are ungrounded in their internal experience. If there is no safety in relationship, then, as social beings, our survival is too precarious. Whatever internal capacities we might have, there is no room for play. In psychoanalysis, we hope to help those who are ungrounded in their internal experience find sufficient safety in relationship to withstand encounters with otherness and build the capacity to play. In these efforts, recognizing ebbs and flows of vitality through our feelings in the counter-transference can be a significant marker of the presence or absence of the person with whom we hope to engage.

In this work, it is important to recognize failures in our understanding as potential markers of a lack of cogency in the stories we are being told. We know the importance of narrative coherence in identity development, and that, at the extreme, lack of coherence can result in psychosis. And yet we can mistake our lack of comprehension for a failure of attention in ways that invite us to cover over the gap rather than inquiring into it, in this way colluding with self-erasure. Even very bright, creative young people can be driven mad as they search for themselves in others or in accomplishments. That search is doomed to fail until they can find someone who insists that their own subjective experience has to be the beginning point of the journey. This means that we must be willing to be present in our own failures in attention or understanding, so that finding meaning together remains at the forefront of the work.

Taking a stand implicitly, through our engagement, about the importance of being able to track experience together in real time in order to build our capacities for understanding is particularly important when working with those whose development has been impeded by trauma. Such experiences encourage a moving on rather than a working through, acting as though one can manage as a way of desperately trying to be up to the challenge. Because of the difficulty of holding hope and also of communicating experience that is largely ineffable and beyond words, metaphors are profoundly important in working with such individuals. Metaphors breathe life into the work because they are, of essence, play*ful*: they cannot be taken in directly, but rather must be *played with*. Such playfulness requires the ability to regulate one's affect so that grief can be faced rather than denied. Coming back to life can be painful. One young woman, whose creative engagements had increasingly become the type of fantasy-making Winnicott (1971) alludes to, noted: "I've been living in a hallucination of what's outside the window. I made up life. I made up the truth. But this is where I am. And it hurts."

In sharing the patient's metaphors, I try to participate in the enterprise of meaning-making, trying to dream through the sessions along with her in the fashion described by Bionian field theorists such as Ferro (2009) and Civitarese (2005). Allowing the veneer to slip enables this young woman to encounter more of herself—and with it, her pain—through which process she begins to come alive sufficiently to feel anything at all beyond the abject and nameless pain she was suffering when we first met. She worries that she is getting worse, but also has the sense that she is getting better. "You've been numb," I say, "And it hurts to come back to life." Recognizing the truth of her experience, and finding ways to anchor those truths into her life story, both help her to make sense of herself in a new and different way. Rather than trying to find the right meaning that will mark her as valuable, she struggles to be more present in precisely those moments that most engender her fear. Knowing that something is at stake becomes an index of her valuation, which, in turn, marks her as the subject of the conversation.

A Case

For those whose histories have pushed them outside of the narrow margins of what is acceptable within the confines of the family story, truth and reality can be both precious and precarious. I worked with one young woman who had become increasingly dysregulated in relation to the story that could not be told. "Virginia" described her mother as wonderful and loving, creating opportunities for enjoyment for her children. What she had not been able to tolerate, it seemed, was to face whatever might disturb that lovely family narrative. An extremely bright and talented young woman, Virginia's development became increasingly waylaid in ways that her parents could not make sense of. They tried to find help for her, but failures built upon failures, leaving them frustrated and likely also frightened. By the time I met her, the parents' story had become one in which Virginia's "madness" was a tragic presumption. Their efforts to assist her, then, resisted her efforts to register her own traumatic narrative.

Initial engagements with the family took the form of painful confrontations between two stories utterly at odds with one another. The mother politely tried to sit through the daughter's urgent efforts to inform the parents about the sources of her distress but finally, in exasperation, appealed to the therapist to stop her daughter from attacking her. I suggested that, although the parents felt as though they had already heard Virginia's story, her own experience seemed to be one of repeating a story that had not been able to register in either parent's mind. My assertion of the legitimacy of Virginia's perspective, which might be quite different from the mother's own, made it possible for two different stories to be told. It was only at that juncture that we were able to begin to consider the conditions under which a conversation between two different minds might evolve.

There are truths that are as difficult to hear as they might be to tell. For Virginia's parents, it was difficult to face the possibility that their child might have been injured while under their care. Although they affirmed their desire to give their daughter whatever she needed, their inability to break through their own resistance to taking in Virginia's perspective made them utterly unavailable to her as resources. Further, the parents' lack of recognition of the source of her distress had left Virginia unable to more cogently recognize her own. It was only when a previous therapist had noted symptoms of early trauma that Virginia had begun to be interested in her symptoms beyond seeing them as impediments to functioning in the world. That recognition had afforded the grounding that Virginia needed in order to begin to register them, see them as potentially meaningful, and begin to make sense of those symptoms within the context of her own life story.

Virginia's nascent recognition of the sources of her distress helped her to make better choices in spite of her disequilibrium. She was able to resist, for example, the diagnosis of schizophrenia when that was offered as a way of making sense of her symptoms that did *not* recognize the story *behind* those symptoms. At that juncture, Virginia was able to *oppose* the medicalized truth with the truth of her experience, insisting that the diagnosis did not make sense because it failed to take into account her trauma history. That insistence helped Virginia find a therapist who recognized that the abuse history *did* make a difference in terms of how her story was told and how one might proceed. Putting together the story of her abuse, and the ways in which her repression of that abuse had undermined her efforts to build a life, became the foundation on which self-knowledge and identity could more solidly be built.

Applying our Knowledge

Virginia's case shows how important the meaning structures through which we contextualize an individual's experience can be to the eventual outcome of the work. Because so many of our patients have experienced early relational difficulties in spite of their parents' best intentions, my work at the Austen Riggs Center helps me to appreciate the importance of the early negotiation that Winnicott (1971) refers to as the *capacity to use an object.* This term marks the developmental juncture at which the young child begins to recognize his or her autonomy in relation to caregivers who can be rejected or even hated and yet with whom he/she can still sustain a relationship. Much like the transition from symbolic equation to symbol usage, this passage marks the child's capacity to creatively engage as an autonomous being with others who are also free agents. This essential separateness that is a precondition for actual engagement between two individuals marks a crucial crossroad we encounter in working with any individual who has lost his/her way. This is the juncture that Bion (1967) marks in his paper on memory and desire, and that Lacan (1978) points to in his metaphor of *the subject caught by the desire of the other,* of needing to be open to what we might discover beyond whatever answers we have found. Those of us who take responsibility for another's development in any way must always remind ourselves whose life we are fighting for, so that we do not undermine the other's nascent development through our own desire.

The fact of difference is an essential grounding point that must be negotiated in order for an autonomous self to develop. We often try to avoid such confrontations through superficial pacts that elide difference and, in that process, also obstruct development. Joining a group can be a way of avoiding having to think through, for ourselves, some of the complications that might inhere in any position we take up. It is also a way of aligning ourselves with authority in a way that precludes the development of our own internal authority (see Tuckett, 1988). We may defer to authority as an assertion of value, without necessarily thinking through the ramifications of the position we have taken.

At Riggs, the principle of *examined living* puts me up against the reality of limits and the problem of other people's minds, needs and values that might be quite different than my own, helping me to more effectively live in a world where my sense of truth or justice is not always met by others of like mind. Psychoanalysis is predicated upon an appreciation for the ways in which meanings are nested and may become entrenched in idiosyncratic patterns that can be hard to get hold of. Bion (1963) extended Klein's (1935, 1946) ideas about early defenses to highlight ways in which unconscious needs and anxieties can drive behavior, using concepts such as splitting and projective identification as lenses to view pressures that drive behavior in groups. At Riggs, the lens that focuses on our patients' engagement in the interpersonal world forms an essential counterpart to the intrapersonal exploration that occurs in individual psychotherapy.

Because the patients have all become waylaid in their lives to some extent, they tend to have entrenched ideas about authority, either deferring to it or opposing it in ways that make it difficult for them to recognize and make use of their own legitimate authority in relation to their lives, wellbeing, and desires. To counter these tendencies, or at least make them more visible, we rely on ideas culled from Lacan (1977) regarding the analytic *Third*, the importance of having a third perspective through which to contextualize an understanding of the dyad (Muller, 2011); and also the *Subject caught by the desire of the Other*, the tendency to look for answers from an external authority rather than making use of and refining one's own internal sensibilities *in relation* to that external data (Charles, 2012). Experiences at group relations conferences help us to better recognize the patterns at play in our community, and concepts such as *task* and *role* help us to locate ourselves in relation to the larger whole, and to think about how to speak as a responsible member of the community from whatever role we find ourselves in at that particular juncture in relation to the task at hand (Obholzer & Roberts, 1994). That type of lens can be extremely useful when working with others who might think very differently from the way we do, encouraging more respectful and more productive engagement.

I find that the psychoanalytic lens is a powerful tool that affords potentially useful vantage points to help us more constructively face the terrible poignancy of the tremendous need in this world where we see so much that breaks our hearts. Along with my work at Riggs, which has afforded me a great deal of learning about groups and sociocultural pressures, I also continue in my roles as Co-Chair of the Association for the Psychoanalysis of Culture and Society, and member of Section IX (Social Responsibility) of Division 39 (Psychoanalysis) of the American Psychological Association, each of which has a social mission at heart. In each of these groups, we try to use the psychoanalytic lens in ways that illuminate cultural and social issues and also work towards change. I take that commitment to social change and social justice seriously, and try to bring forward what I learn through my work at Riggs into other settings, for example, in my work as a consultant to educators in New South Wales, Australia, who are working with Aboriginal preschool children living in conditions of trauma, abuse, chaos and neglect.

Gunawirra

My work with Gunawirra shows me first-hand the important role that opportunities for creative engagement can play in the lives of young traumatized children. Gunawirra attempts to provide healing by interventions focused on primary prevention and empowerment for preschool children and their families. In these efforts, psychoanalytic consultants help to support the work being done in preschools throughout New South Wales. Through such efforts at containment, we try to provide the possibility of vicarious posttraumatic growth rather than traumatization and burnout (Charles, 2015).

The Aboriginal culture has been largely decimated by the "Stolen Generations" of children sent to residential schools where they were forcefully cut off from family, language and traditions, and were also often abused. The assault was so pervasive that, for most Aboriginals, the cultural ties that bind home, family and community were left utterly broken, leaving trails of trauma and neglect behind.

Trauma leaves holes in our experience, disrupting the ability to make sense of our own life story. Identity development depends on sufficient access to parental mind and memory to be able to develop a coherent narrative. For people with roots in more than one culture, the ability to integrate disparate aspects of identity is crucial. In many countries, including my own, complicated histories of oppression and denigration have plagued succeeding generations, with abjection inflicting shame that conditions identity development. Individuals on each side of these divides carry their own particular burdens, implicated in what has occurred but often unable to see a means towards repair. Stewart (2014) shows ways in which the stains of abjection occlude and obstruct identity development in us all, erupting in the crises of violence that have broken through the denial characterizing the pre-Obama years in the U.S.

Similarly, for all Australians, there is a legacy of cultural burdens compounded by denial, disruption, and silence. The relatively recent recognition by the Australian government of the harm done to Aboriginal people provides a bridge whereby healing might occur if we can meet the challenges posed by the traumatic conditions of high poverty, substance use and domestic violence ongoing in Aboriginal communities, fed by the *sequelae* of the intergenerational transmission of unresolved mourning.

In spite of the increasing recognition and respect for the Aboriginal culture in Australia, the identity development of Aboriginal children is impeded by the complex history that has disrupted the cultural legacies from their ancestors. The history of rejection, denigration, and persecution has disrupted the transmission of life stories for the Aboriginal people, obstructing the passing along of cultural traditions that aided survival and quality of life in previous generations. That disruption makes it difficult for parents to pass along to their children a cultural legacy that would help them to develop a healthy, resilient sense of self, made further problematic by the internalization of shame (Charles, 2014b, c). That direct transmission is important and is currently obstructed by the prevalence of internalized shame. Through "embodied simulation," we take in information directly from experiences of being with our elders about how the world works, which also tells us how to see *ourselves* in the larger cultural narrative. Recognition of these less conscious forces helps us to provide opportunities for children to explore and work through such entanglements. Children are resilient, and play is the work of the child. In our interventions, we found that even very traumatized preschool children were able, through creative expression, to identify aspects of their native culture in ways that invite pride and strength.

Our recognition of ways in which shame may be impeding positive identity development can help us to find ways to assist the child in building another story alongside his/her current picture of reality, one that marks respect and value for the rich cultural traditions that are also part of the Aboriginal heritage. Children in devalued positions in the culture tend to feel that they are not the person who can be valued. Abjection must be actively countered by the adults who can contextualize and soften the harshness of those forces. As Winnicott taught us, the child must be able to look into the mirror of the human face and find himself reflected there with respect, interest, dignity, and with love.

Atkinson (2002) talks about the trauma trails that have broken into the song lines of a culture rich in a deep appreciation for the basic experience of being in and cherishing the world. That is the place we would like to invite the child into: that still place inside, where we can be in touch with our basic sense of what feels good and what feels bad, and learn to move accordingly. Adults need to be able to hear some of what has become silenced, and to recognize that disruptive behavior may be an attempt to break into the surface conversation that has left the child's needs and feelings hidden.

Psychoanalysis is fundamentally a theory of development, a way of trying to understand what goes wrong (and right!) for the person. Freud developed a method of listening very carefully, to try to make sense of what was said and what was left unsaid, or perhaps spoken in ways beyond words. Increasingly, child researchers show us that, with children, it is the "beyond words" that is often most important in making sense of what children may be trying to tell us. Much as a dream or a story can allow us to tell difficult truths indirectly, symptoms can allow us to tell truths that can't be spoken, either because we do not have the words or because those words are not recognized or valued by the family or community.

In my work with the teachers, I have tried to adapt what I have learned from the psychoanalytic and developmental literatures in ways that might be useful in their work, highlighting how children often show us, through their symptoms or their play, something about the truths that cannot yet be named. Being willing to let children show and then tell us their story at their own pace, in their own way, helps them to *discover* that story and, in the process, learn to make use of, and believe in, their own capacities. In this way, we support the development of reflective function, helping to build the foundation for a stronger self, a self that will be more resilient in the face of life's challenges.

Showing teachers how identification processes happen directly helps them to recognize that in listening attentively and respectfully to the children, they are teaching them to be respectful not only to others but also to themselves. The *process* of learning is much more important than the actual content. Through our actions, children can learn that their thoughts, experiences, and feelings *matter*, and they can also encounter respect for the power and richness of their own heritage and cultural traditions, to help detoxify the internalized shame that has been passed along the generations.

As consultant, my job is to recognize the value of the work so that the therapists and teachers can sustain their engagement with children suffering from ongoing abuse and neglect. I highlight the importance of providing engagement at the level of play, trying to accept the child's language and limits without forcing meanings into words beyond the child's capacity. I help the adults to recognize ways in which expressive arts can help the child to find ways of speaking about their troubles that can be seen and heard, thereby building a stronger, more coherent and pride-filled sense of identity. This is the type of play we want to encourage, play that helps the child to recognize her own internal experience in context and build a story that makes sense. To help this process, the teacher must accept the story *as it is being told*, to become a reflective mirror in which the child can respectfully find him/herself.

As we work with children who are too traumatized or inhibited to play freely, we hope that *our interest* may invite greater *playfulness* in the child. In the art therapy project, we found that even the most traumatized children were able to make use of our play space in ways that helped to put their development back on track. Art and other opportunities for creative expression can be a fundamental first step that provides the conditions through which other learning may then proceed.

I am working with Jill Bellinson on an edited volume that compiles some of this information specifically for early child educators, adapting information from the developmental, attachment, and play therapy literatures to be relevant to the teacher in the classroom (Charles & Bellinson, forthcoming). Such information helps to ground teachers working under such difficult conditions, thereby potentially strengthening their relations with the children and with one another. Research affirms the importance of a secure relationship through which the child can learn to play his/her way through developmental challenges, to try the world on for size, and to figure out how the pieces fit together and how relationships work, rightfully at the center of the drama, building an idea of *the way things work* in his world. Our willingness to be curious, playful, and to make false starts tells the child that it is all right to try and fail, that mistakes are a part of learning. That openness helps children to make their own meanings and find answers within themslves, so that they can learn to make use of their own internal signs and signals; to recognize patterns; to locate desires; and to make choices.

Conclusion

In working with individuals struggling so valiantly against over-whelming odds, the most salient aspect for me has been to support their work by helping them to see that it is, indeed, important. *Learning to use our minds without losing touch with our hearts* is an important part of this process. We psychoanalysts find ourselves often working at—or even outside—a crazy edge of experience. We hope to encourage the possibility of growth, reflectivity, and creativity by providing spaces in which such development can take place. In this work, recognizing the limits of what we can and cannot do helps those we work with to accept their limits as well and, through such acceptance, perhaps begin to derive pleasure from their own development and productions. No matter how limited or nascent, there is satisfaction in growth, if one can be sufficiently present to play with it, and one can only be playful if there is sufficient safety in one's surroundings. In our various roles, it matters to engage at the utmost human level, to hold the struggling human beings with respect, so that hope is embedded in our care, as people learn to work their problems through as best they can and experience a sense of mastery, pride, and connection in that process.

I have been working for some years with a woman struggling with psychosis. She goes places I cannot follow, sees things I cannot see. Her perceptions have a great deal of acuity, although there are times when I may read the signs differently. We have learned to lumber along together unevenly, as she moves past the place where I am able to be actively helpful to her. I often feel utterly inept in her presence, and yet my respect for her efforts keeps her coming back in spite of the very real limits of what I can offer. How we humbly offer what we can, even in the face of its utter insufficiency, is, I think, the hope of a society in which our patients, students—and our children—may surpass us as we first shelter and support, and then let them free to fly off as they can and seek shelter when needed. I think we need be very cautious in this medicalized and increasingly rigid, constricting and dichotomizing world, in which we might cut off precisely the nascent creativity that might, ultimately, save us from ourselves, if we can set our fear to the side and try to stand on the side of hope and possibility, and listen to the voices that are hardest for us to hear.

References

Abraham, N. (1975). Notes on the phantom: A complement to Freud's metapsychology. In N. Abraham & M. Torok, *The Shell and the Kernel* (N. T. Rand, ed. & trans.; pp. 171–176). Chicago: University of Chicago Press, 1994.

Apprey, M. (1993). The African-American experience: Forced migration and the transgenerational trauma. *Mind and Human Interaction,* 4:70–75.

Atkinson, J. (2002). *Trauma Trails: Recreating Song Lines: The Transgenerational Effects of Trauma in Indigenous Australia.* North Melbourne: Spinifex Press.

Beebe, B., & Lachmann, F. (1994). Representation and internalization in infancy: Three principles of salience. *Psychoanalytic Psychology,* 11:127–165.

Bion, W.R. (1963). *Experiences in Groups and Other Papers.* London & New York: Routledge.

——— (1967b). Notes on memory and desire. *Psychoanalytic Forum,* 2:271–280.

Charles, M. (2011). System pressures, ethics, and autonomy. In: E. Plakun (Ed.), *Treatment Resistance and Patient Authority: The Austen Riggs Reader,* pp. 174–197. New York: Norton.

——— (2012). *Working with Trauma: Lessons from Bion and Lacan.* New York: Jason Aronson.

——— (2014a). Trauma, Fragmentation, Memory and Identity. In M. O'Loughlin & M. Charles (Eds.), *Fragments of Trauma and the Social Production of Suffering.* Lanham, MD: Rowman & Littlefield, pp. 25–44.

——— (2014b). Trauma, Childhood, and Emotional Resilience. In N. Tracey (Ed.). *Transgenerational Trauma and the Aboriginal Preschool Child: Healing through Intervention.* Lanham, MD: Rowman & Littlefield, pp. 109–131.

——— (2014c). The Intergenerational Transmission of Trauma: Effects on Identity Development. In N. Tracey (Ed.). *Transgenerational Trauma and the Aboriginal Preschool Child: Healing through Intervention.* Lanham, MD: Rowman & Littlefield, pp. 133–152.

——— (2015). Caring for the caregivers: Consulting with therapists in the trenches. Special Issue: M. Akhtar, Guest Editor, *Psychoanalytic Inquiry.* 35:682–695.

Charles, M., & Bellinson, J. (forthcoming). *Building Lives: Incorporating Developmental Theory into Early Childhood Education.* London & New York: Routledge.

Charles, M., & O'Loughlin, M. (2013). The complex subject of psychosis. Special Issue: Psychosis, M. Charles, Guest Editor. *Psychoanalysis, Culture, and Society,* 17(4):410–421.

Civitarese, G. (2005). Fire at the theatre: (Un)reality of/in the transference and interpretation. *The International Journal of Psychoanalysis,* 86:1299–1316.

Ferro, A. (2009). Transformations in dreaming and characters in the psychoanalytic field. *The International Journal of Psychoanalysis*, 90:209–230.

Klein, M. (1935). A contribution to the psychogenesis of manic-depressive states. *In Love, Guilt, Reparation and Other Works, 1921–1945* (pp. 262–289). London: Hogarth Press, 1975.

———— (1946). Notes on some schizoid mechanisms. *In Envy and Gratitude and Other Works, 1946–1963* (pp. 1–24). London: Hogarth Press, 1975.

Lacan, J. (1977). *Écrits: A Selection*, A. Sheridan (Trans.). New York: W. W. Norton.

———— (1978). *The Four Fundamental Concepts of Psycho-Analysis*, A. Sheridan (Trans.), pp. 174–186. New York: W. W. Norton.

LaCapra, D. (1999). Trauma, absence, loss. *Crit. Inq.*, 25:696–727.

Liotti, G. (1999). Disorganization of attachment as a model for understanding dissociative psychopathology. In: J. Solomon & C. George (Eds.), *Attachment Disorganization.* New York & London: Guilford Press.

Main, M. & Hesse, E. (1990). Parent's unresolved traumatic experiences are related to infant disorganized/disoriented attachment status: Is frightened and/or frightening parental behavior the linking mechanism? In: M. Greenberg, D. Cicchetti, & E. M. Cummings (Eds.), *Attachment in the Preschool Years: Theory, Research, and Intervention* (pp. 161–182). Chicago: University of Chicago Press.

Muller, J. (2011). Why the pair needs the Third. In: E. Plakun (Ed.), *Treatment Resistance and Patient Authority: The Austen Riggs Reader*, pp. 97–120. New York: Norton.

Obholzer, A., & Roberts, V.Z. (1994). *The Unconscious at Work: Individual and Organizational Stress in Human Services.* London: Routledge.

Segal, H. (1957). Notes on symbol formation. *International Journal of Psycho-Analysis*, 38:391–397.

Stewart, A.R. (2014). Witnessing horror: Psychoanalysis and the abject stain of lynching photography. *Psychoanalysis, Culture & Society*, 19:413–434.

Tuckett, D. (1998). Evaluating psychoanalytic papers: Towards the development of a common standard. *International Journal of Psycho-Analysis*, 79:431–448.

Volkan, V.D. (2001). Transgenerational transmissions and chosen traumas: An aspect of large-group identity. *Group Analysis*, 34:79–97.

Winnicott, D.W. (1971), *Playing and Reality.* New York: Basic Books.

Moral Injury and Healing: Contemporary and Ancient Lessons

Nancy Sherman

Georgetown University

Author Note:

Nancy Sherman, Ph.D., is a distinguished University Professor and Professor of Philosophy at Georgetown University, with affiliate appointments at the Center on National Security and the Law at Georgetown University Law Center and Georgetown's Kennedy Institute of Ethics. She is also a Guggenheim Foundation Fellow.

Nancy Sherman

Abstract

In this chapter, I examine moral injury in the context of military service. Moral injury occurs when a person suffers severe moral conflict, trauma, or anguish due to real or apparent moral transgressions or falling short of personal, professional, and moral ideals. I consider moral injury through the double lens of contemporary soldiers and lessons from ancient Greek warriors, with an eye to moral healing or repair through compassionate self-empathy. I begin with clarification about my conception of moral injury and repair. I then turn to two contemporary cases that deal with shame, guilt, and compassionate self-empathy. The first concerns the shame that results from failure to compassionately help noncombatants caught in war even in cases where this failure is non-culpable and unavoidable. The second addresses the guilt that follows the death of fellow soldiers, often coupled with and complicated by the burden of unreasonable self-expectations. I introduce Sophocles' Ajax to shed important light on the cases.

Moral Injury and Healing: Contemporary and Ancient Lessons

The notion of moral injury resonates with many service members and veterans. For some, the term feels safe, non-stigmatizing and non-clinical, inviting reflection about the moral burdens carried in war and the awful moral conflicts that can come with donning the uniform. More specifically, the term points to the moral dimensions of psychological anguish too often eclipsed in more traditional and narrower diagnoses of posttraumatic stress as a fear-conditioned response to life threat. My own work in a series of books has been to reflect on this resonance through in-depth interviews with service members, whether in thinking about issues of the appeal of ancient Stoicism for warriors (Sherman, 2005), or responses to moral luck in the fog of war (Sherman, 2010), or what philosophers call "reactive attitudes," that is, emotions constituting how individuals hold themselves and others to account (Sherman, 2015).

In this chapter, I want to revisit the notion of military-related moral injury, with an eye to moral healing or repair through compassionate self-empathy. Specifically, I want to consider moral trauma through the double lens of contemporary soldiers and lessons from ancient Greek warriors, the latter as portrayed by an ancient Greek general, who more famously was a tragedian—namely, Sophocles. The plan is this: I begin with clarification about my conception of moral injury and repair. I then turn to two contemporary cases that deal with shame and guilt, and compassionate self-empathy. I introduce Sophocles' *Ajax* to shed important light on the cases.

Moral Injury

First, we need to clarify terms. I use the term *moral injury* to identify an experience in which a person suffers severe moral conflict, trauma, or anguish to do with real or apparent moral transgressions and/or falling short of personal, professional, and moral ideals. I focus here on moral injury in the context of military service (though, moral injury needn't be restricted to military contexts), whether in a war zone or not. The injuring or damaging can be "by self" from the point of view of agent, "to self" from the point of view of victim, or "to another" from the point of view of a close-up bystander of what is done by or to others. It is important to note that the occasions for such moral injury need not be physical acts involving killing, maiming, collateral harm, torturing, or atrocities and grotesqueries associated with war. That view of moral injury in military service as arising only from deadly or highly assaultive and physically visceral experiences is simply too limiting. The contexts are far more wide-ranging, and include interpersonal transactions (physical *and* verbal) to do with real or perceived deep betrayals, profound breaches of good will, and violations of dignitary respect (as in acts of exploitation, discrimination, scapegoating, and so on). That said, my emphasis is not on a list of representative external conditions that are necessary or sufficient causes for moral injury. Rather, my interest is in the nature of the anguish itself, as a reactive attitude or emotion, albeit triggered by and directed at a wide range of external and intrapsychic circumstances.

In talking about reactive attitudes, I draw on the seminal 1962 essay of P. F. Strawson, "Freedom and Resentment" (1962) and the fertile philosophical literature that essay spawned.[36] Following in that tradition, I argue that moral injury is felt and often publicly expressed by a host of negative reactive attitudes that constitute a sense of holding self and others morally to account in terms of certain implicit or explicit norms and ideals. Those emotions include: *guilt, shame, resentment, moral disappointment, moral indignation,* and a *sense of moral betrayal.* Additional, more globalized negative feelings expressive of moral injury might be *moral despair, moral anxiety,* or *moral disillusionment,* though these emotions do not record that same sense of moral reproach or blame that the first set do. Moral healing is a process of *moral recovery* or *moral repair* that involves, again, in a constitutive way, positive emotions of holding persons to account. These positive reactive attitudes include such emotions as trust, hope in persons, forgiveness, and a sense of compassionate empathy that positions one to move beyond the raw sense of hurt and blame.[37]

It is clear that I am thinking about moral injury and repair as a philosopher and not as a clinician.[38] Though I have psychoanalytic research training, I do not see patients and do not view my work as clinical. Moreover, as I have suggested, clinical diagnoses can be unduly restrictive, especially those to do with the DSM *(Diagnostic and Statistics Manual)* designed by the American Psychiatric Association as a diagnostic guide for insurance-filing purposes. The original PTSD diagnosis *(DSM III, 1980)*, while a remarkable breakthrough

---

36. To name a few: (Macnamara, 2011, 2012, 2013a, 2013b, 2015; Watson, 2004).

37. I discuss this fuller range of healing emotions in more detail in *Afterwar* (Sherman, 2015).

38. For a good clinical study of military moral injury, in the context of therapy protocols for military trauma, see (Litz, 2016).

in the diagnosis and treatment of neurasthenia and war (as well as rape-related) psychological trauma, nonetheless bears the marks of its behaviorist era in its view of trauma as primarily a fear-conditioned response to life threat, characterized primarily by symptoms of re-experiencing, avoidance, and arousal/hypervigilance. Recovery typically involves a desensitization of the fear response, often through a combination of exposure techniques and cognitive behavioral therapy.[39] While I do not dispute the prevalence of PTSD in military-related trauma or the effectiveness of various forms of exposure or cognitive behavioral therapy, I do question viewing the fear response as the ubiquitous traumatic response to war, whether one is agent, victim, or bystander.[40] War, by any sane reckoning, is filled with moral ambiguity and epistemic indefiniteness, with causes that are often only dubiously just but not manifestly unjust, and moral fog that rolls in all too thick, especially in today's population-centric wars where enemy uniforms are largely absent and combatants and noncombatants shift in and out of role in a 24-hour period. An uptick in challenges in discerning the particulars can mean a diminution in agency and give an open hand to tragic moral luck. All of this is a contributor to the moral and psychological stress that modern warfare wreaks on the psyche. But add to this the moral injuries that can come from interpersonal violations—betrayals from command or buddies, from moral exploitations of various kinds, sexual assault, predation, and harassment that aren't specific to the military or war, but are often exacerbated by the tension of deployments at home or abroad and the hierarchy of male command in a deeply misogynistic military.[41] The seeds for moral injury in military service abound.

The term *moral injury* is in fashion now, but it has a well-worn history in British writing. Bishop Joseph Butler, lecturing in Rolls Chapel, London, in the 1720s, devoted his eighth of fifteen sermons to "Resentment and Forgiveness of Injuries," where by "injury," "as distinct from pain or loss" or mere "hurt" or "mere harm" or "suffering," he means to call his listeners' attention to "moral wrong" or "in-

---

39. For discussion, see (Litz, 2016).

40. *DSM-5* adds important new criteria to the symptom list that include persistent and exaggerated negative beliefs, or negative mood states. But shame and guilt experiences are combined in a single criterion, and the notion that each is a distinct kind of reactive attitude to holding persons accountable is eclipsed by the idea of a persistent mood state (American Psychiatric Association, 2013).

41. For further discussion of gender-related moral injury, see chapters 5, 6, and 7 of *Afterwar* (Sherman, 2015).

justice" or "cruelty" incurred by the "injurious person," and rightly met with resentment and indignation (Butler, 1792). For a Christian, taught to turn a cheek and love the enemy, Butler's good news was that the boiling of the passions here was not itself a manifestation of the "dreadful vices of malice and revenge," but a "generous movement of mind" necessary for moral protest in the image of a divine God and humanity. David Hume and Adam Smith, in more general ways, anticipate the idea of moral injury and reactive attitudes, such as resentment, in their theory of moral sense. For they argue that it is constitutive of our human nature to have attitudes produced by our moral assessments of conduct and behavior, *i.e.*, holding persons to account, through praise or blame, for compliance to or aspiration toward specific norms.[42]

Consider the following case to help understand the contours of moral injury.

The Wounds of Shame and the Healing of Self-Empathy[43]

Army Major Jeffrey Hall deployed to Iraq twice, commanding infantry and artillery units (at the time, at the rank of captain) near Baghdad and Fallujah.[44] He signed up for the Army at 17, and at 40, despite having implemented versions of COIN (counterinsurgency operations) in those last deployments—serving as mayor of a local advisory council of elders, painting schools and laying sewers, outfitting scores of children with shoes (who never having worn them before had no clue that shoes, or their feet, had a right and a left), and risking life to bring food and medical care to families in need—he still thinks what he should do in armed conflict, and what he is good at and trained to do as a soldier, is engage and destroy an enemy.

And yet that was not what his war in Iraq was about. Once Baghdad fell in 2003, he found himself deep in softer and more cultural methods of warfare, often inadequately supported, and unclear of the cause or mission. He often felt betrayed by his command, and as a result, he, in turn, was forced to betray those who counted on him.

---

42. For further discussion, (Bennett, 2008, pp. p. 67, 68).

43. For the following discussion through to the end of this chapter, I draw on extracts (c.5000w) from pp.78–97 & 101–103 from Ch.4, "Recovering Lost Goodness," from *Afterwar: Healing the Moral Wounds of Our Soldiers* by Sherman, Nancy (2015) by permission of Oxford University Press, USA.

44. I first interviewed Jeff Hall in September 2010 and several times later that year and thereafter. I am also grateful to his wife, Sheri, for conversations about moral injury.

Stateside, he was diagnosed with severe, near suicidal posttraumatic stress disorder (PTSD) and with the support of his wife and his commander at home, sought treatment at Walter Reed Army Medical Center. As he puts it, "You have to understand. My PTSD had everything to do with moral injury. It was not from killing, or seeing bodies severed, or blown up. It was from betrayal, from moral betrayal."

One incident stands out. In his first deployment in 2003, a civilian family driving home from church in Baghdad's Mansour district crossed a cordon and got caught in the crossfire of a U.S. attack on a high-value target. Hall's unit didn't carry out the attack, but he was near the scene at the time. The mother and son were evacuated from the car, though they died shortly thereafter. The father was instantly killed, his body parts strewn over the road. Hall and a buddy gathered up the fragments and rolled them up in a rug that they then loaded onto an ambulance. "It was collateral damage that happens and that is probably justified in war," Hall says philosophically. "The car just turned a corner at the wrong place at the wrong time." But in his mind what followed was not at all justified or unavoidable, and it is that aftermath that unravels him.

Shortly after the accident, Hall got orders from his battalion headquarters to find the surviving family members and begin to make amends. He found the home and a young daughter and elderly uncle, who had stepped in as guardian. Over *chai* the family made it clear that what they wanted most was the return of the bodies for a prompt burial. Hall set to work, but his efforts were stymied at every turn. His battalion was partnered with the Coalition Provisional Agency (CPA), Paul Bremer's American occupation administration set up to govern Iraq after the fall of Baghdad, and incompetence, by many accounts, ran deep.[45] Hoping to cut through the bureaucracy, Hall drove to the morgue himself and located the bodies. But the CPA wouldn't release them without official paperwork authorized and signed by the Iraqi Ministry of Health. So began the wait of over a month for the bodies.

In the meantime, Hall's commander called to inform him that the CPA had issued solace money for the family. With cautious excitement, Hall drove to battalion headquarters to pick up the money; finally, he'd have something positive to show the uncle and daughter. He was speechless when he opened the envelope and counted the bills. It was a piddling $750. He let his commander know how he felt:

---

45. For an excellent account, see (Chandrasekaran, 2006).

"Sir, they lost a father, a mother, and a son. And a car that is probably as important to them as the other losses." He handed the money back to the commander in disgust: "You go pay them with this!" The commander, cocooned for much of the war inside Sadam's former palace in the Green Zone, was unmoved. Hall had an unequivocal order to deliver the money.

And so, he did. In silence, he handed the uncle the envelope and watched as he counted the bills, and then flung them to the ground. "I deserve whatever this man does," Hall recalls thinking. "If he slaps me in my face, I will take it. I will just take it." But the uncle just stood up, turned his back to Hall, and walked out of the room, the money still strewn on the floor. With the young girl's eyes glued on him, Hall put on his helmet, snapped his chinstrap, and left the house, covered in shame.

But the ordeal, and the shame, wouldn't end. The bodies were finally returned to the family, unembalmed and rotted beyond recognition by the scorching desert heat. The family had one last request of Hall. They needed death certificates to finalize the burial. And so Hall returned to the Ministry of Health and was given the certificates. On each was stamped in bold red letters: "ENEMY." "Can't you give me something that doesn't have "enemy" stamped on it?" Hall beseeched. "No," the official curtly replied. "They are enemies. They are considered enemies."

The incompetence of Hall's superiors verges on the comedic, but the profound moral injury that Hall suffered verges on the tragic.[46] Disarmed of much of his usual arsenal as a warrior, he needed more than ever to be able to trust his own basic goodness and have some assurance that he could compassionately help these noncombatants caught in war. However much it is a part of the just conduct of a soldier to minimize collateral damage in war and ameliorate its effects, for Hall, the duty was more basic; it was an intimate duty to a family he had come to know and care for. He felt thoroughly impotent in the role. He felt profoundly betrayed by his command and coalition and humiliated that their massive incompetence forced him to betray innocents who had suffered so grievously. When he says the injury was worse and more lasting than what he suffered from seeing the detritus of war for three years, what he means, in part, is

---

46. There may be comedic elements in the incredible incompetence that characterized much work off the Coalition Provisional Agency: "You couldn't invent more comedic war narratives," Rajiv Chandrasekaran (2006) said in a seminar at the Wilson Center, September 2011, reflecting on his own research and writing about that period of the war in Iraq.

that the betrayal by command put him in a position of feeling trapped and helpless, much more powerless and captive than he had ever felt in facing enemy fire. He was stripped defenseless, with nowhere to go. That shame haunted him until one day back home on base at Fort Riley, Kansas, he simply couldn't put his combat boots on. Suicidal feelings and ideas took over. It was at that point that a new, far more benign commander than his previous one got him help. Empathy and self-empathy were a critical part of the healing.

The idea of self-empathy may strike some as odd. As an epistemic notion, empathy is typically directed at another and is a vehicle for understanding how to see the world from his/her particular corner. As an affective mode, it is a way of being able to share someone else's emotion and so have congruent feeling. But what work does empathy do when directed at self? Even if we are never *fully* in sync with our own minds and emotions, for most of us, there isn't the same kind of gap within us as there is between us. The idea of empathizing with oneself, some might say, is redundant. I argue in this chapter that this is not so. Even if we are already in sync with many aspects of ourselves, there are still corners we don't peek into because their contents are too alien, so possibilities for change are thereby closed off. Self-empathy (or what I am interested in, therapeutic self-empathy) can play a role in peering into those corners and opening doors. It can be an important part of recovering a sense of lost goodness. It can be a way of calling out to oneself that one is hurt and in need of attention and response.[47]

Put this way, self-empathy can be construed as a kind of positive reactive attitude, alongside trust and certain forms of hope in persons—in ourselves and in others. These emotions, each in their own way, and whether directed at the self or others, expose vulnerability and call out to others about one's needs, dependence, aspirations, normative expectations, and so on—and they seek a response. With trust, we call upon another to tend to our interests when we cannot. With hope, we call upon another to aspire to heights that we may not expect him/her to reach without our setting the challenge. And with self-empathy, too, we call upon ourselves to re-evaluate our past actions, and to show mercy and understanding where we could not before. Sometimes we "grow" responsiveness in those we engage through our emotional calls. This is often true in the case of trust,

---

47. Here, I am influenced by the work of (Kukla & Lance, 2009) and (Macnamara, 2012) on Strawsonian models of reactive attitudes. See (P. F. Strawson, 1993).

where if we are a bit wise with regard to whom we trust for what and when, our very act of trusting may elicit and reinforce another's trustworthiness.[48] Something similar may happen in the case of therapeutic self-empathy. We uncover our hurt to ourselves, and in that acknowledgment can sometimes elicit resources for responding to and ameliorating the suffering. In the case of punishing guilt, in empathetically reviewing the very evaluations that are at the core of our self-reproach, we may find room to hold ourselves to account in a more compassionate and equitable way. Rather than focusing on the fact that we have fallen short of some standard to which we hold ourselves, as we do when we take up the perspective of the accuser, we learn to empathize with our imperfect selves: we take up the perspective of the accused, of one who genuinely attempted to meet the endorsed standard, but failed through no fault of his/her own.

We shall come to the various dimensions of self-empathy and their healing powers. But first I retell another story of shame, this one an ancient tale. And then I turn to a contemporary story of guilt that opens the door for self-empathy.

Ajax's Shame

I first met Major Hall at a reading of Sophocles' *Ajax*, performed by the Theater of War before a mostly military audience.[49] The play is another story of shame, with disastrous outcome. Ajax is stripped of his *timê*, his honor and status, when the Greek chiefs vote to award Achilles' armor—a prize given to the best fighter—to Odysseus rather than him, despite his legendary status. As Homer chronicles in the *Iliad*, Ajax was "the bulwark of the Achaeans" in their fight against Troy, "giant" in size, "powerful and well-built," "the giant god of battle," unrivaled as a fighter (Homer, 1990, III, lines 270–290, VII, lines 242–332).[50] In a famed duel with Hector, he is easily the victor. His own warrior mettle is storied, god-like, but so too is his father's. He is the son of Telamon, who battled the Trojans alongside Heracles and who for his mettle was awarded the Trojan king's daughter, Hesione, as a war bride.

---

48. See (Jones, 2012).

49. For more on the Theater of War, and the larger umbrella theater group under the direction of Bryan Doerries, see: (*Outside the Wire*, 2011); see also (Healy, 2009).

50. For a wonderful account of lessons to be learned from a retelling of the Ajax story, see (Woodruff, 2011).

In the play, Ajax's shock and shame of losing a prize comparable to his father's becomes part of a more generalized, psychological
break. He has lost all face before those who matter: "I will return
from Troy having earned nothing. How could he [my father, Telam-
on] stand to even look at me?" (Sophocles, 2007, lines 464–5) In a
pique of blazing rage, he sets out to take revenge on Odysseus and his
troops, and to prove once and for all his unmatched skill as a swords-
man. But the goddess Athena blinds him and he flails his sword in
the dark, mistaking barnyard animals for his rival: He "hacked at
this chief and that chief," recounts Athena. And after tiring of the
slaughter, he took the rest of the beasts captive and tortured them.
Ajax "comes to" in a bloodbath of butchered carcasses and mutilated
livestock. He mocks the sight of himself: "Look at the valiant man!
The brave heart! The one who unflinchingly faced the enemy! You
see the great deeds I have done to harmless beasts? Oh, the ridicule
runs riot against me!" (Sophocles, 2007, lines 364–7).

There is ironic distance,[51] but it fails to insulate. Ajax's self-eval-
uation couldn't be more unforgiving. He seems to look on at himself
as someone in the past. But his past is not *past*. It consumes him in
the present. In an unparalleled moment in Greek tragedy, this great
Greek general falls on his sword on stage. In this particular staging of
the play, before a community that has come to know suicide all too
intimately, the scene brought a hush like few moments I have known
in theater. Ajax was in the room, in Major Hall and in many others,
who felt they had lost their identity as warriors, and then their good
name.

Here, the work of psychoanalyst Melvin Lansky is pertinent and
well worth mentioning. Lansky, who has worked extensively with
Vietnam War veterans, writes insightfully of stages that lead up to
a violent, impulsive act, such as suicide, and the role of shame as a
precipitant.[52] Though Lansky's discussion is not focused on Sophocles' *Ajax*, the stages he describes have interesting correlates in the
play and underscore the power of the play for understanding suicidal
impulses and the role of shame as a causal factor:

1. In the first stage, turbulence and shame erupt from a
   "narcissistic wound" that exposes one's own "limitations."
   In our play, Ajax is passed over for the all-critical prize, to

---

51. On narrative and ironic distance, see (Goldie, 2007; 2011, p. 87).

52. See (Lansky, 1995, p. 1086).

which he believes he is entitled. This injury to his ego throws him into a narcissistic rage.

2. Next, there is a "dissociative" break that may follow the upsurge of shame. As Lansky puts it, "In more protracted cases, the patient often reports a disorganized, fragile, paranoid state of mind." Similarly, for Ajax there is madness induced by a god: "Never in your right mind/Would you, Telamon's son,/ Go so far as to slaughter livestock./The gods must have driven him mad!" sing the Chorus (lines 182–5). "I can darken the sharpest eyes," Athena boasts to Odysseus (line 85).

3. The dissociative break is followed by an impulsive act, with the impulsive actor "oblivious" to its consequences. Ajax finds himself in a delusional state: "He thought he was bathing his hands in your blood," Athena tells Odysseus (line 43). Mad with rage, Ajax is unaware of his environment and the objects he acts upon.

4. The agent's consequent "reaction to the act," often "conscious remorse or guilt," can mask the shame of dissociating and of the impulsive act. Surveying the massacre he has executed, Ajax bemoans: "You see the great deeds I have done to harmless animals" (line 366). So, Ajax's wife, Tecmessa, reports: "He has been laid low by this evil. He won't eat or drink or say anything. He just sits in the midst of his butchery" (line 320–25).

5. Finally, there is a tenuous and manipulated reaching out to loved ones in response to the intimidation of self-harming. So Ajax demands that Tecmessa bring to him their son for a final encounter: "Lift him up to me here. The sight of fresh blood will not frighten him—Not if he is truly his father's son. Now he must begin to be broken in and hardened to the ways of his father." (lines 545–550). In Ajax's case, shame piles on shame—the barnyard massacre piles on top of the loss of the coveted and anticipated prize—leading to the final, irrevocable act.

The experience of shame—as Ajax's and Hall's stories, ancient and contemporary, show—is about being seen and about having nowhere to hide.[53] Greek etymology is a reminder. *Aidôs* is related to *aidoia*, genitals. To be ashamed is to be caught without your figleaf.[54] The audience can be real or imagined. When Aristotle says, "eyes are upon you," he should not be read literally (Aristotle, 1984, *Nicomachean Ethics*, II.6 1384a35–1384b1). That is how shame *feels*.

"I Was Never Going to Be the One-Stop Intel Analyst for the Whole Army"

Consider another case, this one to do more with guilt than shame, and involving a student of mine. I turn to this case, for the guilt led, in critical ways, to healing through self-empathy. Tom Fiebrandt served in Iraq between July 2001 and December 2005.[55] At twenty-one he was a young sergeant and a team leader of a group of intelligence analysts attached to an Army cavalry squadron of 410 men in Tal Afar, a desert town not far from Mosul, about 40 miles from the Syrian border. As cavalry, his unit served as the "eyes and ears" of the battalion, collecting and sorting intelligence critical for a dynamic picture of the current battlefield. The unit was a "bridge" between those inside and outside the wire, with Fiebrandt himself spending much of his time outside, talking to troops and locals, and drawing and re-drawing a visual, first-hand picture of the vicinity and its dangers. He knew how tall buildings were on different streets, where snipers could lurk, where you did and didn't want to be. He became the point guy to whom noncommissioned officers and officers alike turned to get their information. As he put it, with modesty but candor, his superiors "had confidence in his competence."

About three months before his deployment was up, he was ordered to take a few days of "R and R" (rest and relaxation) in Qatar before returning to the States for a longer two-week leave. Fiebrandt was reluctant to abandon the unit so close to the end of their deployment, but an order was an order and leave-time was mandatory anyway. He was stressed of late, "bouncing inside and outside the wire," as he put it, and at some level, he knew that a break was probably a

---

53. For a penetrating study of the ancients on shame, see (Williams, 1993).

54. Susan Brison has raised the question with me as to whether shame must have this sense of being exposed, in addition to the sense, I discuss later, of falling short of an ideal. She suggests that these may be two very different features of shame, and the latter is a more central part of the concept.

55. I interviewed Tom Fiebrandt in Fall 2010. I came to know him through a class I taught at Georgetown that fall on the ethics of war.

good idea.

En route to Qatar, he learned that his unit was about to run a cordon and search operation in the southeast corner of the town Tal Afar, which had become a major smuggling hub, with weapons pouring in from unsecured borders with Syria. It was now time to flush out the weapon caches and insurgents with a strong show of troop forces and a door-to-door raid. What Fiebrandt didn't know was that as part of the preparation, one of the platoons, headed by Lt. William Edens, a close friend, had been ordered to scout out a potential egress route at the backside of the city where a wall of troops could be mounted to block insurgents fleeing the raid into the desert. It was during this preparatory drive-through that an Improvised Explosive Device (IED) struck Edens' vehicle, killing him and two others. Fiebrandt learned about the incident a few days after he arrived in Qatar. It hit him hard: "What bothered me was that it was in an area that I knew very well. It was in a part of the city that you really had to see in order to visualize. And I had this lurking suspicion that my soldiers, who had never actually, personally been there, didn't really have a grasp on all the information that I felt I did. In some way, I almost felt responsible for not being there to provide them with the information that may have potentially resulted in a different outcome. So, it is rough. It is a difficult thing for me to process.... So here I was sitting by a pool, and I hear this. It was—I don't even know how to describe it. It was—devastating."

Had Fiebrandt been there, he is sure he would have recommended against Edens' taking that road. He knew that back area of the city was especially dangerous and that no unit vehicles had traveled down that road for good reason. He would have urged more reconnaissance on the routes and potential alternatives. "Whether or not I would have been successful in getting that to become the battle plan, I don't know." But given that he was relied on for this kind of information, he had a good chance of making the case. In his mind, he let down his command as well as his friend. What happened, as he puts it, "reflected poorly" on him. He "faults" himself for not being there, and though he is "frustrated" that his unit members "didn't have the same clout" as he did and couldn't "pick up the slack" in his absence, he doesn't fault them for failing to make the call.

Significantly, it is just this sense of feeling that he is the only guy that can do the job and that it is a job that requires constant vigilance, without gaps and breaks, that both hounds him and ultimately opens the way for self-exculpation. The fact that he didn't *choose* to take the leave—that he was acting on an order—only gets him so far. The real exculpation comes some three to four months after the incident, when his deployment is over and he reflects on the incident in connection with whether he should re-enlist and return to Iraq after what would amount to a longer period away. He now sees, somehow, that the demand he put on himself to be quasi-omniscient, to keep constant vigil on the changing battlefield, as he puts it several times, without "gaps in his knowledge," is unsustainable. He reconstructs the thinking: "Well, God, I thought to myself, if I am not here in a two-week period of time and things go to hell in a hand basket... what is the situation going to be like when I get back, having been away longer? I am going to be less equipped to handle any further situations, because now I have a real gap in my knowledge. So, all of this was coalescing at the same time, and it took me a while to sort of realize that I couldn't be the person that was there all the time. I could only be in one spot at a time. I could re-enlist and I could stay in the job. But ultimately, I am never going to cover the whole country. I was never going to be the one-stop intel analyst for the whole Army. Maybe my role was actually very small."

Looking on from the outside, we might say, "Well, of course." However well Fiebrandt served in his role and however critical he was to the safety of his unit, he wasn't there that day, wasn't at fault for not being there that day, and wasn't at fault for not briefing his unit in advance about a mission that he didn't even know was going to take place. Yet for Fiebrandt, it was an epiphany to see that holding himself responsible was grandiose. It required too idealized a sense of his role, responsibilities, and duties, and too idealized a set of expectations and injunctions about how he was supposed to function. And yet the unreasonableness of the demands he held himself to only dawned on him with time, when he realized their absurd implications—that he was expecting of himself something close to full omniscience and omnipresence, a constant vigil on the battlefield that could produce an accurate, automatically refreshed picture without gaps, breaks, and breaches. He chuckles as he thinks about the absurdity of it all and of the *reductio* that it took to get him to realize it. But, it is a tentative laugh. He still knows the pull of those expectations, and what it is like to be in their grip. He may no longer endorse the evaluations so intimately related to the feelings, but when he says, "I kind of fault myself," "I almost felt responsible for not being there," he still can put himself in the mindset of what it was like to endorse those evaluations and feel their tugs. He is now at a point where he has moved on. But he got there only through an honest moral struggle about what it means to be vigilant as an intel guy. There were limits to his knowledge and frailties that he had to accept, however they compromised his agency. Like many soldiers I have spoken to, Fiebrandt doesn't easily volunteer the word "guilt." His words are "fault" and "responsibility." But, it is clear that he is talking about self-blame.

I tell this story to illustrate the function of guilt, here, as a way of working out the boundaries of moral responsibility. There is genuine *intellectual* figuring out. The emotion of guilt is not just recalcitrant (Brady, 2009, p. 429). Fiebrandt is not sure what he believes, and he is not going to let himself off the hook until he is sure. The rub, of course, is that having "to be sure" quickly spirals into intellectualization and rationalization, an inventing of reasons. In short, it becomes primitive thinking that mixes rational processing with the illogicality of wishful/magical thinking and presumptions of omniscience. There are elements of this in Fiebrandt's thinking.[56] Without any inkling of the planned raid, Fiebrandt had no reason to inform his commanders of potential dangers before he left for R and R. Yet he repeatedly put himself back in the reporting chain as if he knew, or should have known, what would become relevant only later. Similarly, there was little reason for him to have pointed out that particular street to Edens, though projecting forward he helps himself to what is now the salience of that piece of knowledge and faults himself for failing to share it earlier. He faults himself for an epistemic stance he couldn't easily have had then.

But my point is what Fiebrandt was going through wasn't *just* that. He was also thinking, as he put it: Was he like the homeowner who never quite got around to putting a fence around the backyard pool and then one day discovers a child has wandered into the pool and drowned? Or was he more like the cop who might have had helpful information but was legitimately off-duty at the moment and nowhere near the scene of danger? In the end, he seemed to think he was more like the cop than the homeowner, but accepting that required a lengthy, psychological process of surmounting his self-reproach. It required accepting his limits and the bad luck of being up against them then. It required self-empathy.

---

56. Similarly, a therapist who works with soldiers recently told me of a patient who repeatedly went over the site of where he lost a buddy, homing in over and over on the spot on Google maps, working out how he could have prevented the death if he only took this route rather than that.

More on Self-Empathy

Much has been written on empathy in the past three decades, and so I will be brief in this prelude to self-empathy.[57] Empathy is a term of fairly recent academic coinage. It comes into usage at the turn of the 20th century with the translation by Titchner of the German word *Einfühlung*—to enter into a feeling, a term itself first used by Robert Vischer in 1873 in the context of the psychology of aesthetics and developed by Theodor Lipps in the context of how we know other minds.[58] Two prominent models of empathy have emerged in recent years, somewhat in competition in the psychological and philosophical literature. The first is empathy as vicarious arousal or contagion. The key historical figure is David Hume and his notion of sympathy, though what he means is what we would now call empathy, a mechanism that allows us to "catch" another person's affect. We know others' emotions by coming to feel qualitatively similar or congruent emotions. Hume's metaphor is intuitive: We are attached, as if by a cord, with movement at one end reverberating at the other, causing a fainter impression of the original feeling (1968/1739, pp. 316–324). The second camp, led by Adam Smith, conceives of empathy in more robust, cognitive terms (2000). Empathy (again, "sympathy" is his term) is a process that engages imagination, requiring simulation and the taking up of roles or perspectives. We come to know another's emotions by trading places "in fancy," as Smith puts it, and coming to "beat time" with their hearts (2000, 4, I.I.1). But Smith insists that the swap is not only situational, but also dispositional:[59] We not only stand in another's shoes. We try to become them in their shoes: to "enter, as it were, into his body and become in some measure the same person with him" (2000, 3, I.I.1).[60]

---

57. For my own overview of the subject with lengthy references and discussion of the literature, see especially (Sherman, 1998a, 1998b, 1998c).

58. For discussion, see (Eisenberg & Strayer, 1987), (Lipps, 1903), and (Titchener, 1909). For Freud and his interest in empathy, see (Pigman, 1995) and (Freud, 1986, p. 325).

59. For reflections on becoming another, see Bernard Williams' "Imagination and the Self," in (Williams, 1973).

60. On the notion of "becoming" the other person and the therapeutic work of empathic resonance, the writing of psychoanalytic theorist Heinz Kohut is highly instructive. See (Kohut, 1971, 1977, 1984). Note, for Smith, there is an ultimate interest in moral judgment and the fittingness of the emotion, and this requires a bringing back of that empathic connection to one's own bosom (Smith, 2000), in a way that can both facilitate moral insight but also distort empathy with a projection from our own home base.

How do these models fare with respect to *self*-empathy, and in particular, its role in surmounting overly harsh self-reproach? One obvious worry for the contagion model is that it suggests a picture of empathy as a repetition of the same stuck, often intrusive feeling, and risks retraumatization as a secondary effect of the repetition (even when the repetition is in the service of mastery and self-understanding).[61] The idea of emotional fixity or stubbornness is part of a more general worry that the philosopher Peter Goldie raises about the inbuilt biases of emotional construals (or ways of "seeing as") that predispose us to judgments (in the way perceptions do), but in some cases, predispose us to what we don't believe.[62] As he puts it, emotional subjects tend to confirm rather than disconfirm their evaluative construals: "The feeling directed toward the object of the emotion, and the related perception of the object as having the [evaluative] property, tend to be *idées fixes* to which reason has to cohere. The phenomenon is a familiar one: when we are afraid, we tend unknowingly to seek out features of the object of our fear that will justify the fear" (Goldie, 2004, p. 99).[63] So, we have an epistemic tendency to build an "epistemic landscape" that coheres with an evaluation and feeling. We lock ourselves into a specific emotional take. Self-empathy, as a contagious re-experience of emotion, may exacerbate a tendency that we already have and that itself requires intervention.

Similar worries emerge for the simulation view of empathy, for it would require that we take up again the very perspective from which we are trying to free ourselves. In the cases I detailed above, the emo-

---

61. See Freud on repetition compulsion in (Freud, 1974, p. 293). Also included in the symptoms of post-traumatic stress are intrusive recollections. For a very helpful discussion of posttraumatic stress and its treatment, see (Wilson, Friendman, & Lindy, 2001). Note, there has been a move afoot, with some momentum from the Army, to drop the "D" in PTSD (Posttraumatic Stress Disorder) because of the stigmatizing effect of the term. The argument is often made that service members returning from war with limb losses do not have "limb disorders." Why should those returning from war with psychological stress have disorders? There are other terminological shifts aimed to "normalize" the response to stress. For a history of PTSD and its inclusion in the Diagnostic and Statistics Manual III in 1980, see (Herman, 1992).

62. "Construal" is Robert Roberts' term for the cognitive content of an emotion. For how Roberts distinguishes that notion from a stricter judgment, see, for example, (R. Roberts, 2013).

63. This is similar to Brady's view with respect to recalcitrant emotion, that because emotions tend toward a "capture and consume" mode, through emotional engagement, we sometimes waste attentional resources on problems already solved. See (Brady, 2007).

tional subject's focus is framed by guilt and shame that "capture and consume attention," (to use Brady's felicitous term).[64] Self-empathy requires dwelling again in that perspective, and so re-experiencing the same emotions. In the case of traumatic emotions, it may involve retraumatization.

These objections may be limited, but they make clear that if a notion of self-empathy is to be part of a model of emotional and moral growth, something more than simulating and re-experiencing traumatic events and emotions (whether through narration or other representational forms, *e.g.,* artwork or dance) is required. Here, not surprisingly, the notion of empathy in psychotherapy is helpful. Psychotherapy of various stripes, and especially psychodynamic models, depend on a patient's revisiting and reliving painful emotions, characteristically in the context of an empathic listener who can both bear compassionate witness to the pain and, through various interventions and gentle corrections of bias, interpretations or reframings, help break the repetition and defenses. The therapist's empathy involves the "tracking" of a patient's emotion, sometimes through her own congruent reenactments or countertransferences,[65] and at other times more cognitively. But it also typically involves a conveyed sympathy – compassion, trust, rapport, and a nonjudgmental stance that help build a "working alliance" (Greenson, 1967). Empathy, in this rich context, involves access but also benevolence and trust.[66] The stance is both protective and transformative, helping the patient safely to remember, revisit, and feel painful reactions to traumatic events, as well as to reconstrue what happened in ways that may involve fairer self-judgment and less rigid notions of success and failure that ultimately help loosen self-destructive feelings.

All of this is relatively familiar stuff. Less familiar is the notion of self-empathy and what role it can play in moral healing, not as a competitor or replacement for second-person empathy and its role in formal or informal therapy, but as something additional that has an important place in its own right.

One way to think about self-empathy is as a conceptually or causally derivative notion. We look at ourselves as if from outside,

---

64. See (Brady, 2009, pp. 423, 425–426, 428–429).

65. See (Chused, 1991) and (McLaughlin, 1991).

66. And so the therapist is not just a blank screen or withholding (or "abstinent"), on the traditional Freudian view. For a discussion, see (Sherman, 1998b) and (Sherman, 1995).

from a spectatorial point of view. Adam Smith develops the stance: "Whatever judgment we can form concerning [our own conduct], accordingly, must always bear some secret reference, either to what are, or to what, upon a certain condition, would be, or to what, we imagine, ought to be the judgment of others" (Smith, 2000, p. 161, III.I.1) So an individual may come to self-empathy by internalizing a second personal instance of it, as when he/she learns a measure of self-empathy through the empathy of a therapist toward him/her. In this case, he/she may internalize another's stance. But people may also internalize their own stance toward others. So, a rape victim in a support group may come to feel self-empathy only after first feeling empathy toward others in the group who were similarly victimized. "Oh my, God, that's what happened to me," she might come to say to herself.[67] The recognition of experiences similar to her own and the ensuing empathy toward others may enable her now to look at herself through new eyes. Second-person empathy, both the receiving and giving of it, may thus prepare one for first-person empathy. One gains an outside perspective on oneself that is qualitatively different from the punishing and shaming stance that has held one hostage until now. Veteran support groups may similarly enable self-empathy through the validating experience of empathizing and being empathized with.

In thinking about self-empathy, it is useful to turn to Aristotle's remarks about self-love (or self-friendship) in *Nicomachean Ethics* IX.8. He is aware that the idea of self-love may be a bit strained, both because it requires that we stand as subject *and* object towards ourselves,[68] but, more important, because it connotes a problematic sort of selfishness. However, there is room for a good kind of self-love, he insists, that is the capacity of the self to listen to practical reason with equanimity. He associates this kind of self-love with nobility and the sacrifice characteristic of virtue and practical wisdom, and contrasts it with the baser kind of self-love that involves taking material advantage for oneself.

However, in the soldiers' stories that are my focus, there is no shortage of nobility and sacrifice. If anything, that aspiration for virtue is too hard-driving, giving way to too much self-punishment when luck runs out. Even so, Aristotle's idea of finding the right way

---

67. I thank Susan Brison for this point.

68. After all, there is only one chapter on this odd kind of friendship in a discussion that that goes on for 26 chapters (at least in the Nicomachean Ethics).

to befriend oneself is useful here. The best kind of friendship—that of character friendship, he tells us—is an arena for character critique and moral growth (IX.12 1172a),[69] which like all friendship, requires positive feelings (*philias*) toward one's object and feelings of good-will (*eunoia*).[70]

Self-empathy, as I am imagining it, involves a similar kind of self-friendship and requires a minimal measure of good will or com-passion. I am also imagining it in the service of moral growth and, in the cases I have limned of moral repair, of being called forth when one has held oneself accountable in a way that begins to seem unfair, or at least requires further reconsideration and reassessment of the nature of that accountability. And so the self-empathy I have in mind emerges as part of a moral process and is *earned* as a counterweight to overbearing self-judgment. This helps deflect various popular im-ages of self-empathy as essentially self-kindness or self-compassion, a going-gentle-on-oneself, or, relatedly, the kind of self-esteem that is a contrived boost to undo self-deprecation, or a narcissistic self-ab-sorption, in which the gaze turns too much to self and not enough to others.[71] But equally, I am not thinking of self-empathy as a minimi-zation of self, a putting of self in its place, as Cicero redacts the Ep-icurean teaching: these are "the restrictions under which all humans live," (2002, *Tusculan Disputations*, 3.77) "you are not the only one to have this happen," (2002, *Tusculan Disputations*, 3.78) "to endure these things is human" (2002, *Tusculan Disputations*, 3.34). The Epi-curean teaching, in essence, is that distress occurs when we direct our attention toward something we regard as evil and regard as a relative-ly *great* evil compared to goods measured against it. The Epicureans hold that we are masters of our own attention, and so we can prevent this kind of stress by directing our attention to pleasures of various kinds, or to the minimization of our woes by focusing on those of others.[72] This is not the kind of self-empathy I have in mind. I am en-visioning self-empathy as an emotional attitude that predisposes one to a fairer self-assessment, especially, in the cases I have focused on, where luck and accident and power ceded to others squeeze out one's

69. See also (Sherman, 1997), ch. 5.

70. See (Aristotle, 1984), Nicomachean Ethics, VIII.2 for the criteria of friendship.

71. See (Neff, 2003).

72. See Graver's useful discussion of the Epicurean position in (Cicero, 2002, p. 99).

moral efficacy or cast doubt on one's goodness.

As a kind of felt reactive attitude, self-empathy operates by drawing us in, in the way that *emotions*, not less-charged mental states, do, reining in our attention on what is morally salient and significant to our moral agency and well-being.[73] One way of thinking about Tom Fiebrandt's experience is that he entreated himself to look back at the specific evaluations in his self-condemnation and the need for reopening the case. He went back to the very scenes that caused so much pain and assessed them from a new perspective that time and distance allowed. In the to-and-fro dialogue of expressed reactive attitudes, overwrought guilt calls on the self to consider the reasonableness of showing ourselves some compassion and empathy in the same way that resentment asks those who have transgressed us to now give us reasons for reassurance or trust.[74] The call in each case has the standing to expect a reply.

As suggested, the notion of self-esteem doesn't get at this reparative idea, but neither does self-respect. The underlying notion behind self-respect is that one is not servile or subordinate to others, but rather an equal among equals. Yet someone may have no doubt about that, stand in no need of its reaffirmation, and yet still need a fairer hearing about whether "could-have-done's" entail "should-have-done's" in the case of guilt feelings, or about how fixed or severe the damage done to self is in the case of shame feelings.

This reparative or therapeutic view of self-empathy presupposes the possibility of narrative distance and what Peter Goldie has called a "narratable" conception of self: "We are able to deploy in thought and feeling a narratable conception of oneself: with a narratable past, which one now remembers, interprets, and evaluates in various ways; with a present; and with a narratable future, about which one can make plans, have hopes and aspirations, and so on. This conception of oneself is the narrative sense of self" (2011, p. 86).[75]

---

73. See (Sherman, 1997, p. 68) on the idea that emotions are ways of tracking, in defeasible ways, the morally relevant news. See also (Hurley & Macnamara, 2010).

74. See (Walker, 2006, pp. 42, 73; Williams, 1995). Just as blame "asks" a transgressor for "acknowledgment" of one's standing, so too does self-blame ask one's condemner for acknowledgment of the hurt and reconsideration of the charges. On the call-and-response nature of reactive attitudes, see (Macnamara, 2012).

75. For a sharp and lively criticism of the idea of a narrative self, see (G. Strawson, 2004).

One is "in effect seeing oneself as another" (Goldie, 2011, p. 86). And this creates an evaluative and epistemic gap essential to re-appraisal and reevaluation: "One now knows what one did not know then; […] one can now take an evaluative stance which differs from the stance that one then took" (Goldie, 2011, p. 87).

My notion of self-empathy adds to this narratable conception of self an ability to see from beyond or outside without radical dissociation or alienation from the old self and its ways of seeing *and* feeling. That is part of the force of the notions of affective and cognitive re-engagement. In this sense, self-empathy allows for self-reintegration (a kind of connectedness), rather than serial reinvention or radical conversion. Though we may have psychologically and emotionally moved on, we can still remember how we saw and felt things. We can still be affected, even if slightly, in some way. As I am imagining it, in a case like Prior's, he can still feel a bit of the bite of the old guilt. It doesn't rattle him any longer, but in narrating the story, he is nonetheless affected by the remembering, in some way as he once was. That is not all he feels with respect to the events. He now sees circumstances far more completely and his emotions reflect those changed appraisals. But it is not just that he is now *tolerating* what he used to feel or think or *accepting* and *owning* it for what it was, as therapists might put it. Rather, he also knows how it feels, as if in *muscle memory*. That is a part of his self-empathy. Similarly, in Hall's case, we can imagine him experiencing a flush of shame as he retells the story and brings to mind the faces of the father and daughter or hears the commander's intonation as he gives him the order to deliver the envelope. The shame is no longer intrusive and paralyzing, as it is in posttraumatic stress. But it is still accessible. Self-empathy, as I am using the term—in addition to a compassionate, less judging regard—involves this kind of affective, empathic access.[76]

Obviously, the degree of access will depend on how changed a person's psychological makeup has become. Access exists along a continuum. When the narrative distance is great, an individual may

---

76. See (Schechtman, 2001), whose work I came upon in revising this paper. She invokes Richard Wollheim's notion of "event memory," as discussed in *The Thread of Life* (1984), which, as she explains, "is not a cold cognitive relation to the past, but one which is thoroughly infused with affect" (248). Wollheim, when describing his World War II soldier years, recalls driving by mistake into the German lines in August 1944: Having described the event and the memory of it, he says, "and as I remember feeling those feelings, the sense of loss, the sense of terror, the sense of being on my own, the upsurge of rebellion against my fate, come over me, so that I am affected by them in some such way as I was when I felt them on that remote summer night"(Wollheim, 1984, p. 106).

be able to remember only coldly and cognitively, with little emotional valence. He/she isn't much alive to how circumstances felt then. At this extreme, a limit to self-empathy has been reached, at least for a while.

Self-empathy is not self-forgiveness

Some readers may have the nagging thought that what I have been after all along is not self-empathy, but self-forgiveness.[77] Isn't it forgiveness that can really heal the guilt-wracked soul?

Even if a notion of *self*-forgiveness is coherent in cases where one has transgressed against another, it seems an ill-fitting notion when there is no real intentional wrongdoing for which to demand forgiveness. True, as a more general idea of forswearing anger and blame,[78] it may have its place in the surmounting of self-reproach, irrespective of whether that reproach is deserved or not. But even so, self-forgiveness doesn't expose the more complex evaluative and affective mechanism I have been keen to explore, of surmounting certain emotions with compassion while preserving empathic access to them.

And why is that access important and worth preserving? I suspect it is because I don't believe that difficult conflicts and the emotions that express them are ever so completely resolved that all residue of such conflicts disappear. Self-empathy is a way of remaining attuned to those tugs and pulls as they morph into new shapes on new landscapes. It is a compassionate form of keeping self-vigil. That said, we may also need self-empathy in the cases where we have, in fact, transgressed or acted morally wrongly, and forgiveness, toward self or from others, doesn't seem quite right—perhaps because the wrongdoing was so heinous (and unforgivable).

To sum up, in thinking about self-empathy I have focused on moral injuries that may *seem* only apparent because the wrongs are only apparent. But the injuries are no less real; and the soldiers' suffering no less real. Soldiers routinely impose moral responsibility on themselves in the face of factors that make light of their own agency, whether flukish accident, the tyranny of bureaucracy and public indifference, unreliable intelligence, or all too lethal high-tech and low-tech weaponry. All this begs for healing, in part, through the consolations of self-empathy that allow one to touch the past in a way

---

77. For the coherence of that notion, see (Goldie, 2011).

78. See (Calhoun, 1992; Goldie, 2011; Griswold, 2007; R. C. Roberts, 2003).

that doesn't devastate, and to see a future filled with some sense of trust and hope in self and others.[79]

---

79. I wish to thank Francisco Gallegos for early help in researching this chapter and Kris Bradley for help with citations and references. Also, I thank Christina Biedermann, Susan Brison, and Jessica Stern for helpful comments on various drafts. I thank Trip Glazer and Katherine Ward for research assistance at various points in the life of this chapter.

References

American Psychiatric Association. (2013). *Posttraumatic Stress Disorder Diagnostic and Statistical Manual of Mental Disorders* (5th ed.). Arlington, VA: American Psychiatric Publishing.

Aristotle. (1984). The Complete Works of Aristotle: the Revised Oxford Translation. *Bollingen series* (71: 2).

Bennett, J. (2008). Accountability. In M. McKenna & P. Russell (Eds.), *Free Will and Reactive Attitudes: Perspectives on P. F. Strawson's 'Freedom and Resentment'* (pp. 47–68): Ashgate.

Brady, M.S. (2007). Recalcitrant Emotions and Visual Illusions. *American Philosophical Quarterly,* 44(3), 273–284.

——— (2009). The Irrationality of Recalcitrant Emotions. *Philosophical Studies: An International Journal for Philosophy in the Analytic Tradition,* 145(3), 413–430.

Butler, J. (1792). Sermon VIII: Upon Resentment. *Fifteen sermons preached at Rolls Chapel: to which is added six sermons preached on publick occasions:* Printed for F. and C. Rivington.

Calhoun, C. (1992). Changing One's Heart. *Ethics: An International Journal of Social, Political, and Legal Philosophy,* 103(1), 76–96.

Chandrasekaran, R. (2006). *Imperial life in the emerald city: inside Iraq's green zone.* New York: Alfred A. Knopf.

Chused, J.F. (1991). The Evocative Power of Enactments. *Journal Of The American Psychoanalytic Association,* 39(3), 615–639. doi:10.1177/000306519103900302

Cicero. (2002). *Cicero on the Emotions: Tusculan Disputations 3 and 4* (Graver, M.Ed.). Chicago: University of Chicago Press.

Eisenberg, N., & Strayer, J. (1987). *Empathy and its development.* Cambridge; New York: Cambridge University Press.

Freud, S. (1974). *Standard Edition of the Complete Psychological Works of Sigmund Freud* (J. Strachey, Trans.). London: Hogarth Press.

——— (1986). *The complete letters of Sigmund Freud to Wilhelm Fliess, 1887–1904* (Masson, J. ed.). Cambridge: Harvard

University Press.

Goldie, P. (2004). Emotion, Feeling, And Knowledge of the World. In Solomon (Ed.), *Thinking About Feeling: Contermporary Philosophers on Emotions* (pp. 91–106). New York: Oxford University Press.

———— (2007). Dramatic Irony, Narrative, and the External Perspective. *Philosophy: The Journal of the Royal Institute of Philosophy,* 60(Supp), 69–84.

———— (2011). Self-Forgiveness and the Narrative Sense of Self. In C. Fricke (Ed.), *The Ethics of Forgiveness: A Collection of Essays*: Routledge.

Greenson, R. R. (1967). *The Technique and Practice of Psychoanalysis.* New York: International Universities Press.

Griswold, C.L. (2007). *Forgiveness: a philosophical exploration*: Cambridge University Press.

Healy, P. (2009, November 22). The Anguish of War for Today's Soldiers, Explored by Sophocles. *The New York Times.* Retrieved from: *http://www.nytimes.com/2009/11/12/theater/12greeks. html?pagewanted=all*

Herman, J.L. (1992). *Trauma and Recovery*. New York: BasicBooks.

Homer. (1990). *The Iliad* (R. Fagles, Trans.). New York: Penguin.

Hume, D. (1968/1739). *A Treatise of Human Nature*. London: Oxford University Press.

Hurley, E., & Macnamara, C. (2010). Beyond Belief: Toward a Theory of Reactive Attitudes. *Philosophical Papers,* 39, 373–99.

Jones, K. (2012). Trustworwthiness. *Ethics, 123*(1), 61–85.

Kohut, H. (1971). *The Analysis of Self.* Madison, CT: International Universities Press.

————(1977). *The Restoration of the Self.* Madison, CT: International Universities Press.

———— (1984). *How Does Analysis Cure?* Chicago: University of Chicago Press.

Kukla, R., & Lance, M.N. (2009). *"Yo!" and "Lo!" : the pragmatic topography of the space of reasons*. Cambridge, Mass.:

Harvard University Press.

Lansky, M.R. (1995). Shame and the scope of psychoanalytic understanding. *American Behavioral Scientist, 38*(8), 1076–1090. doi:10.1177/0002764295038008004

Lipps, T. (1903). Einfühlung, Innere Nachahmung und Organempfindung. *Archiv für gesamte Psychologie,* 1, 465–519.

Litz, B., Leslie Lebowitz, Matt. J. Gray, and William Nash. (2016). *Adaptive Disclosure: A new Treatment for Military Trauma, Loss, and Moral Injury.* New York and London: Guilford Press.

Macnamara, C. (2011). Holding Others Responsible. *Philosophical Studies,* 152, 81–102.

——— (2012). "Screw You" & "Thank You. *Philosophical Studies, 130*(2).

——— (2013a). Reactive Attitudes as Communicative Entities. *Philosophy & Phenomenological Research,* XC (No. 3), 546–569.

——— (2013b). Taking Demands Out of Blame. In D. J. Coates & N. A. Tognazzini (Eds.), *Blame: Its Nature and Norms* (pp. 141–161): Oxford University Press.

——— (2015). Blame, Communication, and Morally Responsible Agency. In R. Clarke, M. McKenna, & A. M. Smith (Eds.), *The Nature of Moral Responsibility: New Essays* (pp. 211–236). New York: Oxford University Press.

McLaughlin, J. (1991). Clinical and Theoretical Aspects of Enactment. *Journal of American Psychoanalytic Association,* 39, 595–614.

Neff, K. (2003). Self-Compassion: An Alternative Conceptualization of a Healthy Attitude Toward Oneself. *Self & Identity,* 2(2), 85.

Outside the Wire. (2011). Retrieved from *http://www. outsidethewirellc.com/*

Pigman, G.W. (1995). Freud and the history of empathy. *The International Journal Of Psycho-Analysis,* 76 (Pt 2), 237–256.

Roberts, R. (2013). Justice as an Emotion Dispositon. In J. Deigh (Ed.), *On Emotions: Philosophical Essays* (pp. 14–28). New York: Oxford University Press.

Roberts, R.C. (2003). *Emotions: an Essay in Aid of Moral Psychology.* Cambridge, UK; New York: Cambridge University Press.

Schechtman, M. (2001). Empathic Access: The Missing Ingredient in Personal Identity. *Philosophical Explorations: An International Journal for the Philosophy of Mind and Action,* 4(2), 95–111.

Sherman, N. (1995). The Moral Perspective and the Psychoanalytic Quest. *The Journal of the American Academy of Psychoanalysis,* 23(2), 223–241.

———— (1997). *Making a Necessity of Virtue: Aristotle and Kant on Virtue.* New York: Cambridge University Press.

———— (1998a). Concrete Kantian Respect. In E. F. Paul, F. D. Miller, & J. Paul (Eds.), *Virtue and Vice* (pp. 119–148). New York: Cambridge University Press.

———— (1998b). Empathy and Imagination. *Philosophy of Emotions, Midwest Studies in Philosophy,* 22, 82–119.

———— (1998c). Empathy, Respect, and Humanitarian Intervention. *Ethics and International Affairs,* 12, 103–119.

———— (2005). *Stoic Warriors: The Ancient Philosophy Behind the Military Mind.* New York: Oxford University Press.

———— (2010). *The Untold War: Inside the Hearts, Minds, and Souls of Our Soldiers.* New York: Oxford University Press.

———— (2015). *Afterwar: Healing The Moral Injuries Of Our Soldiers.* New York, NY: Oxford University Press.

Smith, A. (2000). *The Theory of Moral Sentiments.* New York: Prometheus.

Sophocles. (2007). Ajax (P. Meineck & P. Woodruff, Trans.) *Four Tragedies* (pp. 1–62). Indianapolis: Hackett.

Strawson, G. (2004). Against Narrativity. Ratio: *An International Journal of Analytic Philosophy,* 17(4), 428–452.

Strawson, P.F. (1962). Freedom and resentment. *Proceedings of the British Academy,* 48, 1–25.

———— (1993). Freedom and Resentment. In J. Fischer & M. Ravizza (Eds.), *Perspectives on Moral Responsibility.* Ithaca: Cornell University Press.

Titchener, E.B. (1909). *Lectures on the experimental psychology of the thought-processes.* New York: Macmillan.

Walker, M.U. (2006). *Moral Repair: Reconstructing Moral Relations after Wrongdoing.* New York: Cambridge University Press.

Watson, G. (2004). *Agency and Answerability.* New York: Oxford.

Williams, B. (1973). *Problems of the Self.* Cambridge: Cambridge University Press.

———— (1993). *Shame and Necessity.* Berkeley: University of California Press.

———— (1995). *Making Sense of Humanity.* Cambridge: Cambridge University Press.

Wilson, J., Friendman, M., & Lindy, J. (2001). *Treating Psychological Trauma and PTSD.* Guildford CT: The Guilford Press.

Wollheim, R. (1984). *The Thread of Life.* Cambridge MA: Harvard University Press.

Woodruff, P. (2011). *The Ajax Dilemma: Justice, Fairness, and Rewards.* New York: Oxford University Press.

Literature as Witness:
Trauma and Hope in Toni Morrison's *God Help the Child*

Evelyn Jaffe Schreiber

The George Washington University

Author Note:

Evelyn Jaffe Schreiber, Ph.D. is a Professor of English at The George Washington University. She is Immediate Past President of the Toni Morrison Society. As a trained educator at the United States Holocaust Memorial Museum, she works with groups from the FBI, ICE, State Department, state law enforcement, and schools.

Contact information:
eschreib@gwu.edu; Schreiber.evelyn@gmail.com

Evelyn Jaffe Schreiber

Abstract

Dori Laub's work with Holocaust survivors describes how the disintegrated self that trauma produces can be rebuilt with the help of "testimony" to an "external listener" (50). According to Laub, survivors "need [...] a totally present listener who creates the holding space for them [...T]estimony is the healing of the wound by shaping and giving shape to an experience that's fragmented, a healing way of pulling fragments together" (48). This listener, Laub argues, needs to come "from outside to help create an internal audience" (49). Toni Morrison's most recent novel, *God Held the Child*, illustrates the possibility of moving through trauma to claim a worthy self through this process of testimony. Both Bride and Booker, the novel's protagonists, reconstruct past traumas by telling their stories in the holding space they create for each other. Together, Bride and Booker reconstruct their traumas to gain agency and self-esteem by "bearing witness" to their representative African American testimonies. In this way, Morrison's novel becomes the holding space for African American trauma.

Literature as Witness: Trauma and Hope in Toni Morrison's
God Help the Child

Dori Laub's work with Holocaust survivors describes how the disintegrated self that trauma produces can be rebuilt with the help of "testimony" to an "external listener" (50). According to Laub, survivors "need [. . .] a totally present listener who creates the holding space for them. [. . . T]estimony is the healing of the wound by shaping and giving shape to an experience that's fragmented" (48). This listener, Laub argues, needs to come "from outside to help create an internal audience" (49). Toni Morrison's most recent novel, *God Help the Child*, illustrates the possibility of moving through trauma to claim a worthy self through this process of testimony. Both Bride and Booker, the novel's protagonists, reconstruct past traumas by telling their stories in the holding space they create for each other. Together, Bride and Booker reconstruct their childhood traumas to gain agency and self-esteem by "bearing witness" to their representative African American testimonies. In this way, Morrison's novel becomes the holding space for African American trauma.

Morrison's novel revolves around Bride and Booker, but Morrison is also interested in the traumas of all of the characters and narrators she presents: Sweetness, the high-yellow mother who gives birth to a "blue-black" child Lula Ann; Sofia Huxley, the school teacher sent to prison for abusing her young pupils; Rain, the sexually abused runaway discarded by her mother and rescued from the streets by the hippie couple Evelyn and Steve; and Queen, Booker's aunt who lives alone after abandoning her children and splitting from seven "husbands." These damaged people, through their interactions with Bride and Booker, articulate their own personal demons and their attempts to move beyond them. Some of these individuals serve to elicit testimony from Bride and Booker by stimulating repressed memory so that Bride and Booker "know" what is repressed in order to work through layers of familial, personal, and societal traumas. I will review key events in the novel to demonstrate Laub's theory of testimony, Lacan's idea of subjectivity, and African American connections to testimony, to explain how Bride and Booker gain personal agency.

Morrison begins and ends this novel with the voice of Sweetness, the "high-yellow" mother who rejects her dark-skinned child, Lula Ann, the protagonist otherwise known as Bride. Sweetness articulates her own trauma that results from Lula Ann's problematic deep black color: "It's not my fault. So you can't blame me[. . . S]omething was wrong. Really wrong. She was so black she scared me. Midnight black, Sudanese black" (3). Sweetness explains that her Grandmother had passed for white, underscoring the generational and cultural trauma caused by the stigma of racial othering. Sweetness elaborates that in a segregated culture, "the lighter, the better" (4). Her Grandmother passed because "[. . .]how else can we hold on to a little dignity? How else can you avoid being spit on in a drugstore [. . .]?" (4). When Lula Ann's light-skinned parents see their new baby, her color is a mystery. "It broke our marriage to pieces," Sweetness claims, chagrined that her husband couldn't bring himself to touch the child (5). Sweetness even considers smothering the baby. She had to be strict, knowing how her daughter's "color is a cross she will always carry. But it's not my fault." (7) After two chapters from Bride's point of view, Sweetness resurfaces to try and make amends, and to verbalize her own trauma, which she has never told her daughter: "I wasn't a bad mother, you have to know that, but I may have done some hurtful things to my only child because I had to protect her. [. . .] All because of skin privileges." Looking back, Sweetness realizes that "What you do to children matters. And they might never forget" (43). With this direct address, Morrison sets up the reader as the outside witness for Sweetness, calling upon the reader to accept her testimony and address her trauma and the trauma she has heaped upon her daughter. Thus, the reader must grapple with the national problem of racial othering and the trauma that ensues for the black community. The prevalent American racial hatred towards black people provides an overarching societal trauma that negatively impacts the development of an integrated self. Colorism ignites the trauma that Sweetness and Bride inherit. Bride's journey takes her from a fragmented self to an integrated subject through her testimony, which connects her to the historical and ongoing trauma of the African American community. In turn, Booker must be able to live with his brother's horrific mutilation and death, rather than carry it as a burden that prohibits him from living his own life with integrity.

Jacques Lacan's theory of subjectivity further explains Laub's process of creating a sense of self to alleviate trauma. Lacan suggests that a subject is born into the "Real" as a "body in pieces," or a fragmented self (*Seminar* 54). During what Lacan calls the mirror stage, the subject visualizes an imaginary self that reflects a perfect, unified, and totalized image. When the mirror stage ends, the subject's sense of unity crumbles because imaginary wholeness is always being undercut by social and cultural forces outside the self (*Écrits* 2–4). For black people in American culture, a unified self of the imaginary stage is difficult when society values whiteness, because, as Kaja Silverman writes, "only certain subjects have access to a flattering image of self, and [. . .] others have imposed upon them an image so deidealizing that no one would willingly identify with it" (29). The gaze of the white Other, and one's own lack in its presence, perpetuates fragmentation, fear, and trauma for black characters.

Lacan suggests, however, that individuals can move from a socially constructed object to a subject with an internalized knowledge of cultural erasure. Laub's internal listener, to whom the survivor can testify, is important for the movement into Lacan's subject position. As Laub claims, "the formation of narrative [needed for subjectivity] only happens within an internal dialogue. And a listener temporarily takes the place of that internal other, that addressee" (48).

Morrison chronicles how Bride and Booker develop Laub's internal listener to become Lacan's integrated subjects, who can give what Geneva Smitherman calls "verbal witness to the efficacy, truth, and power of some experience that all blacks shared" (58). Testimony, in this last communal sense, has a particular connection to African American culture, through the church, music, and community suffering. Susan Hubert describes how personal experiences relate to communal ones, with the church providing the avenue for sharing. She notes that the "importance of the individual's relationship to the community has been emphasized throughout the history of African-American Christianity, in part because of the influence of African religions" (45). Further, in the "context of the African-American church, the primary narrative of life-in-community is the testimony" (46). According to James Cone, "the purpose of testimony is not only to strengthen an individual's faith, but also to build the faith of the community" (12).

Music provides another source of community healing. Vikki Visvis claims that "Black music [. . .] brings latent memories to the fore, integrating dissociated recollections into consciousness" (258). Further, as "a model of testimony, black music not only affects the individual but also implicates a community, and the collective facets of this form of testimony are specific to the African American community" (266).[80] A third connection of black lives to testimony comes from the agency provided by those who have documented on record their physical and psychological abuse within white culture.

---

80. Yvonne Atkinson argues that the call/response dynamic, connects with "Witness/Testify, another part of the word-of-mouth facet of the African American community" (22-23).

Kidada Williams describes how "Testifying about racial violence was a crucial factor in African Americans' individual recovery and their collective resistance to white supremacy because whenever victims related their experiences of this violence, they created witnesses to their trauma" (Williams, 5). These testimonies on public record created acts of resistance that formed a "collective black body" out of suffering individuals (Williams, 10).

Interestingly, in *God Help the Child* Morrison revisits her first novel, *The Bluest Eye*, wherein Pecola's community brands her as ugly for having dark-black skin and being impoverished. Unlike Pecola and her community members, who are all doomed to accept the hopeless weight of racial othering, Lula Ann reinvents herself as Bride, a cosmetics guru who shines as an exotic black beauty, dressing only in white to highlight her ebony skin. In contrast to the bleak landscape of her first novel, *God Help the Child* suggests hope for claiming a lovable self. But the road is not easy. Bride's early childhood traumas erupt and attempt to erase her self-esteem. Craving her mother's love, the eight-year-old Lula Ann testifies in court by pointing to a teacher accused of child abuse. Although she herself was not abused, her testimony, along with those of other girls, convicts Sofia Huxley. This lie produces the effect Lula Ann dreamed of:

> I glanced at Sweetness; she was smiling like I've never seen her smile before [. . .]. As we walked down the courthouse steps she held my hand, my hand. She never did that before and it surprised me as much as it pleased me because I always knew she didn't like touching me. I could tell. Distaste was all over her face when I was little and she had to bathe me [. . .] I used to pray she would slap my face or spank me just to feel her touch. (31)

Bride's guilt about lying and sending the teacher to prison prompts/motivates her to try to make amends 15 years later, when Sofia makes parole. Yet when Bride offers her cash and airline tickets to make up for time in prison and the loss of a teaching career, Sofia explodes with physical violence towards Bride. This eruption has its seeds in Sofia's own childhood trauma from living in a home of punishment, obedience, and silence, an environment that her husband replicated. As she cries about her imprisonment for the first time, Sofia realizes that Bride has gifted her "the release of tears unshed for fifteen years. [. . .] Now I am clean and able" (70). Her encounter with Bride, an empathetic listener, allows Sofia to verbalize the childhood pain dormant in her unconscious: "Beating her, kicking and punching her freed me up more than being paroled. I felt I was ripping blue-

and-white wallpaper, returning slaps and running the devil Mommy knew so well out of my life" (77). This violent encounter with Bride provides Sofia with the space to finally verbalize her early trauma.

At the same time, during Sofia's beating, Bride "reverted to the Lula Ann who never fought back" and when it was over "like a whipped puppy I just crawled away afraid to even whimper" (32). When Bride tells Booker about the episode, he deserts her, claiming that she is "not the woman I want" (8). These words wound Bride, and leave her feeling "erased" (13): "I told him every single thing about myself; he confided nothing" (11). "I spilled my heart to him; he told me nothing about himself. I talked; he listened" but "Then he split [. . .] dumping me exactly as Sofia Huxley did" (62). Bride thought that "his complete understanding of me" was important in their relationship, and confided only to Booker about her childhood (62). Because there has been no dialogue, only a one-way flow of information, Booker rejects her.

To regain her former equilibrium, Bride realizes that she must "discover what she was made of—cotton or steel—there could be no retreat, no turning back" (143). On her journey, the stable, loving white couple Steve and Evelyn, along with the wounded child Rain, enable Bride to develop empathy for other people during her forced convalescence in their remote and rustic cabin. Next, it is Booker's aunt, Queen, who guides Bride in her quest to confront Booker and get to the meaning of his rejection. Queen provides the outside voice necessary for Bride to build an inner one when she admonishes: "You come all this way and just turn around and leave?" Gaining strength, Bride proclaims, "You're absolutely right! Totally right! This is about me, not him. Me!" (152). Bride realizes that "she had been scorned and rejected by everybody all her life. Booker was the one person she was able to confront—which was the same as confronting herself, standing up for herself. Wasn't she worth something? Anything?" (98). Confronting Lacan's Real, Bride gathers her disparate pieces.

Bride physically attacks Booker so that he cannot escape a confrontation. They slap each other and Bride breaks a bottle over his head—both use physical touch to initiate connection. Having collapsed, Bride can confess to Booker that she lied under oath and wrongly convicted her teacher just so "my mother would hold my hand [. . .] And look at me with proud eyes, for once" (153). This truth provides Booker with the insight into Bride's actions he has lacked and enables him to verbalize his own trauma around his brother's death that caused him to desert her: "My brother, he was murdered by a freak, a predator like the one I thought you were forgiving" (154). By holding on to their childhood traumas, neither Bride nor Booker has ever fully lived in the present. Bride realizes that she never knew Booker or asked about *his* story—only her own. It is only when Bride and Booker enter into a dialogue where they listen to each other's pain and commit to working together to heal each other that they can move forward. Bride will come to terms with her traumatic past in order to build self-love, and she will learn to love Booker for the wounded person he is, rather than an idealized partner who can rob her of her subjectivity when he shuts her out. While Bride's mother made her feel shame for her blackness, Booker tells Bride that her color is simply a "genetic trait—not a flaw, not a curse, not a blessing nor a sin" (143). Bride reflects how "While talking to him certain things I had buried came up fresh as though I was seeing them for the first time" (53). Their exchange releases repressed memories.

When Queen returns to see how the wounded lovers are doing, she asks Booker what caused their initial split. He responds, "Lies. Silence. Just not saying what was true or why [. . .] About us as kids, things that happened, why we did things, thought things, took actions that were really about what went on when we were just children" (155). Queen not only listens to Booker, but she also asks hard questions in the safe space of her love for him. "She told her truth. What's yours? [. . . Your brother] must be worn out having to die and get no rest because he has to run somebody else's life [. . .] Did you ever feel free of him?" (156–157). As Queen leaves Booker to sort things out with Bride, she worries that "They will blow it [. . .] Each will cling to [. . .] some long-ago trouble and pain life dumped on their pure and innocent selves. And each one will rewrite that story forever, knowing the plot, guessing the theme, inventing its meaning and dismissing its origin" (158). Despite this fear, both Booker and Bride *do* ultimately process what Queen has unearthed, and can finally get out of their endless cycle of mindlessly reliving trauma. Robert Jay Lifton describes Booker's situation when he explains that for a survivor and witness,

> the only way one can feel right or justified in reconstituting oneself and going on living with some vitality is to carry through one's responsibility to the dead. And it's carrying through that responsibility via one's witness [. . .] that enables one to be an integrated human being once more. (12)

Booker carries on this responsibility by writing a note to his dead brother to articulate his pain at Adam's passing and his guilt at his own survival: *"[I] miss the emotion that your dying produced a feeling so strong it defined me while it erased you leaving [. . .] I apologize for enslaving you in order to chain myself to the illusion of control"* (161). Bride, in turn, "having confessed Lula Ann's sins [. . .] felt newly born. No longer forced to relive, no, outlive the disdain of her mother and the abandonment of her father" (162). Now, "[t]hey worked together like a true couple, thinking not of themselves, but of helping somebody else" (167). When Bride tells Booker she is "pregnant and it's yours," Booker replies, "It's ours." (174), solidifying his commitment to work on a future together. Further, he "offered her the hand she had craved all her life, the hand that did not need a lie to deserve it, the hand of trust and caring for—a combination that some call natural love" (175). Bride finally gets the loving hand her mother refused to give her.

But Morrison does not leave us with this sentimental ending. She closes the novel with the voice of Sweetness still rationalizing her treatment of her blue-black daughter and articulating the trauma she herself suffered from the gaze of white culture at Lula Ann's birth: "I know I did the best for her under the circumstances. When my husband ran out on us, Lula Ann was a burden. A heavy one but I bore it well" (177). Sweetness challenges Bride and Booker to do better, as they are about "find out what it takes, how the world is, how it works and how it changes when you are a parent. Good luck and God help the child" (178). While readers listen to Sweetness' skepticism about the world she has known, they also witness Bride and Booker's successful breakthrough, and the possibility in store for their future progeny. Having verbalized their traumas and pieced together their shattered selves, Bride and Booker have given testimony to what was unknown on a conscious level.[81] Together, Bride and Booker, assisted by their community, have reconstructed their traumas to gain agency and self-esteem. For both of them, testimony that leads to the development of an inner listener has provided necessary healing. They both move from objects to subjects, reclaiming selves that were shattered, and reaching subject status through the dialogue of their inner and outer voices.

---

81. Cathy Caruth finds that what "returns to haunt the victim [. . .] is not only the reality of the violent event but also the reality of the way that its violence has not yet been fully known." (*Unclaimed* 6) Geoffrey Hartman claims that trauma is "an experience that is not experienced, that resists or escapes consciousness." (Hartman 214)

References

Atkinson, Y. (2000). Language that Bears Witness: The Black English Oral Tradition in the Works of Toni Morrison. *The Aesthetics of Toni Morrison: Speaking the Unspeakable.* Ed. Marc C. Conner. Jackson: UP of Mississippi. 12–30.

Caruth, C., ed. (2014). *Listening to Trauma: Conversations with Leaders in the Theory and Treatment of Catastrophic Experience.* Baltimore: Johns Hopkins UP.

——— (1996). *Unclaimed Experience: Trauma, Narrative, and History.* Baltimore: The Johns Hopkins UP.

Cone, J. (1986). *My Soul Looks Back.* Maryknoll, NY: Orbis.

Hartman, G. (2014). Words and Wounds: An Interview with Geoffrey Hartman. Caruth. *Listening.* 213–235.

Hubert, S.J. (1998). Testimony and Prophesy in *The Life and Religious Experience of Jarena Lee. The Journal of Religious Thought* 54/55.2/1, 45–52.

Lacan, J. (1977). *Ecrits: A Selection.* Trans. Alan Sheridan. New York: Norton.

——— (1991). *The Seminar of Jacques Lacan: Book II, The Ego in Freud's Theory and in the Technique of Psychoanalysis 1954–1955.* Ed. Jacques-Alain Miller. Trans. Sylvana Tomaselli. New York: Norton.

Laub, D. (2014). A Record that Has Yet to Be Made: An Interview with Dori Laub. Caruth. *Listening.* 47–78.

Lifton, R.J. (2014). Giving Death Its Due: An Interview with Robert Jay Lifton. Caruth. *Listening.* 3–22.

Morrison, T. (2016). *God Help the Child.* New York: Vintage International.

Silverman, K. (1996). *The Threshold of the Visible World.* New York: Routledge.

Smitherman, G. (2000). *Talkin that Talk: Language, Culture, and Education in African America.* London: Routledge, 2000.

Visvis, V. (2008). Alternatives to the "Talking Cure": Black Music as Traumatic Testimony in Toni Morrison's *Song of Solomon. African American Review* 42.2, 255–268.

Williams, K.E. (2012). *They Left Great Marks on Me: African American Testimonies of Racial Violence from Emancipation to World War I.* NY: NYUP.

Law & Order: TV, Poetry & Process

Jane Shore
The George Washington University

Jane Shore, M.F.A., is a Professor of English at The George Washington University, where she teaches Creative Writing.

She has received fellowships from The John Simon Guggenheim Foundation and The Radcliffe Institute; she was an Alfred Hodder Fellow at Princeton; a Goodyear Fellow at The Foxcroft School; and she twice received grants from The National Endowment for the Arts and was a Jenny McKean Moore Writer-in-Residence at The George Washington University.

Jane Shore

Abstract

In 2003, there was a murder-suicide in my home in Chevy Chase, DC. A few months after the event, I began watching *Law & Order.* I was studying it so as to "learn something" from it. I had to watch because I wasn't there—the show was a way to show me what dead bodies looked like. I steeped myself in it. For me, the trauma was "acted out" by watching the show. It is reassuring because most of the time the good guys win. I watched it for 12 years. Recently, my therapist said to me about my TV habit, "Do you think you are retraumatizing yourself?" I decided to write a poem that originally began with the therapist's question. But I cut that. So the therapist, the very person who prompted the poem, had to be repressed. In a way, as so often in writing, the poem took over and left triggering questions behind. On the advice of my readers, I also removed some very angry or psychological language, words like "psychopath," "addict," and "obsessed." I'll present the poem and my process of writing it.

Law & Order: TV, Poetry & Process

In July 2003, there was a murder-suicide in my home in Chevy Chase, DC. My husband, Howard, and I and our fifteen-year old-daughter were away for the summer in our house in Vermont. My best friend in DC, who had spare set of keys, found the bodies eight hours after she got the call for help left in the early morning on her voicemail. The caller, a fellow poet and single mother of a two-year-old boy, an acquaintance of ours, someone we did not know well enough to yet call a friend, had agreed to housesit until September, when the new semester of school began. She was between teaching jobs and estranged from the child's father, a prominent poet. Her parents lived in Silver Spring, close by. Our big furnished house, rent-free, would be a calm place for her to catch her breath before moving with her son to Atlanta to teach. My husband and I could empathize with her, having been academic gypsies for much of our working lives. We could do a good deed and have a worry-free summer, too, because among other reasons, an empty house in DC attracts burglars.

Six months later, in February 2004, the murder-suicide was the cover story in *The Washington Post's* Sunday Magazine. My husband and I declined to be interviewed for the article. But in October, three months after the event when we were back in DC, we did let Susan Stamberg record us talking about our experience as part of her NPR six-part series called "No Place Like Home." The title of our interview was "Reclaiming a Haunted House." Shell-shocked, Howard and I reluctantly agreed to do it; Susan was someone we knew, who lived in our neighborhood, and we thought it could be therapeutic and signal our far-flung friends that we were okay. The ground rule of the interview was that we NOT talk about the mother and her baby. Many details were then, as they still are now, unknown to us. Though at times I am curious, I still haven't made any effort to research more thoroughly what happened that day.

By 2005, I had quickly written three poems about the aftermath of this tragedy, which my family euphemistically referred to as "what happened in our house." Having written these poems, I thought I was done with the subject. I presented them at my plenary talk during the last DC *Listening to Trauma Conference* in 2010, and they are published in my books *A Yes-or-No Answer* and *That Said, New and Selected Poems* (Houghton Mifflin Harcourt, 2008 and 2012.) These poems are about the things we found in our house when we returned there in the fall, three months after the murder-suicide, items that our close friends (who cleaned up and threw out and boxed up what seemed obviously not ours) had missed: her face soap in my soap dish, her jewelry on my dresser, her clothes hanging in my closet, plus dozens of loose keys from my daughter's keychain collection that her boy had played with, that turned up in odd places—weeks, and sometimes months after we "re-possessed" our house.

I tried to escape (like a lot of people do) by watching television, but almost every show was about murder or violence. Likewise, I could not watch the news. Watching *Law & Order*, however, was strangely solacing and "safe." It has an enduring formula: the first half-hour is always "Law," the cold open when the police find the victims, followed by the procedural when the perpetrators are appre-hended. The second half-hour is always "Order," that is, the typical courtroom drama when the killers go to court and are sentenced for their crimes. Mostly, the good guys win. Cases are resolved. There's closure. This formula works well, and the show and its franchises still continue to be hits—turn on any cable-connected TV and you are likely to run into an episode of *Law & Order.*

But for me, watching *Law & Order* was personal: I was studying the show to *"learn something"* from it. I *had* to watch it, you see, because I wasn't there to witness the horrifically bloody scene or its aftermath in person. The show could show me, among other things, what dead bodies look like, as I had never seen a corpse. The trauma was "acted out"; I could vicariously relive it numerous times and absorb its details, and perhaps begin to heal myself. I became a *Law & Order* slut: I didn't discriminate between *Law & Order: Criminal Intent, Law & Order: SVU,* even the pirated *Law & Order: UK.* The original *Law & Order* is known in the trade as "the mother ship." All in all, for 12 years after "what happened in our house," I compulsive-ly watched and re-watched the shows and their reruns.

My husband, Howard, was of course very concerned about me. He was baffled as to why I would watch this specific violence, re-played, that kept reminding me afresh of the murder-suicide. He wouldn't, he *couldn't*, join me on the couch and share my blossom-ing obsession—murder as spectator sport. Luckily, we are different people. And he had his own way of eventually writing about it, as a chapter in a memoir, and his own way of working it out.

Twelve years after the murder-suicide, during one of our ses-sions, my therapist said to me about my TV habit, "Do you think you are maybe retraumatizing yourself?" And when she did, it was as if I literally heard that unique *Law & Order "doing-doing"* sound, the iconic aural punctuation that signals a change of scenes. Although my dozen years of watching had perhaps served its initial purpose, in my almost dozen years of therapy talking about it, I had never considered that what had once solaced me might now be having a damaging effect on me. And so, the first drafts of this new poem, "Law & Order," began with my therapist's question, but this was a line that I eventually cut from my poem. As I will later discuss, the word "retraumatizing" is a difficult word to use in a lyric poem. So the therapist, the very person who had prompted me to write my poem, had to be repressed! In this way, as so often in my writing, the content of the poem took over and left its triggering idea behind.

*

With very few exceptions, my poems are autobiographical, written in the first person. But I, like many poets, also write poems sometimes using a persona, a mask, as described in T.S. Eliot's essay, "Tradition and the Individual Talent." A persona allows me to explore complicated subject matter and emotions, and provides distance between the "writer-Jane" from the "person-Jane"—the one who experienced the subject matter first-hand. If there were no separation or distance between the two, I'd write my poetry the same way I might write a diary entry or a letter. Using a persona gives me permission to say things that I, as Jane Shore, might not—or dare not—say. It allows me to go deeper than I might ordinarily—I can pretend to be someone else thinking and observing. And I have some wiggle-room to play with the facts.

*

So far, as of this writing, I have forty-seven revisions of "Law & Order." In some drafts, I changed just a word or a line. I cut and pasted sections of the narrative, testing to see where particular images worked best. I sometimes scrapped ideas that I loved. Here and there, the tone was off—my narrator was too sarcastic or angry or jokey.

I wrote the first twenty versions of the poem using shorter lines, about half the length of its current lines. The shorter lines made my poem twice as long, and made it hard for me to keep track of my "plot." Shorter lines kept stalling the poem and short-circuiting my ideas. Short lines made the poem appear to lack *gravitas*. I was reminded of the postcard the poet James Merrill wrote me about my first book, *Eye Level*, which comprises mostly long, very skinny poems, using only a few words per line. Merrill said, "You're writing these large narrative poems, and it's like eating a huge meal with a doll's spoon." Here is an example:

> LAW & ORDER #29
> What happened in our house
>
> If, as my therapist said, I was
> re-traumatizing myself,
> channel surfing every night
> to find an episode or two
> to accompany my insomnia,
> then rerunning it in my head,
> did seeing many corpses,
> even if they were only actors
> pretending to be dead, and fake
> blood, deaden and desensitize me?
> There was Law & there Order
> connected by the ampersand,
> the halves fit into the neat box
> the circle of an hour,
> tamed and digestible. consumable, an *amuse bouche*.
> What happened in our house
> was not a made-for-TV drama.
> We were hundreds of miles away.
> So I had to picture the striped
> black & yellow crime scene tape
> festooning our front door,
> the typed note she propped
> on the sideboard telling why
> she had to kill her child & then
> herself, both her wrists slashed
> instead of handcuffed.
> I wasn't there & couldn't imagine it.
> Instead, I studied the detectives
> whipping out disposable gloves
> & cops kicking doors down
> to get to the bodies, and later
> wisecracking at the remains.
> Compelled to watch them all,

all the series, the thousand episodes,
like a birder adding to my life list.
I absorbed the spatter patterns,
angle of the knife—pooled blood
seeping through the beige kilim
& into the floor joists.
It really happened in our house,
in our dining room, between
the window & the table, where,
for years thereafter, we couldn't
bear to eat a meal. We hopscotched
over invisible chalk outlines
of their bodies. That was years ago.
Since we sold that house, & moved,
no psychopaths have crossed my path.
Perhaps that's why I'm still addicted,
assured that, at the end of the hour,
justice will be served, the actors
will rise up from the bloody floor,
change back into their street clothes,
& go home to the suburbs
where no fingerprints, no clustered
oval smudges delicate as the dust
from moth wings, climb the walls
& furniture & wooden shutters, drawer pulls,
everywhere they touched.

When I doubled # 29's line length and put the poem in tercets—three-line stanzas—it suddenly <u>snapped</u> into shape—the new line length and new overall shape of the poem magically reined in the out-of-control story plus the troubling emotions surrounding it (#47.) This new form and shape <u>anchored</u> the poem, tamed it. I do not typically write in traditional verse forms, like sonnets or villanelles. While I'm not a formal poet, I do use a lot of subtle patterning, resembling much of what goes on in traditional verse. Except for an occasional rhyming poem, I'm really a free-verse poet. Paradoxically, when writing #47, although I was most constrained by the tercets, I felt very free. I had room to play. I like the way "Law & Order #47" now looks on the page. It is pleasing, symmetrical. It is a container, and it contains. How a poem looks visually is very important to me—the shape telegraphs and mimics different psychological states

Jane Shore

of mind. I like neatness, order. Writing in tercets forced me to trim
each individual line and give each stanza its own integrity, each one
a chunk that further advances the narrative.

LAW & ORDER #47

We let someone we barely knew housesit one July.
She was unsettled, between jobs, with a baby.
My husband and I thought it was a *mitzvah*, a good deed.

When it happened, we were five hundred miles away.
So I had to picture the black & yellow crime scene tape
festooning our front door, & knives & the typed note

propped on the sideboard telling why she killed her boy
& then herself, the slashes on her wrists like bloody handcuffs.
I didn't want to imagine it. Instead, I studied TV cops

kicking doors down to get to bodies variously posed,
though they were only actors pretending to be dead,
I watched detectives pulling on disposable gloves

& smoking & wisecracking within earshot of corpses.
Channel-surfing on cable, I watched, piecemeal,
all twenty seasons of *Law & Order,* the original series,

five-hundred-fifty-six episodes, like a birder adding
to my life list. I learned forensics & spatter patterns;
how blood, seeping through the floor, soaked the joists.

It really happened in our house, in our dining room
between the window & the table where, afterwards,
we couldn't bear to eat a meal. We hopscotched over

the invisible chalk outlines of bodies; we erased
the dusted fingerprints, shadows climbing the walls;
we replaced our family portraits with lithographs of trees.

Since we sold that house & moved, I'm still watching
reruns, hoping for a different outcome.

One where, at the end of the hour, justice will be served,

the dead will rise up from the bloody floor
& change back into their street clothes, & return
to houses exactly as they left them.

*

Once I had the voice figured out and the three-line stanzas in place, I had to deal with the bloody facts. Literally. There was a lot of blood. How was I to portray the horror of the scene without exploiting it and playing up its shock value, thus cheapening my poem? There was a lot of physical damage to the house—a large section of the dining room floor had to be replaced. Rugs had to be disposed of. I was told that the mother used two large kitchen knives and that she stabbed her child thirty-plus times, piercing his lungs, heart, and forearm. One account says that she slit his wrists. One account said that she gave him a bottle of milk laced with drugs earlier that morning. After she killed him, she then stabbed herself multiple times and slit her own wrists. She lay on the dining room floor next to her child and died, in the position where my friend found them. The murder-suicide was certainly premeditated because she had bought these knives herself. She did not use my kitchen knives, although my friends who cleaned up later threw away one or two because the knives (inadvertently) had blood on them. Drafts of my poem wrestle with how much or how little of this nightmarish imagery to use. These were facts. I didn't make them up. I had to find a way to balance my horror and disgust versus my curiosity and fascination with the gore. My poetry-friends who saw versions of "Law & Order" made many comments that influenced the final version of my poem. Their suggestions helped me decide which lines and images to use, how long to linger over details, and how far to push them. They helped me to calibrate my anger and horror, and to control the poem's tone.

For example: the image of the slashed wrists. This simile came to me instantaneously as a visual image. Slashed wrists might look *as though they were* handcuffed. It took me many drafts to get this line just right. Ironically, toying with the words distanced and distracted me from their actual meaning. By taking the actual time to craft the image, I had a chance to absorb it (feel it more deeply) on a visceral level. This particular image is very important to me beyond the visual and the visceral: I want to imply (without saying it directly) that the mother *is a criminal* for murdering her child. It's as though she has been arrested. She's both the perp and the victim. And she's hand-cuffed, so she can't do further harm. And, if she is handcuffed, it is a kind of justice for her child, who was an innocent.

My poet-friends told me to play down the blood. They reminded me that what she did was "an act of desperation." They said, "Don't be too ghoulishly interested in the blood or the edge of empathy will be lost." They also said that the very act of watching the show *Law & Order* was a way for me to sort out the fantasy from the reality of what happened. I used fantasy (imagining what happened, retracing images and scenes that I did not witness in person) to approach the reality of what did happen.

How can the narrator be both horrified and angry, yet sympathetic? Her nest has been violated. Her own family was wounded. Like the murdered boy, the poem's narrator's daughter is a child, too, and a victim: she must live in the house and process the tragedy that took place there. The little boy slept in her bedroom. Like him, the daughter is an innocent. Then there is that complicated knot to untangle: how much empathy should she have toward the murderer? Should she identify with the mother? Can she imagine feeling both desperation and rage so strong that she could commit the unthinkable, kill her child and herself? Yes, for a micro-second, perhaps, she *can* imagine it. As her therapist said, how many times does an angry or frustrated mother say (in a pejorative sense) "that she could just kill her kid"? But the narrator is not mentally ill as the killer was, to *literally* kill her child.

*

On the advice of my fellow poet-critics, I removed some very angry and/or psychological language: precise words like "psychopath," "addicted," "hooked," and "obsessed." Though the opening lines for a long time were, "If, as my therapist said, I was retraumatizing myself,"—my ear couldn't get around how unnatural and unmusical and clunky the word "retraumatizing" sounded to my internal ear, how awkward it was to say out loud; the way it looked on the page and took up too much room. It's a word in a language that I might use in my everyday talk, but how knowledgeable and savvy do I want my poem's narrator to be? Do I want her to use psychological jargon? To use "retraumatize" and "addicted" and "obsessed" and other such lingo sets up an expectation that the narrator speaks the same language as the therapist. *I* know what the word "retraumatize" means (I was analyzed back in the 1970s.) But I want my narrator's language and diction to come from her own experience, I want to take her off the couch. Therefore, I systematically removed language that presupposes a psychoanalytic vocabulary.

I believe that, when writing a poem, it's important to "know just enough" about a subject. If you know too much about it in an academic or analytic sense, or have too much research rolling around inside your head, the ideas in your poem don't have room to grow. When writing certain poems, it's important for me to be a little stupid or naïve. It is important for me not to know (beforehand) how my poem will end. Like the reader, I want to discover the subject and content along the way. If I already knew the ending when I started, there would be no need for me to write my poem. My poem would feel like an outline for a paper. I would be writing an essay, perhaps, and not a poem. I need to discover *along the way* what a poem is truly about, and find its *emotional center* for myself.

Its emotional center is "what I didn't know I knew." Once I find the poem's emotional center, it can leave its surface level and speak from its core. Hitting the emotional center is, for me, always a revelation, a surprise—and the payoff. The high. If I merely stay on the surface, if I don't discover what deeper thing I want to say, then I will have failed. When that happens, I'll put my poem away until I am ready to wrestle with it again, and perhaps be able to hit the bullseye.

*

Our house was haunted, but not in the ghostly sense. My family members were secondary victims. Writing this essay, I am still revising my poem. I still have questions about word-choice: saying the detectives were "pulling on" their disposable gloves rather than "whipping them out" in an earlier draft in which the language seemed too colloquial. The line about my narrator's needing to watch the episodes "like a birder adding to my life list" seemed too lighthearted to one of my poet-friends. For now, I am keeping it until I can think of something better. Right now, though, I want to show the compulsive nature of needing to accumulate, acquire, to add up the episodes the way a birder commodifies his experience, the same way my narrator wants to "master" the series' content.

*

I wish I could have used the phrase, "a cold open," as in the draft that began with the line, "Every episode of *Law & Order* begins with 'a cold open,' that is, the discovery of a body or bodies."

*

I'm still thinking about how to better use the dusted fingerprints, which was an indelible image that greeted us on our return home. The grey smudges of dusted fingerprints showed up in many surprising places in our house. In earlier drafts, the poem's last lines were, "their dusted fingerprints, smudged ovals of gray, like the powder from butterfly wings, climbed the walls & windows & tabletops, everywhere they touched." That image of the butterfly wings is perhaps too pretty, too poetic, to use in this gritty a poem, although it can be said that the butterfly is a symbol of rebirth. Yet for me, seeing these fingerprints was eerie: they somehow *reanimated* the mother and her son, set them in motion. I could imagine them going about their daily chores with their fingerprints serving as a map of their actions, which was truly disturbing to me.

*

In earlier drafts, I used the word "and" to separate "Law" and "Order," instead of the ampersand. One of my poet-critics remarked that an ampersand looks like a twisted body. What a fantastic image that is, one which I tried to use as a simile in my poem, but I couldn't make it work! There was no room for it and that observation would require more sentences of explanation to make it fit. Stylistically, because I used an ampersand in the title, I decided to use ampersands throughout the poem, wherever I encountered an "and." This may be a bit gimmicky, but it's edgy too, and adds a little something extra to the tone.

*

I mentioned before that my poems are autobiographical. I always try to tell the truth, sticking to what really happened. But I am not averse to lying when necessary, if it enhances my poem. If a room is red, but a blue room better suits my poem (either because the word "blue" rhymes with other sounds in my poem or because the color blue creates a visual cue that a red room might not) I always go the poem's way. After a while, the poem has a mind of its own, so to speak. As long as what you say is "essentially true," you can stretch the truth.

*

This essay not about "what happened in our house." It is about the process of writing a poem about "what happened in our house." It is about translating experience into art. While I continue to unravel the tragedy through therapeutic means at my own pace, unlike my poem, I do not have closure. My experience in real life does not tie up neatly in a bow. There are things about the event I do not want to say publicly. I still need to protect my privacy.

*

Every poem presents its own puzzle to be solved by writing the poem. Paul Valéry wrote, "A poem is never finished, only abandoned." At the time of this writing, I still consider "Law & Order" unfinished. I'll continue to tweak its language and strive to make every line as good as the poem's best lines, until every word and image is as perfect as it can be. Then I'll abandon it.

*

The jury's still out on if writing "Law & Order" will eventually help me understand and absorb the trauma and the tragedy of "what happened in our house." Revising my poem, however, is like hitting the replay button. It's no small irony that the act of writing, itself, is a kind of retraumatizing.

Appendix: early drafts of "Law & Order" with some poet-critics' comments:

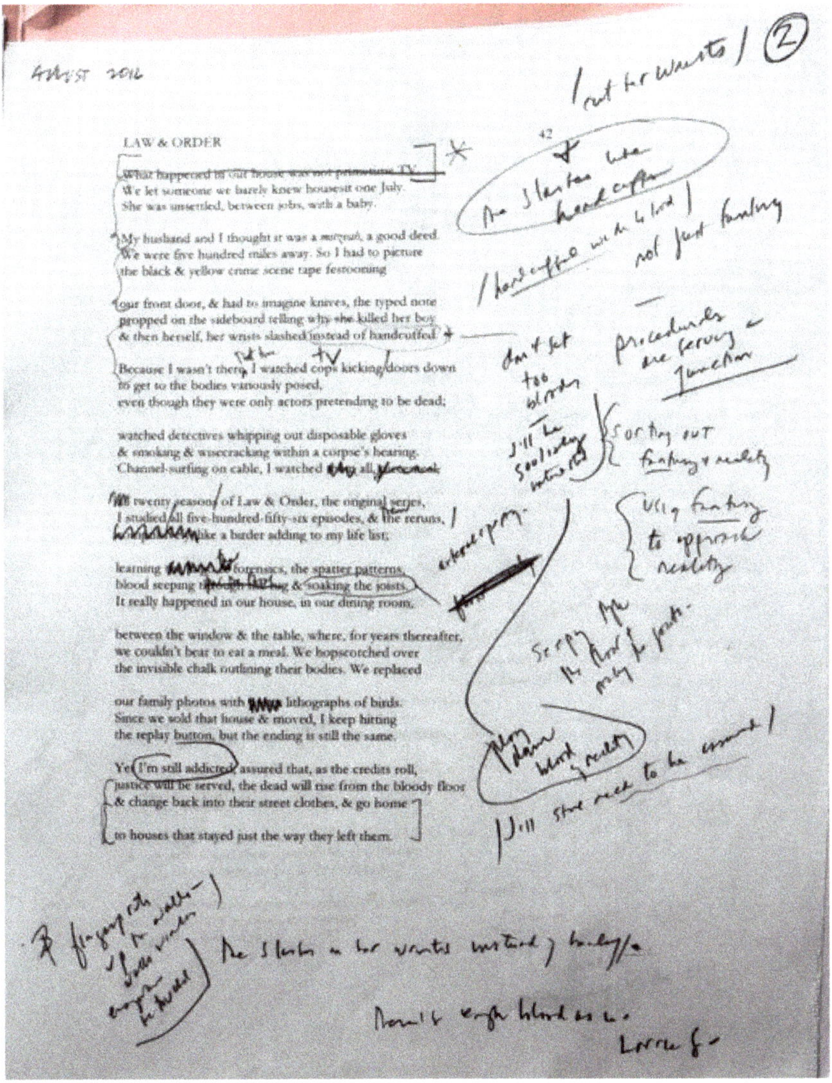

AUGUST 2016

LAW & ORDER

42

What happened in our house was not prime-time TV.
We let someone we barely knew housesit one July.
She was unsettled, between jobs, with a baby.

My husband and I thought it was a mitzvah, a good deed.
We were five hundred miles away. So I had to picture
the black & yellow crime scene tape festooning

our front door, & had to imagine knives, the typed note
propped on the sideboard telling why she killed her boy
& then herself, her wrists slashed instead of handcuffed.

Because I wasn't there, I watched cops kicking doors down
to get to the bodies variously posed,
even though they were only actors pretending to be dead;

watched detectives whipping out disposable gloves
& smoking & wisecracking within a corpse's hearing.
Channel-surfing on cable, I watched all

twenty seasons of Law & Order, the original series,
I studied all five-hundred-fifty-six episodes, & the reruns,
like a birder adding to my life list;

learning forensics, the spatter patterns,
blood seeping & soaking the joists.
It really happened in our house, in our dining room,

between the window & the table, where, for years thereafter,
we couldn't bear to eat a meal. We hopscotched over
the invisible chalk outlining their bodies. We replaced

our family photos with lithographs of birds.
Since we sold that house & moved, I keep hitting
the replay button, but the ending is still the same.

Yet I'm still addicted, assured that, as the credits roll,
justice will be served, the dead will rise from the bloody floor
& change back into their street clothes, & go home

to houses that stayed just the way they left them.

[handwritten marginal annotations throughout, largely illegible]

313

Jane Shore

LAW & ORDER   46

We let someone we barely knew housesit one July.
She was unsettled, between jobs, with a baby.
My husband and I thought it was a *mitzvah*, a good deed.

We had an alibi. We were five hundred miles away.
So I had to picture the black & yellow crime scene tape
festooning our front door, & knives & the typed note

propped on the sideboard telling why she killed her boy
& then herself, her slashed wrists like bloody handcuffs.
I couldn't imagine it. Instead, I watched the TV cops

kicking doors down to get to bodies variously posed,
though they were only actors pretending to be dead,
I watched detectives whipping out disposable gloves

& smoking & wisecracking within earshot of corpses.
Channel-surfing on cable, I watched, piecemeal,
all twenty seasons of Law & Order, the original series,

five-hundred-fifty-six episodes, like a birder adding
to my life list. I learned forensics & spatter patterns.
how blood, seeped through the floor, had soaked the joists.

It really happened in our house, in our dining room,
between the window & the table where, for years thereafter,
we couldn't bear to eat a meal. We hopscotched over

the invisible chalk outlines of bodies, we erased
dusted fingerprints, oval shadows climbing the walls.
We replaced our family portraits with lithographs of birds   flowers

But since we sold that house & moved, I'm still hooked,
still watching reruns, hoping for a different ending.
One where, at the end of the hour, justice will be served,

the dead will rise up from the bloody floor
& change back into their street clothes, & go home
to houses that stayed exactly as they left them.

Nanette C. Auerhahn, Ph.D., is a clinical psychologist in private practice in Beachwood, OH. She is a candidate at the Cleveland Psychoanalytic Center, where she teaches in the Psychoanalytic Psychotherapy Program. Dr. Auerhahn has taught at Yale, Stanford, and Case Western Universities, as well as the California School of Professional Psychology in San Francisco. She received her Ph.D. in 1980 from Yale University and was a postdoctoral fellow at Stanford University. Dr. Auerhahn was the recipient of fellowships from the National Science Foundation, the Mark Kanzer Foundation, the Stanford Humanities Center, and Stanford's Institute for Research on Women and Gender. She has been a researcher with the Fortunoff Videoarchive for Holocaust Testimonies at Yale University and a consultant at the Cleveland Rape Crisis Center, the Case Western Reserve University Counseling Center, Bellefaire Jewish Children's Bureau, Mt. Sinai Hospital, Laurelwood Hospital, and Menorah Park Center for Aging. Dr. Auerhahn has written numerous articles on trauma; her writing was awarded the Cleveland Psychoanalytic Center Essay Prize in 2011 and 2016.

Arthur Blank Jr.,M.D., a psychoanalyst and psychiatrist in private practice in the Washington, DC area (Chevy Chase), was on the psychiatry faculty at Yale for four decades, is now Clinical Professor of Psychiatry at The George Washington University, and teaches at the Washington Baltimore Center for Psychoanalysis. In the 1970's he was one of a handful of clinicians who called attention to the role of trauma in war veterans (Vietnam), and came to Washington to serve as the national director of the community-based counseling centers for war veterans (Vet Centers) of the Department of Veteran Affairs. During his tenure as director, the Vet Centers nationwide saw about 500,000 Vietnam and other war veterans for psychotherapy and counseling. At VA headquarters, he was instrumental in the initiation of the National Vietnam Veterans Readjustment Study, the National Center for PTSD, and other developments. He served on the PTSD Committees for DSM III-R and IV, and has published papers on unconscious flashbacks, the nature of traumatic stressors, and the longitudinal course of PTSD. He maintains a general practice in psychoanalysis and psychiatry with a special expertise about the effects of trauma from a wide variety of sources (abuse, war, disasters, accidents, etc.) and is a member of the Advisory Committee to the Secretary of Veterans Affairs, on Readjustment of Veterans.

Cathy Caruth, Ph.D., is Frank H.T. Rhodes Professor of Humane Letters at Cornell University. Trained as a literary critic and theorist, her first books (*Empirical Truths and Critical Fictions: Locke, Wordsworth, Kant, Freud* and a co-edited collection with D. Esch, *Critical Encounters: Reference and Responsibility in Deconstructive Writing*) focused on philosophy, theory, and psychoanalysis. In the early nineties, she began working on trauma and published *Unclaimed Experience: Trauma, Narrative and History* and the interdisciplinary collection, *Trauma: Explorations in Memory.* She has lectured and taught on trauma in more than 25 countries and has worked with clinicians, activists, researchers and scholars from many disciplines and professions. Her most recent trauma-related publications include the monograph *Literature in the Ashes of History* and *Listening to Trauma: Conversations with Leaders in the Theory and Treatment of Catastrophic Experience*, a collection of 13 interviews she conducted with psychoanalysts, psychiatrists, hospital group leaders, activists, literary critics, and filmmakers about their intellectual, clinical, and personal experience with trauma. She has most recently prepared a twentieth-anniversary edition of *Unclaimed Experience* with a new Afterword that responds to academic debates in the field.

Marilyn Charles is a staff psychologist at the Austen Riggs Center and a psychoanalyst in private practice in Stockbridge, MA. She is also a Training and Supervising Analyst at the Chicago Center for Psychoanalysis, and on faculty at Harvard Medical School, Boston Graduate School of Psychoanalysis, and Universidad de Monterrey. She is actively engaged in mentoring, creating professional opportunities, creating opportunities for dialogue between diverse groups with common interests, and promoting community involvement for those in the helping professions, including her consultation work with Gunawirra in Sydney, Australia. Research interests include creativity, psychosis, resilience, and the intergenerational transmission of trauma. Marilyn serves as Contributing Editor of *Psychoanalysis, Culture, and Society* and is a member of the editorial boards of numerous psychoanalytic journals. She has presented her work nationally and internationally, publishing more than 100 articles and book chapters and six books: *Patterns: Building Blocks of Experience; Constructing Realities: Transformations Through Myth and Metaphor; Learning from Experience: a Guidebook for Clinicians; Working with Trauma: Lessons from Bion and Lacan; Psychoanalysis and Literature: The Stories We Live; Introduction to Contemporary Psychoanalysis: Defining Terms and Building Bridges;* and an edited volume with co-author Michael O'Loughlin: *Fragments of Trauma and the Social Production of Suffering.* She is currently working on two edited volumes: *Women and Psychosis* (with Marie Brown) and *Building Lives: Incorporating Developmental Theory into Early Childhood Education* (with Jill Bellinson).

Françoise Davoine, Agrégée de lettres classiques, PhD in sociology, is a faculty member at the École des Hautes Etudes en Sciences Sociales. She led, with Jean Max Gaudillière, a weekly seminar on "Madness and the social link" for 40 years, until his death in 2015. A member of the ex École Freudienne founded by Jacques Lacan, she worked as a psychoanalyst for 30 years in public psychiatric hospitals and free outdoor consultations, and continues to work as a psychoanalyst in private practice. A member of ISPS U.S. and an Erikson Scholar at the Austen Riggs Center, Stockbridge, Massachusetts, she has presented at conferences in Europe, the U.S., and Latin America. Her articles and books in English include *Wittgenstein's Folly* (YBK Publishers), *History Beyond Trauma* (Other Press), *Mother Folly,* (Stanford) and *Fighting Melancholia: Don Quixote's Teaching* (Karnac). To be published: *A Word to the Wise! Don Quixote's Return to Fight Perversion* (Karnac).

Allen Dyer is Professor of Psychiatry and Behavioral Sciences, Vice-chair for Education, and director of the Global Mental Health program at the George Washington University. His major interests are Global Health and Mental Health, Medical Ethics and Professionalism, cancer survivorship, spirituality and health, and clinical care. Formerly he was Senior Health Advisor at the International Mental Corps. Previously he has been on the faculty at Duke University, Albany Medical College, where he served as Associate Chair of the Department of Psychiatry and Chief Medical Officer of the Capital District Psychiatric Center, and East Tennessee State University, where he served as Chair of the Department of Psychiatry. He received his A.B. and Master of Medical Science at Brown University, his M.D. and his Ph.D. from Duke. The Ph.D. is in medical ethics from the department of religion. While still a resident at Duke, he began his tenure on the APA Ethics committee and the AMA Council on Mental Health. He is the recipient of several awards, including: Attending of the Year, Nancy C.A. Roeske Award in Recognition of Outstanding and Sustained Contributions to Medical Education, An Award and Recognition for service to the Iraqi people, and the Bruno Lima award of APA for disaster psychiatry. He served on the editorial board of the *Encyclopedia of Bioethics.* He is a Distinguished Life Fellow of the APA (DLFAPA).

M. Gerard Fromm, Ph.D., is Distinguished Faculty in the Erikson Institute of the Austen Riggs Center and Assistant Clinical Professor, Yale Child Study Center. Dr. Fromm has taught at, and consulted to, a number of psychoanalytic institutes across the country. He is President of the International Dialogue Initiative, an interdisciplinary group that studies the psychodynamics of societal conflict, Past President of the International Society for the Psychoanalytic Study of Organizations, and has directed or served on the staff of Group Relations Conferences in the United States, Canada, Europe and Israel. He maintains a practice of psychodynamic organizational consultation, including as a partner in College Health and Counseling Service Consulting. His books include the edited volumes, *Lost in Transmission: Studies of Trauma across Generations* and *A Spirit That Impels: Play, Creativity and Psychoanalysis* and a volume of clinical papers, *Taking the Transference, Reaching toward Dreams: Clinical Studies in the Intermediate Area.*

Nancy R. Goodman, PhD, is a training and supervising analyst with the Contemporary Freudian Society, Washington DC, and the IPA. She has served as Chair of all Institute Committees. Many publications reflect her interest in trauma and symbolizing processes as well as female development and enactments. Publications include the following edited volumes: *Finding Unconscious Fantasy in Narrative, Trauma, and Body Pain: A Clinical Guide* (with Paula Ellman); *The Courage to Fight Violence against Women* (with Paula Ellman); *Battling the Life and Death Forces of Sadomasochism: Clinical Perspectives* (with Basseches & Ellman); and *The Power of Witnessing: Reflections, Reverberations, and Traces of the Holocaust* (with Marilyn Meyers). She is Museum Director of the online Virtual Psychoanalytic Museum: www.virtualpsychoanalyticmuseum.org with IPBooks. She maintains a psychoanalytic practice in Bethesda, Maryland.

James l. Griffith, MD is Leon M. Yochelson Professor and Chair in the Department of Psychiatry and Behavioral Sciences. As a psychiatric educator, Dr. Griffith developed a psychiatry residency program at George Washington University that has been distinguished for its curriculum in cross-cultural psychiatry, global mental health, mental health policy, and psychosocial care for medically ill patients. In his clinical research, Dr. Griffith has published extensively on family-centered treatment of psychosomatic disorders and chronic medical illnesses, including a book, *The Body Speaks: Therapeutic Dialogues for Mind-Body Problems*. A second book, *Encountering* *the Sacred in Psychotherapy*, articulated methods for engaging the spiritual and religious resources that people bring to clinical settings. His most recent book, *Religion that Heals, Religion that Harms,* addressed destructive uses of religion and ideology in clinical settings and received the Creative Scholarship Award from the Society for the Study of Psychiatry and Culture. Currently, Dr. Griffith provides psychiatric treatment for immigrants, refugees, and survivors of political torture at Northern Virginia Family Services in Falls Church, VA. He has received the Human Rights Community Award from the United Nations Association of the National Capital Area, and the Margaret B. and Cyril A. Shulman Distinguished Service Award from the George Washington University Medical Center, both for the training of mental health professionals and the development of mental health services for survivors of political torture in the Washington metropolitan area. As an educator, he has received the Distinguished Teacher Award from the George Washington University School of Medicine and Health Sciences. He has been selected by the Washington Psychiatric Society as its 2003 Psychiatrist of the Year and for its 2014 Distinguished Service Award. Most recently, he was selected by *Washingtonian Magazine* as a 2015 "Top Doctor in Washington."

Dr. Harold Kudler received his M.D. from Downstate Medical Center, trained in Psychiatry at Yale and is Adjunct Associate Professor at Duke. From 2000 through 2005, he co-chaired VA's Special Committee on PTSD, which reports to Congress. He has served on the International Society for Traumatic Stress Studies Board of Directors, co-led development of joint VA/Department of Defense Guidelines for the Management of Posttraumatic Stress, and advised on *Sesame Street's* "Talk Listen Connect" series for military families. From 2006 to 2014, he co-led the North Carolina Governor's Focus on Returning Military Members and their Families and, in 2012, was appointed to the North Carolina Institute of Medicine. From 2004 to 2014, Dr. Kudler was Associate Director of the VA's Mid-Atlantic Mental Illness Research, Education, and Clinical Center (MIRECC) on Deployment Mental Health. In July, 2014, he joined VA Central Office in Washington DC where he serves as Chief Consultant for Mental Health Services.

Dr. Dori Laub was born in Cernauti, Romania on June 8, 1937. He was a practicing psychoanalyst in New Haven, Connecticut who worked primarily with victims of massive psychic trauma and with their children. He was Clinical Professor of Psychiatry at the Yale

University School of Medicine and Co-Founder of the Fortunoff Video Archive for Holocaust Testimonies. He obtained his M.D. at the Hadassah Medical School at Hebrew University in Jerusalem, Israel and his M.A. in Clinical Psychology at the Bar Ilan University in Ramat Gan, Israel. He was Acting Director of Genocide Study Program (GSP) at Yale for the years of 2000 and 2003. Since 2001, he served as Deputy Director for Trauma Studies for the GSP. Dr. Laub published on the topic of psychic trauma, its knowing and representation in a variety of psychoanalytic journals and co-authored a book entitled *Testimony—Crises of Witnessing in Literature, Psychoanalysis, and History* with Professor Shoshana Felman.

Robert Jay Lifton, Lecturer in Psychiatry at the Columbia University College of Physicians and Surgeons and distinguished Professor Emeritus of Psychiatry and Psychology at the City University of New York, has written books and papers on such subjects as Nazi doctors (their killing in the name of healing) and genocide; nuclear weapons and their impact on death symbolism; Hiroshima survivors; Chinese thought reform and the Chinese Cultural Revolution; psychological trends in contemporary men and women; and the Vietnam War experience and "atrocity-producing situations." Recent work includes medical complicity in torture and in connection with the war on Iraq; and a comparative study of nuclear and climate threats. He has developed a general psychological perspective around the paradigm of death and the continuity of life, with emphasis on symbolization and the "formative process," and on the malleability of the contemporary or "protean" self. Among his books are *Death in Life: Survivors of Hiroshima* (which won a National Book Award); *The Nazi Doctors: Medical Killing and the Psychology of Genocide; Home From the War: Learning from Vietnam Veterans;* and most recently, *Witness to an Extreme Century: A Memoir.*

Marilyn B. Meyers, Ph.D. is on the faculty of the Washington School of Psychiatry, where she teaches and supervises in the postgraduate Clinical Program on Psychotherapy Practice. She is past Chair of the Clinical Program and Chair of Admissions. She is past President of the Section on Couples and Families of the Division of Psychoanalysis (39) of the American Psychological Association. She is co-editor and co-author with Dr. Nancy Goodman of *The Power of Witnessing: Reflections, Reverberations and Traces of the Holocaust (Trauma, Psychoanalysis and the Living Mind),* (Routledge, 2012). Her other publications include: "When the Holocaust Haunts the Couple: Hope Guilt and Survival" in *Psychoanalytic Perspectives* *on Couple Work, 2005*, and "Am I my Mother's Keeper?; Certain Vicissitudes in the Mother-Daughter Relationship Concerning Envy" in *The Mother-Daughter Relationship* (Jason Aronson, 2008). She is particularly interested in the effects of relational trauma on attachment throughout life. In addition, she has presented papers internationally on the use of film to illustrate the aftermath of massive trauma and the intergenerational transmission of Holocaust trauma. She maintains a private practice in Bethesda, MD.

Evelyn Jaffe Schreiber, Ph.D. is a Professor of English at The George Washington University. Her book, *Subversive Voices: Eroticizing the Other in William Faulkner and Toni Morrison*, examines identity and race via the theory of Jacques Lacan and cultural studies and was awarded the Toni Morrison Society book prize. It was a finalist for the MLA award for best first book, 2003. Her book, *Race, Trauma, and Home in the Novels of Toni Morrison*, is an interdisciplinary study of trauma in Morrison's fiction and was published in 2010. It was awarded the Toni Morrison Society Book Prize and was nominated for the MLA William Sanders Scarborough Prize for an outstanding scholarly study of black American literature or culture, 2011. She is Immediate Past President of the Toni Morrison Society affiliate of the American Literature Association. Her research applies Lacanian and other psychoanalytic principles of identity/subjectivity/agency, trauma theory, cultural studies, and neuroscience to literary texts, with articles on Faulkner, Morrison, Pinter, trauma, stream-of-consciousness, psychoanalytic theory, cultural studies, and multicultural issues. Professor Schreiber teaches a course focused on Washington theatre called "What's New About New Plays?" and a special course on race, identity, and trauma in the works of William Faulkner and Toni Morrison. As a trained educator at the United States Holocaust Memorial Museum, she works with groups from the FBI, ICE, State Department, state law enforcement, and schools.

Nancy Sherman is a distinguished University Professor and Professor of Philosophy at Georgetown University, with affiliate appointments at the Center on National Security and the Law at Georgetown University Law Center and Georgetown's Kennedy Institute of Ethics. She is also a Guggenheim Foundation Fellow. From 1997–1999, she served as the inaugural holder of the Distinguished Chair in Ethics at the U. S. Naval Academy, designing the brigade-wide military ethics course and the Stockdale Center for Ethical Leadership. She has research training in psychoanalysis from the Washington Psychoanalytic Institute and regularly consults

litary and veteran groups in the U.S. and abroad on issues
ics, moral injury, and posttraumatic stress. In October 2005,
man visited Guantanamo Bay Detention Center as part of an
ependent observer team assessing the medical and mental health
re of detainees; in 2011–2012 she attended the Vice Chief of the
J.S. Army's Suicide Prevention Group; in Spring 2015 she briefed
Army Chief of Staff 's research team; in January 2016, she briefed
the Marine Commandant and executive Marine staff on moral injury.
In April 2016, she gave the inaugural nationwide broadcast of grand
rounds for the Department of Veteran Affairs National Center for
Ethics and Professionalism. She is a much sought-after national and
international public speaker.

Jane Shore was born in North Bergen, New Jersey and got her B.A.
at Goddard College and her M.F.A at the University of Iowa. She
is the author of six books of poems: *Eye Level,* winner of the 1977
Juniper Prize; *The Minute Hand*, awarded the 1986 Lamont Prize;
Music Minus One, a finalist of the 1996 National Book Critic Circle
Award; and *Happy Family* (1999). *A Yes-or-No Answer*, published
by Houghton Mifflin Harcourt in 2008, was awarded the 2010 Poet's
Prize. Jane received fellowships from The Guggenheim Foundation
and The Radcliffe Institute; she was a Hodder Fellow at Princeton
University, a Goodyear Fellow at The Foxcroft School, and was twice
awarded grants from The National Endowment for the Arts. Her
poems are widely anthologized, including in *The Norton Anthology
of Poetry*, and have appeared in *The New Yorker, The Yale Review,
Ploughshares,* etc. Her work has been featured on NPR's *All Things
Considered* and read by Garrison Keillor on *The Writer's Almanac.
That Said, New and Selected Poems* was published by Houghton
Mifflin Harcourt in 2012. A Professor in the English Department at
The George Washington University, she lives in Washington, DC and
in East Calais, Vermont.

Myra Sklarew, former president of Yaddo Artists Community,
Professor Emerita, American University and founder of the MFA
Program in Creative Writing, has published 17 books including
poetry, fiction, essays. Forthcoming, *A Survivor Named Trauma:
Holocaust and the Construction of Memory,* SUNY Press. Her poetry
has twice been recorded for the Library of Congress Contemporary
Poet's Series. She was educated at Tufts University, Johns Hopkins
University, Cold Spring Harbor Biological Institute, the Radcliffe
Institute and the National Institutes of Health. She recently presented
a paper, "The (Impossible) Reconciliation of Time," at Rice

University, and is co-editor with Bruce Sklarew of *The Journey of Child Development,* published by Taylor & Francis. Shortly after the end of the 45-year Soviet occupation of Lithuania, Myra Sklarew began traveling to Lithuania, home of her maternal family. Over the years since then, she has come to know survivors, rescuers, witnesses and those of younger generations. "Trauma Made Manifest" makes use of her early work in the neuroscience of memory at Yale University School of Medicine.

www.ingramcontent.com/pod-product-compliance
Lightning Source LLC
Chambersburg PA
CBHW060309030426
42336CB00011B/981